Preventing mental illness in practice

Increasingly, planners and practitioners are considering setting up a greater level of preventive mental health care at a local level. *Preventing Mental Illness in Practice* aims to inform their decisions by describing characteristics of 'good practice', and identifying a number of promising approaches which are described in some detail. The review represents the second stage of a prevention research project set up by MIND (National Association for Mental Health).

The criteria used for identifying good practice are that the project: is targeted towards people known to be at high risk of mental illness; makes maximum use of existing natural, voluntary or community support networks; and supports people in a way that enhances their capacity to control their own life circumstances. The projects selected cover the life stages – from pregnancy and early childhood to old age. They are discussed in the context of relevant research findings which give the rationale for the approach.

Ten different projects or services are described: what is provided, how the target group is engaged, the resources required, management problems, and evidence of effectiveness. Interviews with clients and service providers give colour to the descriptions with personal accounts of why the support has been needed and how, in their view, it meets those needs.

Jennifer Newton, PhD, is a research psychologist and was commissioned by MIND to review the prospects for prevention. Her first book, the highly successful *Preventing Mental Illness*, was a review of relevant research and received critical acclaim. She is currently Research Fellow at the Sainsbury Centre for Mental Health.

Preventing mental illness
in practice

Jennifer Newton

London and New York

First published 1992
by Routledge
11 New Fetter Lane, London EC4P 4EE

Simultaneously published in the USA and Canada
by Routledge
29 West 35th Street, New York, NY 10001

First published in paperback in 1994

Typeset by Witwell Ltd, Southport
Printed and bound in Great Britain by
Mackays of Chatham PLC, Chatham, Kent

British Library Cataloguing in Publication Data
Newton, Jennifer, *1953–*
  Preventing mental illness in practice
  1. Mental health services
  I. Title
  362.20425

Library of Congress Cataloging in Publication Data
Newton, Jennifer, 1953–
  Preventing mental illness in practice/Jennifer Newton.
  p.   cm.
  Includes bibliographical references and index
  1. Mental illness–Prevention.   2. Preventive health services.
  3. Mental health services.   I. Title
  [DNLM: 1. Mental Disorders–prevention & control.   2. Preventive
  Psychiatry.   WM 31.5 N564p]
  RA790.N46   1992
  616.89–dc20
  DNLM/DLC
  for Library of Congress   91–18530
                                                                                    CIP

ISBN 0–415–11993–6

Contents

Acknowledgements

This book was planned by a Prevention Advisory Committee at MIND as a straightforward description of good practice in prevention. It followed a review of research and theory which provided a range of indications about where our best hopes for prevention should lie. In particular, the earlier phase had helped clarify who some of the important target groups should be, what kind of support they needed, and what were some of the essential ingredients of 'good practice'. I was, therefore, simply to talk to key people in service planning and delivery for my target groups about known examples of exemplary innovative provision, then visit these projects or services and describe them. The aim was, of course, to provide information that would help planners or practitioners wishing to improve preventive provision. Like many 'straightforward' ideas this has proved quite complex to write about.

Several people assisted me in searching out examples of the kinds of projects I was looking for. In this respect I would like to thank Dr Ruth Berkowitz, Dr David Challis, Dr Stella Dixon, Dr Ian Falloon, and Mr Paul Robson. Information resources such as Good Practices in Mental Health were particularly helpful at this stage.

I have been delighted by the readiness of all the projects and services I approached to allow my visits and assist me in my task. Those directly involved in the schemes have arranged for me to see at first hand as much of what is offered as possible; have helped to find clients willing to talk to me about their experiences; and have devoted a considerable amount of time to ensuring I gained a full understanding of their work. I am extremely grateful to them: Dr Walter Barker, Ms Shane Billington, Dr Max Birchwood, Ms Anne Jenkins, Ms Sarah Honeywood, Ms Rosemary Luckett, Ms Sue Pettigrew, Mr Robin Saunders, Ms Joanne Smith, Ms Jill Steyne, Ms Dorothy Sutcliffe, Dr Rodney Turner, Ms Peggy Wiseman, and Dr Reginald Yorke. Colleagues of many of these individuals, whose names are too numerous to list, also gave me every assistance and I have enjoyed my time with them.

Clients of these services and projects have been remarkably open and willing to talk to me about their experiences and I am thankful to them for this. I have not used their real names in the text, and have changed some of the identifying characteristics. But to all who remember talking to me – I have greatly appreciated your support.

My research was funded by grants from the Leigh Trust, The King Edward Hospital Fund for London, Thames Telethon, Marks and Spencer Plc, and the Noah Trust, and I would like to express my gratitude to them for this. I have also been fortunate to have the expertise and encouragement to draw upon, of members of the advisory group convened by MIND. I would particularly like to thank Professor George Brown for the numerous opportunities to discuss aspects of this work, and for his longstanding support and encouragement for the project. Vicky Whitfield of MIND has helped me considerably by typing the manuscript, often under pressure of time.

Finally, I should add that views expressed in this book, and the terminology used to do so, will inevitably reflect biases of my own.

Jennifer Newton

Introduction

It is widely believed that a good deal of the personal distress that is commonly labelled mental illness is preventable. A review of some of the recent aetiological research confirms this view, and shows that it is increasingly possible to offer suggestions to individuals, families, practitioners and planners about where our best hopes for prevention should lie (Newton, 1988).

Of course the research workers who have brought these new insights into aetiology would almost certainly take the view that more research is required, and that evaluation of intervention trials needs replicating (and, in some instances, setting up for the first time). But current knowledge is sufficiently impressive that we can at least begin to think about prevention, and about how existing services might be influenced by current research. This book therefore examines existing service provision in the light of insights gained from research, and represents the second of the two stages of the prevention research project commissioned by MIND (the National Association for Mental Health).

By bringing together some basic principles of 'good practice' in preventive care, with evidence from research about how we might hope to prevent mental health problems, the aim has been to identify, from the existing range of health and social welfare services, those approaches to care that hold particular promise for prevention. Some are more innovative than others, of course, and many of the projects visited would not describe their central aims in terms of mental health prevention. Nevertheless, applying criteria for likely effectiveness in prevention brings out a number of issues that will be familiar to service providers accustomed to considering their effectiveness by other means.

The projects are described in some detail, to illustrate what is involved in establishing such a scheme, what resources are needed, how clients are offered help, what that help consists of, and in particular, what has led clients to need that help, and how, in their view, it is meeting those needs. Such evaluation is highly subjective, but can nevertheless prove revealing. Of course, I have tried to choose promising projects which also have systematic evaluative data on effectiveness, but such information is not always available. This lack of material has not been used here as a reason to exclude work which appears to be well justified (in terms of relevant research) as likely to be preventive.

Informing my choice of a scheme as 'promising' are three general conclusions drawn from the literature (Newton, 1988).

1 that aetiological research should be used to identify a group particularly likely to be vulnerable to serious mental illness, so that the programme can be targeted toward this group and planned to reduce vulnerability in a way concordant with that research. This is the 'disease modelling' approach (see Newton, 1988).
2 that the intervention should increase the individual's capacity to control their own life circumstances, and not create dependence upon the service.
3 that services should make maximum use of existing natural, community and voluntary support networks, and involve changes to existing styles of professional support rather than requiring additional numbers of professional personnel.

A brief summary of the thinking behind these conclusions is given below.

TARGETING VULNERABLE INDIVIDUALS

Targeting vulnerable individuals is an approach in which the first step is to use the best available aetiological research to identify some of the factors which characterise people whose probability of experiencing that disorder is considerably raised. A preventive programme is then targeted at this high-risk group. This is the medical model for prevention, and can be contrasted with a health promotion model which targets the general population with measures known to be preventive of disorder for a few and assumed to be health-promoting for the rest. Mental health promotion methods include communication, education, legislation, fiscal measures, organisational change and community development (World Health Organization, 1984). The factors they aim to change are usually assumed to be preventive of a range of disorder rather than of any specific disorder. The two approaches need not conflict, and are often both of value. To take two examples from physical medicine: consider cigarette smoking and cervical cancer, and blood cholesterol and heart disease. A simplistic disease model could look like this:

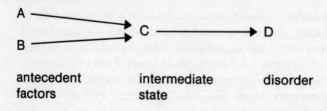

antecedent   intermediate   disorder
factors   state

In the case of cervical cancer we could take antecedent factors A = smoking and B = wart virus. A and B both independently affect C – in this case, 'CIN' levels (an abbreviated medical term for precancerous abnormal cells in the surface layers of the cervix) – which is itself an early indication or precursor of disorder D, cervical cancer. In heart disease and angina, two of the antecedent factors are blood cholesterol and family history of heart disease. These together influence intermediate state C, narrowing of the arteries, which in turn is linked to the development of ischaemic heart disease.

These models are not strictly causal, as the relationships are complex, but they illustrate the sequence of important risk indicators. If we knew nothing about factors antecedent to the disorder, we could only hope to pick up the disorder in its earliest stages and treat it. But as we also know that high CIN levels precede cervical cancer, and high blood cholesterol levels and high blood pressure often precede more serious coronary problems, we can consider screening the whole population periodically for both factors and institute early treatment when found. However, knowledge about factors antecedent to this enables intervention to be planned, in theory at least, in a potentially more cost-effective manner. Leaving aside problems of identification and ethical considerations we could, say, offer more regular screening to women who have had the wart virus, who smoke (and to those who take the pill or who have many sexual partners), and screen other groups less frequently. And we could provide blood pressure tests at more frequent intervals for men over 40, people with a family history of heart disease and so on. And we can use one antecedent factor to narrow the target group (e.g. all who have close relatives with a history of heart disease), and knowledge about other antecedent factors as the basis of the preventive intervention (e.g. advice on diet, smoking, alcohol, stress and exercise). Indeed computerisation in general practice and the development of health record cards covering lifestyle factors may make such a formalised screening a practical possibility in the future. Of course, many issues must be resolved before screening can be justified, and the most important of these is whether preventive measures or the earlier treatment of an abnormality made possible by screening have been shown, in fact, to improve the prognosis.

However, for heart disease and cancer it also makes sense to mount general population health promotion strategies – against smoking, a high consumption of saturated fats and so on. In fact, this is widely considered a more fruitful approach than a targeted one. A health promotion strategy – that is, one which effectively focuses on any factor known to have a causal role in any disorder and encourages the whole population to change their habits – becomes rational for four reasons:

1 there is sound evidence for the target factor having an aetiological role in at least one disorder;

2 the disorder or disorders to which this factor contributes could potentially affect a large number of people, or the disorder currently affects only a relatively small number of people but is usually fatal (e.g. AIDS);

3 the factor targeted is important enough to warrant attention, and the necessary strategies are straightforward enough and cheap enough to mount on a population-wide scale;

4 even those not at risk of developing the specific disorder will not be harmed by the measure.

If any of these do not apply, then it may well be more advisable to wait for people to show early signs of trouble and then treat them, or, better, to revert to the disease modelling approach and use another factor to identify a high-risk group, and provide the measure or message for this smaller group.

This 'disease modelling' approach is the one advocated here for the prevention of mental illnesses. But for some physical disorders, it has been argued convincingly that a health promotion model is preferable. Rose (1981) favours this approach to the prevention of heart disease, and Kreitman (1986) makes a similar case in favour of general population health promotion strategies for the prevention of 'problem' drinking. Both writers describe the difficulty of reaching the mass of people likely to have a problem by selecting out a high-risk group for intervention.

This difficulty where known risk factors have a low predictive accuracy can also be illustrated by the prevalence of Down's Syndrome. Screening programmes are reserved for pregnant women at raised risk of having a Down's Syndrome baby, namely those aged over 37 years, yet the majority of such babies are born to younger women. These examples illustrate the different picture produced by identifying risk on the basis of the *relative* risk of individuals, as compared to that produced from identifying risk according to the actual or *attributable* risk (Rose, 1981). That is, among 40- to 44-year-old women, as many as 13 in 1,000 births will be a Down's Syndrome baby (and the risk to women older than this is 35 per 1,000 births). Among births to women under 30 less than one in 1,000 will be affected by Down's Syndrome. But as only 1 per cent of all births are to women of 40 years or more, they only contribute 13 per cent of the Down's Syndrome babies. Many more babies are born to women aged under 30, so even at their lower relative risk over half (51 per cent) of Down's Syndrome babies are born to women in this age group. This means that even a very successful prevention programme targeting the women with the highest relative risk (women aged 40 or more) can only reduce the numbers of Down's Syndrome births by a maximum of 13 per cent (figures from Alberman and Berry, 1979).

Rose (1981) illustrates this point with coronary heart disease. Death from heart disease among 55- to 64-year-old men increases linearly and steeply with increasing levels of serum cholesterol, but the greatest *number* of deaths do not occur among those with the very highest levels. As Rose concludes, a principle to remember in prevention is that 'a large number of people exposed to a low risk is likely to produce more cases than a small number of people exposed to a high risk. In business the same principle underlies the mass market: profits are larger when small amounts are taken from the masses than when large amounts are taken from the few rich people' (Rose, 1981).

On this basis, Rose argues in favour of mass strategies for prevention, although he is well aware of the inherent difficulties in this. For instance, telling a man he is in a high-risk group for coronary heart disease is a message which may motivate him to alter his diet. He will almost certainly know about smoking and diet in relation to heart disease, but advice that he has a special reason to take this seriously will increase the likelihood that he will take action. Persuading people at low risk to change their diet when there is much less chance of personal benefit will be much harder. This is what Rose calls the 'prevention paradox': 'a measure that brings large benefit to the community offers little to each participating individual.' Social pressure to change behaviour (such as no smoking policies in the work-place) may be more effective in these circumstances than health education.

But do these arguments apply to mental illness prevention? To a certain extent they may do, but one cannot conclude that general-population strategies are the most valuable response. Societal changes such as reducing the level of unemployment, or providing better housing, or facilitating job-share schemes and part-time employment are certainly justifiable in these terms. But there are many other good reasons to argue for such moves aside from their potential for reducing depression. Also, they are not activities that health and social welfare professionals typically have much influence over, or that would have implications for their day-to-day work. In terms of the individual and their immediate environment (that is, in terms of factors which these professions might be able to influence), mental health promotion messages are not straightforward, the strategies would usually not be universally beneficial, and intervention will often be too costly to offer widely.

Furthermore, our knowledge about risk for depression has advanced so that we can now begin to specify a high-risk group into which *most* people likely to get depressed will fall. The majority of cases will *not* be found among low- or moderate-risk groups. Most serious cases of depression in women occur among those who have both existing negative social and negative psychological factors (who have, for example, a poor relationship with a partner *and* low self-esteem) (Brown *et al.*, 1990). It is among such women that a major loss or disappointment is particularly likely to produce depression (men were not studied in this research). In their survey of high-risk women in Islington (working class with children), as many as three-quarters of all onsets of depression occurred among the 23 per cent of women who had both social *and* psychological risk factors (Brown *et al.*, 1990). And, taking the statistics from the other angle, it was found that a large proportion (at least 39 per cent) of these 'high-risk' women did develop depression. If this finding is confirmed in further studies it may soon be possible to use simple screening questionnaires (in GP waiting rooms perhaps), to identify people at high risk of depression. Of course, as much psychiatric disorder tends to follow a relapsing course to some extent, a previous history of mental illness should also be a realistic method by which to identify risk.

This means that it may make sense to target help toward these high-risk groups. For mental health problems it is more logical to do so given the likely costliness of any intervention. The kind of help needed by people vulnerable to mental illness is not comparable to the health education messages currently promoted: give up smoking, lower your intake of alcohol and cholesterol, wear a seat belt and so on. Cost of the test, and the possibility of causing miscarriage in a small proportion of non-affected pregnancies are, of course, the two main reasons why preventive approaches for Down's Syndrome are still targeted, despite the small proportion of cases which are preventable in this way. Amniocentesis, until recently our only available method of detecting Down's Syndrome antenatally, could not be made more widely available without prohibitive cost implications. If there was no risk of miscarriage against which to justify restricting its use, it would have to be limited in some other way, most likely in terms equivalent to 'cost per life saved' assessments currently quoted for judgements about breast screening programmes or coronary heart bypass grafts (i.e. cost per Down's Syndrome life avoided). However, a simple blood test has now become available which looks as though it may give some indication of high risk of Down's Syndrome pregnancy among all age groups so that amniocentesis can be offered to a selected group (according to blood test results) of young women as well as to all older women. This will clearly improve the effectiveness of the screening process without a serious escalation of cost. Such balancing of cost against benefit is fundamental to a consideration of the benefits of health promotion strategies relative to disease modelling approaches.

One of the important issues for a consideration of prevention for mental illness is that although we know many of the antecedent factors, a number of these cannot be considered out of context in order to suggest ways forward for general health promotion. Personal events such as a pregnancy will obviously have quite a different significance depending on whether it was planned and wanted or not. The break-up of a marriage will usually be less distressing to the partner who is leaving to live with someone else than to the partner left alone. And an event, however bad, is typically insufficient to provoke depression without considering factors such as social support.

Social factors underlying psychiatric disorder must be considered in terms of their *meaning* to the individual. It is only in the way the antecedent factors interact that they are significant.

One of the often cited difficulties of health education is that those who most need to take action are the most difficult to reach and to affect. Those who already eat a healthy diet are those most likely to read the articles about the advantages of high fibre and the best choice of cereals and so on. The message is least likely to reach the group with the most unhealthy diets. So too with the efficacy of social intervention. Those most likely to use a newly established mother and toddler group will tend to be the more confident women, and also the ones with good friends to go with them. Unless efforts are made to set up the group in a particularly accessible way to encourage women with less self-confidence or without local friends to join; or unless some outreach/befriending work is done so that such women would know at least one person fairly well if they came, this kind of support will be bound to fall short of its preventive potential.

In a disorder for which it *is* possible to identify a high-risk group into which a *substantial* proportion of cases will fall, it is crucial that if a *costly* intervention is selected, it succeeds with the high-risk group. And to reach those most in need requires knowledge about relevant risk indicators and how they interact, about optimum supportive strategies to engage those particular individuals, and about the kind of support they need most. In short, a return to the disease modelling approach.

HELPING PEOPLE TO TAKE CONTROL OVER THEIR OWN LIVES

In much of the research on aetiology and on the effectiveness of intervention, the issue of powerlessness or helplessness or an expectation of a lack of control surfaces as critical (Abramson *et al.*, 1978; Garber *et al.*, 1979; Brown *et al.*, 1986a; Harris *et al.*, 1990; Rodin, 1986, for instance).

To begin with, helplessness is an important explanatory variable in the causal model of depression developed by George Brown, Tirril Harris and colleagues (see Harris *et al.*, 1990). It helped to explain their finding that a prolonged period of 'lack of care' in the childhood of their female samples was associated with a raised risk of depression in adulthood. Although there were more apparent links along an 'experience' pathway (lack of care often associated with low social class, with an institutional stay, with unintended pre-marital pregnancy and a stressful lifestyle in adulthood), helplessness was thought to be a major reason why the girl failed to break out of such a disastrous cycle. A year or more of neglect, indifference and a low level of control from parents or other main carers was thought to sometimes induce in the child a sense that the world (or her world) was impervious to her own efforts to change it for the better. If 'good' actions bring no reward and negative outcomes continue to be highly probable then perhaps a helpless attitude toward stress and toward long-term difficulties is learnt and persists.

This is in line with the theories of Seligman, Abramson and their colleagues who describe and test experimentally the concept of 'learned helplessness' (Abramson *et al.*, 1978). In Brown and Harris's formulations, such helpless 'cognitive sets' are also contributing factors in influencing the likelihood of girls (who have experienced a childhood lack of care) becoming pregnant unintentionally during their teens, and then in determining how they cope with this event. Girls who allowed themselves to become trapped into single parenthood, or who chose to settle with the child's father 'for the sake of the baby' when they would not otherwise have chosen to do so were more likely to become depressed in the future. This was as much to do with the stressful life circumstances in which they found themselves as their poor mastery or low self-esteem. Helplessness increases the likelihood that one adversity will lead to another. However, helplessness is a cognitive set, not a fixed and permanent personality trait, *and it can change with altered circumstances.* It is influenced by early life experiences, by experiences in later childhood and adolescence, and by circumstances in adult life. Secure, stable and close supportive relationships will enhance self-esteem and coping ability (Brown and Harris, 1978; Quinton *et al.*, 1984) and so will success, achievement, and positive experiences (Quinton *et al.*, 1984).

Depression more often than not develops in people who have been living with major life difficulties for a period of years, or following an event with profound long-term implications of loss. How people deal with these severe events or major difficulties will be linked to their vulnerability or resilience to depression, and an expectation of control is a central component of effective coping. It matters that people act and do not simply react (Rutter, 1985). To be successful, programmes aiming to prevent anxiety or depression, or enrich mental health in some sense must consider the issue of control, and the expectation of control (Rodin *et al.*, 1987).

Rodin's reviews of the research literature show that feelings of control or self-determination are linked to physical as well as mental health (e.g. Rodin, 1986). There are studies linking a lack of control over stress to cancerous tumour growth and proliferation, and to the onset and progression of cardiovascular disease (see Rodin, 1986). Paykel (1979) found that people who had attempted suicide were particularly likely to have experienced an excess of events beyond their control, and also argued that the same kinds of event can lead to a range of physical as well as mental disorder. Rodin (1986) reports that both the immune system and the neuroendocrine system appear to be responsive to changes from controllable to uncontrollable stress. She emphasises, however, that greater control is not always beneficial. Although, for instance, several studies have shown that people who are depressed or feel helpless take longer to recover from illness, or are more likely to die from serious illnesses (see Rodin, 1986), it does not follow that it will be in every patient's best interests to give them more control, say, in their own treatment. Some patients neither expect nor prefer responsibility for medical decisions. It is important to work out carefully the conditions under which exercising control is beneficial and when it is not. Taking an active, involved role in recovery from surgery or illness may aid adjustment at one stage of illness, but not in another.

When one of the central aims of a programme is to enhance control and perceived self-efficacy, this should affect not only the *content* of the intervention programme, but *how* any support is delivered. How an offer of help is made will be an important determinant in whether people seek that help, whether they continue to accept help, and how they feel after receiving it (Rodin *et al.*, 1987). As Rodin and her colleagues point out, the helping process can be undermined if the helper takes on too much responsibility for generating and implementing the solutions, or if helper and client have a different understanding of who is responsible for what. In fact the act of helping can in some circumstances reduce rather than enhance the individual's sense of control and self-esteem. It is also possible that such ambiguities about or imbalances in power will serve to increase the dependency of a client on that service.

Of course enhancing control is not just about helping people to see themselves as masterful rather than helpless. The opportunities, and the perceived opportunities for taking control must also be present. If every effort by a woman to pay off the family's mounting debts were thwarted by her husband's prolific spending on drink, say, her masterful strategies would be unlikely to make her feel better and hence have health dividends. In other settings, opportunities for control may be available, but not encouraged, as in many residential care establishments for the young and the elderly. Preventive programmes should therefore consider the opportunities for taking control, the extent to which exercising control is encouraged and the opportunities made apparent, and the extent to which the individual's personal sense of self-efficacy can be maximised.

MAKING MAXIMUM USE OF NATURAL, VOLUNTARY AND COMMUNITY SUPPORT NETWORKS

Such is the prevalence of mental health problems that any attempt to meet all the need for support through professional specialist personnel would be quite impossible. Estimates of the prevalence of mild psychiatric difficulties which are nevertheless sufficiently troubling to take the sufferer to consult his or her family doctor are almost one in four of the population in any year (Goldberg and Huxley, 1980). Even if a higher threshold is used, such as psychiatric disorder as severe as that treated in out-patient departments, as many as 15 per cent of women and 6 per cent of men in inner city areas may be affected in any one-month period (Bebbington *et al.*, 1981). George Albee, as long ago as 1959, warned that there could never be enough trained mental health personnel to provide treatment for all who needed it, and encouraged the involvement of non-medical personnel and other front line caregivers (clergy, teachers, public health nurses, welfare workers, family doctors) in preventive work undertaken by the proposed Community Mental Health Centres movement. Caplan (1964) made similar proposals. Yet few of the necessary inter-professional links and professional–community links have been widely established. A restrictive filter continues to determine which and how many members of the population can be offered the available support. This is largely according to degree of difficulty, but by no means exclusively. Mode of presentation of symptoms, proximity to treatment services, existence of other supports and many other factors also determine *who* gets treated (Goldberg and Huxley, 1980).

And the cost of services and political commitment toward making them widely available will determine *how many* clients they serve. Clearly one psychiatrist can counsel a very much smaller number of bereaved relatives at a hospice than could a team of volunteers trained by him to take on a befriending and supportive role. Given that resources are finite and the demand for support substantial, programmes of the latter variety have obvious advantages. And in many instances, they can be just as helpful to the individual. Parkes (1981) found that after a brief training and some months of experience in the service, volunteers were able to become as effective as professionals in bereavement counselling. And Eyken (1982), evaluating the mother–to–mother voluntary befriending service Homestart showed that volunteers could often be more stable supporters, in terms of how long they remain involved, and could offer more intensive support than social workers. Although Homestart may be unusual, being particularly well organised and with good training and support for the volunteers, volunteers typically gave two to six hours a week up to their befriending role, and visited (or had a 'caseload' of) up to three women at any one time. This intensity of support is often a great deal more than a social worker can hope to offer.

Of course it is not the intention to suggest that an army of volunteers should be trained to replace professionals in order to save money. The work for which professional training and expertise is required cannot and should not be provided 'on the cheap'. Volunteers should obviously not be used as unpaid professionals. The support volunteers can give is complementary to the professional service, however, and can enable support to be offered to a much larger group.

There are some ways in which the volunteer has an advantage over a professional. Not least of these is reciprocity. Volunteers often derive as much benefit from a befriending role as their 'client'. The self-esteem gained from helping someone else, the sense of being needed, can be as important to the befriender as (or even more important than) the support gained by the client. And when events take a bad turn in the volunteer's life, the support between volunteer and client may reverse direction for a while. There may also be the prospect that the recipient of support can, once her own problems become manageable again, become a befriender herself. If the matching of volunteers to 'clients' is skilful, the volunteer will be similar in many ways to the 'client', enabling greater empathy than is possible in most 'professional–client' relationships. Factors such as these mean that the relationship is likely to be more equal, and there is a greater prospect that the client would see herself as able to cope as well as her befriender has done with similar problems.

There is often the opportunity for greater control for the client over when, how often and what form visits by volunteers take compared to professional support. Brief, unexpected, intermittent visits as are sometimes made by social workers or health visitors, coupled with their perceived authority to remove children deemed to be at risk, may sometimes mean their visits are interpreted more as a threat than a help. And the statutory responsibilities of professionals are bound to mean their relationships with the client must be fundamentally different from that of a friend. Many social workers feel that they must not get 'too close' to individual clients if they are to be able to do their job well. Befrienders, on the other hand, are probably most successful where they do become emotionally involved. Befrienders offer many things which a professional cannot, and vice versa.

Eyken's report discusses in some detail the different qualities of volunteer and professional support. One interesting finding was that a befriender sometimes became an intermediary between the 'client' and statutory services. Clients of the 'mother–to–mother' befriending scheme studied were often highly alienated families, suspicious of professionals, lonely or depressed. They had almost non-existent support networks, or troublesome and negative relationships with extended family ties. Their friendship with the 'Homestart' befriender often led to a much greater take-up of statutory support services subsequently, and to the establishment of a wider informal network of support. Once this was achieved, the befriender was able to begin to withdraw. In short, the most valuable resource of the volunteer is their non-professional role and status. As Eyken describes it, the volunteer role is 'being with', while professionals are more often 'doing to'. Befrienders can sometimes have much greater success in engaging those clients most in need of support.

Beyond the volunteer is the more fundamental and important support network: friends and family. The individuals for whom befriending services can prove valuable are those who have few 'natural' supportive ties, or relationships which are essentially destructive of self-confidence. Many other individuals at risk of mental health problems – in particular those conditions with a biological basis – will have close caring relationships with friends or family. People who have a history of a disorder such as schizophrenia or manic depression often have friends and relations who have tried over a long period to help the individual to recover and remain well. And with diagnoses such as these, of disorders which tend to follow a relapsing course, it has been found that close relationships can play a crucial role in preventing or at least postponing relapse. This evidence is summarised in Chapter 4. As families are often in everyday contact with the disturbed individual, they are clearly in a position to offer more intensive support than any professional, and with advice, education, training and support for themselves they can enhance the prospects that the individual will avoid a major relapse and help them to keep any residual symptoms to a minimum. Time spent in supporting relatives and friends as well as the distressed individual is time well spent. The more fully all parties are involved in the treatment process, the more effective it can be and the less burden ultimately on both psychiatric resources and the family. One of the crucial values of natural networks is that they will continue to be available after the professional support has ceased. They are in a position to ensure gains hold up and continue. This is a point well accepted now by those running pre-school compensatory education programmes. Any help for young children must also involve parents if long-term improvements to behaviour and educational attainment are to be achieved (Bronfenbrenner, 1975).

Finally, there are the so called 'front-line' caregivers (police, community nurses, social workers, teachers, probation officers, family doctors) who already serve as a first port of call for help for people with a range of psychosocial difficulties. It is not realistic to argue for a large increase in their number in order that more time could be devoted to preventive work. Yet with certain changes to their ways of working, they may be able to make a greater contribution to prevention. For example, they could consider and enlist other sources of support apart from their own for their clients, and ensure that their own efforts to be supportive serve to increase rather than decrease the independence and self-efficacy of those they seek to help. The more understanding they have themselves of mental health problems and of how to detect them among their own client or pupil population, and of what voluntary, educational or information resources exist in the local community, the greater prospect they have for offering support or mobilising assistance on their behalf.

In short, mounting preventive programmes entailing one-to-one support greatly increases the target group for mental health and social services support. These services are already stretched to deal with the problems of the population they currently serve. Professionals could not provide support of the order required without an unrealistic increase in their number. Their numbers could never rise sufficiently to service all need, even with the most committed political support and unlimited funds. Neither is it desirable that they should try to do so. Much of the support needed by people vulnerable to mental illness is best provided by 'natural' support networks, the community and lay volunteers. But ensuring that the maximum possible support from such sources is made available has profound implications for the way professionals run their services. They need to continue to devote most of their time to the people with the most marked (and visible) difficulties, for whom their professional skills are clearly required, but they need also to help a much larger group – who don't need their professional skills to the same degree, but nevertheless need help to find effective support. This may be through training volunteers, through setting up support groups which can become self-managed, through offering training and a back-up referral service to voluntary groups, through supporting and advising family carers, through making educational literature on coping with various problems available, through changing the way residential services are managed and so on. Some of these options and others are explored in the following chapters.

Disease models and transitionary periods

In essence, the review which follows is a kind of 'good food guide' for service planners and providers in the field of prevention. However, rather than describing a large number of exemplary programmes, a handful have been presented in some detail, selected as being illustrative of the criteria identified here as determining a 'good' service or project in terms of likely contribution to the prevention of psychiatric disorder. And the choice inevitably reflects a personal bias. I have endeavoured to justify choices on the basis of the three criteria described in the Introduction, and to use evaluation data on the actual service, or from similar projects, to comment on effectiveness. But as with the well-known guide to good restaurants, the experience of the guide when visiting provides a personal critique. It is hoped that such subjective insights will be found valuable by those needing to know more about such services, but without the time to review the field and visit other services themselves.

The evaluation of the projects described leaves much to be desired and, if rigorous criteria for effectiveness in preventing disorder were to be applied, probably all would fail the test. But evaluating services in terms of outcomes such as reductions in prevalence of psychiatric disorder is notoriously difficult, and has led to some disenchantment about how little seems to have been achieved. There are numerous methodological, practical and ethical problems. Take, for example, the time over which health status may need to be monitored. In the case of childhood programmes intended to reduce disadvantage or prevent disorder in adulthood, the evaluation of their success in this respect could take 20 years. Many other events and experiences which also contribute to adult disorder would occur during this interval and would need to be taken into account. Furthermore, keeping track of a sample and their experiences over a long period is difficult and costly. Not surprisingly, those evaluating such programmes usually choose other methods. They either take changes to intermediate factors as indicative of effectiveness (change to the childhood situation attributable to the programme, say), or choose to study those likely to develop disorder (without the service) in the near future (such as people with a history of schizophrenia).

It is also difficult, often, for researchers to find a valid comparison group who do not receive the intervention. People in the same locality with similar problems can rarely be offered the service on a random basis. Even if it is possible to justify withholding a service from a group with equivalent needs, and the service providers agree in principle to do so, several of the comparison group may find similar kinds of support elsewhere; service providers may feel unable to turn down some of the particularly needy cases; and many of those receiving the intervention may drop out. Not infrequently it proves impossible to find an acceptable 'control' group and comparisons between people known to be different in terms of potentially important variables must be made, and this difference controlled for by statistical means.

Research workers sometimes set up their own experimental projects and evaluate these, but even here there can be problems in the translation of a research project to a service: changes are likely to occur in its mode of delivery that will change its effectiveness.

The consideration of the evidence of benefit of the services described in this review must take account of the problems of evaluation. (The above are a few examples but a longer list could easily be made.) If a service copies one which has been proven effective experimentally, or if it is designed to change factors of known aetiological significance to disorder and can demonstrate change in those factors (or data is at least suggestive that it is being effective in these terms), then this is probably the best that can be hoped for. This has been the approach used here, in recognition of the fact that planners and practitioners want findings, want to consider the implication of findings for actions that need to be taken, and want to know what might be involved in taking those actions. It is of little help to them to read detailed comment about the methodological shortcomings, or that more research is needed before conclusions can be drawn when they have to act on the basis of what is currently known or on the best available judgement (Davis, 1987). This is not to suggest, of course, that there is a 'one-way traffic' between research and practice. As indicated earlier, the actual relationship is often an untidy and interesting one, whereby services influence research as much as research informs practice.

In making a judgement here about 'good' practice, two of the criteria used are straightforward. A 'good' programme will be one which helps people to help themselves – assisting them in taking control over their lives. It will do so in a way that makes the maximum use of existing natural, community or voluntary networks, involving professionals in different, often collaborative work practices rather than in a great deal of additional work. However, I have also argued in favour of targeting intervention toward high-risk groups and here is where there is more room for choice. Five 'high-risk' groups have been chosen on which the central five chapters are based. Informing this choice was a consideration for the *time* at which people are most open to influence or, at least, when intervention could potentially achieve most. That is, when the individual's decisions and coping styles may affect their lifestyle for many years to come. Such opportunities are evident when young people leave the family home to set up home lives on their own; when they begin to have children of their own; when facing a crisis or coping with long-term difficulties; when recovering from an acute but relapsing illness; or when becoming too frail to be able to cope alone with day-to-day self-care tasks. Decisions made at such times, and the way the transition is managed, may have effects lasting five, ten or 20 years or more.

Hence the target groups have been selected because of either past experiences or current circumstances which have been described in aetiological research as indicative of a high-risk status for psychiatric disorder; *and* because their current circumstances represent a transitionary period where one course of action rather than another may reduce that risk.

While it is inappropriate to reproduce the review of aetiological theory and research given in *Preventing mental illness* (Newton, 1988), at least some general statements and a 'thumbnail sketch' of the models favoured in that review are needed here in order to justify the choice of services described in the following chapters. For a better understanding of these theories, the research on which they are based, and their further refinement in recent years, the interested reader will need to consult the research papers cited.

In summary, the model developed by George Brown, Tirril Harris and their colleagues at Bedford College on the social origins of depression (latterly reviewed in Brown, 1989), and the research by several teams both here and in the USA on the role of the social environment in relapse rates in schizophrenia were deemed to provide the most promising indications for preventive work (Brown *et al.*, 1966; Falloon *et al.*, 1982; Leff and Vaughn, 1980; Hogarty *et al.*, 1986). In both areas the research is of excellent quality and much of the evidence has held up to replication attempts. In addition, the importance of life events in triggering or provoking a range of psychiatric disorder, and influencing course is also now well accepted and validated by numerous research studies (see Paykel, 1978; Dohrenwend and Dohrenwend, 1974; Brown and Harris, 1989).

SCHIZOPHRENIA

The focus in this review is on the prevention of both relapse and chronicity rather than the prevention of a first onset of schizophrenia; very little is known about the latter. It has now been reasonably well established that social factors like life events and living environment are associated with relapse rates (Leff and Vaughn, 1980; Brown and Birley, 1968; Warner, 1985), and as we know that relapse rates between individuals vary considerably, preventive efforts have focused on the possibility of reducing relapse

rates through social intervention programmes. Follow-up studies to ⌐
show that in this country slightly more than one in four people wl.
experience their first acute episode of schizophrenia appear to recovei
completely. Approximately the same proportion will have lifelong problems of social or intellectual impairment, with many prolonged hospital
stays during psychotic phases. The remainder will follow an intermediate
course with acute psychotic phases interspersed with periods of improvement or recovery. In under-developed countries the course of the disorder
tends to be more favourable, and this has been argued to be because of the
greater opportunities for reintegration and social role rehabilitation in the
non-industrialised world, where there is less stigma and probably more
optimism about the disorder (Warner, 1985). Factors which have been
demonstrated to be effective in reducing relapse rates are neuroleptic
'maintenance' medication (Leff and Wing, 1971; Davis *et al.*, 1980);
reducing the level of emotional tension in the home (or reducing time spent
in face-to-face contact with family members with whom interactions tend
to be high in 'expressed emotion') (Leff *et al.*, 1985); and preparing for
predictable life events (Wing *et al.*, 1964). (The term 'expressed emotion' is
a measure of critical comments, hostility and over-involvement.) The
research in this field is described in Chapter 4. The importance of setting
up a preventive programme as early as possible in the course of this
disorder is increased by the knowledge that in the early years the prognosis
looks worse with each relapse, and is worse the longer the delay before
treatment of the first onset commences. The time at which individuals are
recovering from a first or at least an early acute episode of schizophrenia is
therefore a transitionary period where intervention efforts have the greatest
potential for prevention.

CAUSES OF DEPRESSION: THE BEDFORD COLLEGE MODEL

Increasingly, in recent years, research is confirming the view that depression
is largely a psychosocial condition. Broad concepts like stress and social
support have dominated epidemiological research in this field (Dohrenwend
and Dohrenwend, 1974; Cohen and Syme (Eds), 1985; Gottlieb, 1983). But
the nature of their aetiological role is described most fully by the work of the
Bedford College team, whose model also draws on and synthesises important themes from psychoanalytic and psychological schools exemplified by
theorists such as John Bowlby, Aaron Beck, and Martin Seligman (Brown
and Harris, 1978; Brown, 1989). Their use of sophisticated standardised
assessments of depression, together with detailed but rigorous measure-
ments of the qualitive aspects of stressors and social support have considerably advanced our understanding of this disorder. Evidence to support this
model from other researchers has been accumulating (e.g. Murphy, 1982;
Costello, 1982; Finlay-Jones, 1981). And the importance attached to

external social factors in this model means that it is particularly helpful to a consideration of prevention.

At its simplest level, this model of depression states that adverse life events and long-term marked difficulties can bring about clinical depression in vulnerable women. (A similar model probably applies to men, but less research has been done with male samples.) These two groups of factors will be considered in the current review of intervention, namely 'provoking agents' (life events and difficulties) and 'vulnerability factors'.

Events and difficulties

The importance of events in provoking or triggering psychiatric disorder has long been widely accepted in psychiatry, as the use of terms such as 'reactive' and 'endogenous' indicates. And the research and theory on the nature of their role has a long history. In relation to depression, the core component of an event with the potential to cause the onset of depression in someone who would not otherwise have become depressed (or not for some years) is that it constitutes a marked or moderate long-term threat of loss, and is focused on the individual herself, or jointly with someone else (Brown and Harris, 1978). Events of extreme severity are unlikely to provoke depression if their effect is only short-term (a 10-year-old daughter going missing from school but found safely at the home of a friend later that night, say). However, to understand the extent of the sense of loss, or rejection, something about the individual's beliefs, commitments and any existing social difficulties must be known. Events which can provoke depression almost always threaten some central aspect of identity and self-worth. An apparently minor event may have extremely distressing connotations once the context is fully understood.

In general, for depression, context and meaning are the key elements to consider if making judgements about the likely impact an event may have on a particular individual. The Bedford College team have identified subgroupings of context to provide further insights into the aetiological role of events and difficulties. These groups are described as 'matching' events, in that they are particularly distressing because they threaten a role or an idea to which the person is strongly committed. Or they 'match' a longstanding difficulty, and perhaps therefore finally bring home to the person the hopelessness of the situation they are living with (see Brown et al., 1987). What is also important in this research is that it demonstrates that the same qualities of events which can provoke onset of depression can also cause a worsening in an existing depression, and that there is a reverse process. That is, positive events or, at least, events which hold the prospect of some kind of 'fresh start' can herald the beginning of recovery from an existing depression.

Social difficulties can play a similar role in depression, if those difficulties are marked and longstanding (usually at least two years). They can cause onset of depression in vulnerable women, and a reduction in difficulty can contribute to recovery from an existing depression (Brown and Harris, 1989).

Vulnerability

A vulnerability factor is one which shows little or no effect on its own in terms of causing onset of disorder, but increases risk in the presence of another factor. For depression, that other factor will be a severe event or marked difficulty. The issue of vulnerability is critical – most severe life events are coped with without any serious depressive reaction. Recent research has shown that women very rarely develop depression, however tragic the event, without such vulnerability (Brown *et al.*, 1990). The early model of depression described by Brown and Harris in 1978 showed that of most importance, in terms of vulnerability, was current support. Loss of mother in childhood, that is, past support, was the next most important indication of vulnerability. And although a great deal of research has followed this, and much more is known about both factors, these two remain of central importance. Past loss of mother has now been explained in terms of 'early inadequate parenting', and its role traced through structural environmental factors *and* personality factors, but the importance of parental support in childhood to adult vulnerability to depression is clear (Harris *et al.*, 1986).

Taking current support first, it appears that a close relationship, rather than a network of casual friendships, plays the most important role in protecting against depression for women, although the relative importance of these two kinds of support may be different for men. A close relationship is one with someone the woman sees regularly and in whom she can confide (most frequently a 'marital' partner). The presence of such a 'close other' must also translate into effective support in a crisis in order to be protective. In fact, where a close relationship exists but the woman feels that the support she was expecting has not been forthcoming, that is, she has been 'let down' in terms of receiving support from her partner during a crisis, she will be particularly vulnerable to depression. Where there is no partner, or where the partner is not expected to be supportive during a crisis, the support of another person (usually a woman) who is a close friend or relative can serve a similar preventive role (see Brown, 1989).

While the absence of a supportive relationship may contribute to vulnerability, it seems that the *presence* of an *unsupportive* relationship may play a similar role. Women with a marital relationship characterised by negative interaction (discord, tension, coldness and indifference) were found to be three times more likely to become depressed after a severe event than married women with a better relationship (Brown *et al.*, 1986b).

These findings enable judgements about vulnerability to be made. It does not follow, however, that crisis support mobilised by volunteers, neighbours or professionals will be preventive for those identified as particularly vulnerable. The relationships described as protective were all of long standing. However, women without a close, confiding relationship with a partner were helped by other people named as close. To the extent to which outside efforts to provide support can approximate or become like 'true' friendships it is reasonable to assume that they may well become protective in the face of future crises, if not during the crisis which precipitated the offer of support. Or if the support helps the woman to strengthen an existing, potentially supportive relationship; to establish new close relationships; to change the nature of a relationship characterised by negative interaction; or to break loose from a damaging relationship, it may well play a preventive role, particularly when faced with future life events. And the finding that it was the quantifiable support given by a close other during a crisis – rather than the attachment felt in that relationship – which was crucial means that it cannot be ruled out that the provision of practical and emotional support, even by less close relationships, may have a preventive effect for those lacking more important sources of support.

Furthermore, given the positive effects of difficulty reduction in facilitating recovery, a new source of support with the potential to assist in reducing a longstanding marked difficulty could reasonably be expected to play a role in preventing an existing depression from becoming a chronic condition. Similarly, a new source of support may sometimes bring new hope and the possibility of a fresh start for the woman with an existing depression, and assist recovery.

The quality of current social support may be the single most important factor in determining vulnerability or resilience to depression when facing severe events or coping with longstanding difficulties. But we also know that the quality of support people receive in childhood is an earlier vulnerability factor with considerable importance. If for a period of a year or more the quality of parental care was markedly poor, in terms of neglect, lack of interest and attention, coupled with a lack of control; or if there was a period of sexual abuse; or a marked and persisting antipathy between parent and child, then this 'early inadequate parenting' is also capable of producing a vulnerability to depression in adulthood (see Brown, 1989). It may do so either through a 'personality' pathway or a 'structural' one (or both). That is, the early experiences may lead to a sense of helplessness in childhood and mean that subsequent events or difficulties are not coped with well, and helplessness and low self-esteem become established 'cognitive sets'. The 'structural' pathway links the early experience to an increased risk of institutional care or other alternative care-arrangements, and an increased risk of early marriage or pre-marital pregnancy. This in turn tends to limit the young woman's capacity to further her education or work prospects, meaning continued low socio-economic status is more likely, as is a lifestyle characterised by a high rate of provoking agents. If it were possible somehow to transform the lives of children by miraculously eradicating all kinds of inadequate parenting, research indicates that cases of depression among adult women would be reduced by at least one-third (Brown, 1990).

THE SIGNIFICANCE OF THE RESEARCH

At this point a caveat is warranted. Many of the detailed explanations put forward by these research workers are based on evidence that is still quite tentative, and much needs replicating. The Bedford College model of depression is most applicable to women in the general population. It takes no account of the issue of co-morbidity (people often suffer from a combination of disorders – alcoholism, anxiety, drug dependence, depression), nor of the undoubted efficacy of drug treatment in some instances. It is still considered quite a controversial model of depression by some psychiatrists. The same can be said of the research in schizo-phrenia. However, my own assessment is that the psychosocial data relating to depression and to schizophrenia has sufficient support from research, and sufficient sympathy from clinicians, to justify its use as a means to think about prevention, and to plan experimental studies. The models of depression and of schizophrenia need not be accepted as comprehensive accounts of onset or course in order to be used as a framework for planning various types of intervention. Typically these interventions will, in any case, also be thought to be desirable on more general grounds. But evaluative research on these approaches is needed. The time for such research in the area of schizophrenia was clearly reached nearly 20 years ago, and is probably just being reached where depression is concerned.

But with human problems of the complexity dealt with in aetiological theories of mental illness, evaluation is a difficult business. It is probably wise to move away from the idea of some critical experiment that will settle major issues. Evaluation might more probably focus (as a minimum) on certain general principles of the kind suggested here, such as success in engaging a 'high-risk' group, facilitating individual control as far as possible and providing support in a cost-effective way. At best, where specific principles are applied, more specific outcomes can hope to be measured (improved self-esteem, or reduced emotional tension or 'expressed emotion' in key relationships). Evidence at this level is quite rare, and this is true in the projects reviewed here.

No claim can be made, therefore, that this review is in any sense a definitive evaluation of good practice. It needs to be considered more modestly as a *Good Food Guide* – a highly personal account of apparently innovative and promising services.

OPPORTUNITIES FOR PREVENTION

In using these models of depression and schizophrenia to choose a high-risk group at a point in their lives when support might help them, to some extent, to take a more protected course, there are a number of possibilities. If these are considered chronologically – in the aetiology of depression, one of the earliest social factors we have some information about is quality of parenting. Is it possible to predict which parents will have major parent–child difficulties? Or can a lack of care or inadequate parenting be spotted at an early stage? What kind of help would change the parenting experience for the better? These are the sorts of questions considered in Chapter 1.

But the role of childhood 'lack of care' in adult depression (among women) tends to be mediated by experiences in adolescence and early adulthood, particularly in relationships with men. Early marriage or a pre-marital pregnancy, particularly when decisions about this were made for negative rather than positive reasons, was found to be a common linking factor. Pregnant young women who arranged for a termination or for the baby to be adopted, or had settled with the child's father for positive reasons in addition to bearing his child, were less likely to be found to be depressed, in this research, than those living as single parents or who married 'for the sake of the baby' (Brown *et al.*, 1986a). It was argued that 'helplessness' played a role in determining such coping styles, causing women to be 'trapped' by their circumstances rather than finding a way to step off this 'conveyor belt' of adversity leading to an unsatisfactory relationship; few material resources for starting out in parenthood; often a difficult living situation, with a high rate of stressful events. When young people are known to have had a period of poor parenting, such as those who have spent some of their childhood in institutional care or have had several changes of main caretaker, then support could potentially play a preventive role when they reach the age at which they will be wanting, or sometimes be compelled, to find independent accommodation and to become self-supporting. If they can be helped to find secure homes, to avoid the need to return to live with discordant families whence their problems stemmed, to establish a stable and adequate income, and to avoid unwanted pregnancies, their lives will be much less stressful than otherwise they might be. For this group, who will often have the negative psychological and negative social factors argued to make them particularly vulnerable in terms of the Bedford College model of depression, it should mean that they experience fewer 'provoking agents', and that they have more resources to help them cope with the difficulties that do arise. Managing this important transition well may help them to see themselves as in control of their own lives and make a long-term difference to their risk status. This is the theme of Chapter 2.

Help for young people leaving care in their efforts to establish secure and supported living circumstances of their own should in itself reduce the numbers of unplanned pregnancies. Quinton and colleagues (1984) followed up 80 girls raised in institutions, and found that where they lived after leaving made a substantial difference to pregnancy rates. Ninety-three per cent of those returning to live with discordant families had a child by the time they were interviewed (aged between 21 and 27 years) and many of these were born well before their twentieth birthday. This compared with 51 per cent of those who had been able to stay on in the institution, and 30 per cent of those who had left to live with harmonious families. It was suggested by these authors that the high birthrate for young women in discordant family situations was to a large extent explainable in terms of their need to escape intolerable home lives. Childbearing was seen as a means of escape.

For those young women who do have an early unplanned pregnancy from a relationship with a partner with whom they would not otherwise have chosen to settle, or from a relationship with no prospect of continuing, other sources of support will be particularly important. With a background of poor parenting, they may have few family supports to fall back on. If they do not already have a home of their own they will need considerable practical assistance with accommodation, and support to help them cope with early motherhood. Without reliable support or a memory of good mothering on which to model their own parenting, they remain at high risk of depression and of recreating some of the problems of their own childhoods. These issues are also explored in Chapter 2.

In adulthood most instances of depression, as well as a good deal of other psychiatric illness, follow a period of severe difficulty or a distressing event. Some people, by virtue of their current circumstances or life stage, will be likely to experience a high rate of such events or difficulties, or to experience one event in particular that they will find difficult to cope with. As such, they could be described as being in an 'event-producing situation' (see Newton, 1988). Old age is one such example, often associated with losses to physical health and death of friends and relations. And with increasing frailty may come a loss of independence and opportunity to control one's own life. Many examples of people in 'event-producing situations' can be imagined. A couple with a strong desire to have children, but where the woman has had three consecutive miscarriages, are in an event-producing situation as they try to conceive again. A carer of a close relative suffering a relapsing or terminal illness is likewise in an event-producing situation. These sorts of circumstances could be described as opportunities for anticipatory coping where support may have a preventive effect, particularly if it is clear that there is not an existing 'close other' providing support. For frail elderly people whose natural networks are likely to be diminishing, but whose chronic handicaps or poor physical health have come to mean that they must become dependent upon others to fulfil many of their most basic daily needs, support will obviously be needed. The way in which this support is provided can either increase or minimise their sense of dependency and of being beholden to others. The ideal support will help them to find a lifestyle in which they retain their self-esteem and feel, as far as possible, in control and able to cope. Such approaches are the subject of Chapter 5.

But probably the majority of events which precede psychiatric disorder are not predictable. Support at the time of the crisis may be available from their family or friends. Often, the family doctor is also consulted at an early stage while the individual feels unable to cope with their problems (although they will often consult for physical symptoms allied to this). Of course, at this point support might be considered to be treatment rather than prevention, as disorder in vulnerable people usually follows quite soon after an event. However, crisis support which addresses the origins of the difficulty is generally agreed to be an effective way of assisting people to make changes that will have long-term consequences for recovery, self-esteem, and the occurrence of and management of future crises. General practitioners will also be seeing patients in 'event-producing' situations – the woman with a history of miscarriage who may be seeking the doctor's help to avoid miscarrying again; the carer of a terminally ill relative. These contacts are ideal opportunities for mobilising preventive support. Of course it requires perceptiveness accurately to get to the root of problems presented (particularly when, as is often the case, physical symptoms are described and no reference made to underlying social or emotional difficulties), and to recognise those individuals most vulnerable to depression or other mental illness. The doctor's effectiveness in preventing disorder will depend too on their understanding of the kinds of help which would be most beneficial, and their knowledge of existing sources of help and of whether the mechanisms or resources to mobilise appropriate help are available. These issues are the focus of Chapter 3.

Finally, for schizophrenia, in the absence of more information on aetiology, the only means we have to predict vulnerability is the presence of prodromal signs and symptoms, or the experience of a first episode. Knowledge of social factors influencing susceptibility to a recurrence or a worsening of this disorder means that psychiatric services can plan their rehabilitation programmes and follow-up support to reduce this susceptibility as far as possible. Maintenance medication can reduce relapse rates by over a half (Davis et al., 1980). If, in addition, the individual lives with families rated as low rather than high in terms of 'expressed emotion', then relapse rates are 75 per cent less over a nine-month follow-up period (Vaughn and Leff, 1976). Families can be helped to create the most supportive environment to help their relative recover. Both the individual and his or her family will be better equipped to manage the disorder and prevent a recurrence or a worsening the more they know about it. These issues are the subject of Chapter 4.

A NOTE ABOUT PREVENTION

The concept of prevention used here is defined as action

> intended to reduce the incidence of mental illness amongst people who are relatively free of distressing psychiatric symptoms or who are suffering from symptoms not extensive and severe enough to be defined as cases. They may never before have experienced mental illness or they may have largely recovered from previous illnesses.

> (Newton, 1988)

'Caseness' is usually used to indicate a level of symptomatology measurable on research schedules above a certain threshold – a level which approximates at least to that of most patients seen by psychiatrists in out-patient settings.

This definition corresponds more closely to the lay understanding of the term than the widely used tripartite definition of Caplan (1964), of primary, secondary and tertiary prevention (with which a number of problems can be found (Newton and Craig, 1991). One of the implications of the above definition, with a high threshold for 'caseness', is that intervention with people who have a small number of symptoms will be considered prevention, rather than treatment. It also avoids medicalising the lower end of the spectrum of symptomatology and labelling as disorder what are essentially 'normal' responses to stress. It is natural to feel a certain amount of depression after an adverse life event, or when coping with chronically difficult social circumstances. It is only when the symptoms become more severe or protracted than 'normal' that the depression might be described as disorder. Furthermore, if, as I have suggested above, preventive work is targeted toward those most vulnerable to disorder, then it must be expected that many of the target group will have some symptoms already. This is the logical consequence of using a disease model, if the risk indicators are meaningful. Clearly it would be foolish then to define prevention as work with people who are entirely free from symptomatology. It would rule out work with those most likely to benefit.

Chapter 1

Preventive work with under-fives and their families

Careful research on the origins of mental illnesses like depression has confirmed the long-held views of child psychologists and the common sense lay beliefs that early childhood experiences play a considerable role in creating vulnerability or resilience to later emotional disturbances and psychiatric disorder, particularly depression (Robins, 1966; Harris *et al.*, 1986; Bowlby, 1969, 1973, 1980). Qualities of parenting experiences which appear to be important in the aetiology of depression relate primarily to the warmth of the relationship and the level of control. A low level of control, combined with marked or moderate indifference (neglect, lack of interest and attention) on the part of carers – together termed 'lack of care' – was associated with at least a threefold increase in the risk of depression in adulthood in an in-depth study of these links by the Bedford College team (Brown *et al.*, 1986a). There is also some indication that both sexual abuse in childhood and lasting antipathy from the mother contribute to vulnerability (e.g. Brown, 1989).

These findings about quality of parenting have helped to resolve the confusion arising from research studies on the role of loss of mother (on later depression) which have sometimes produced apparently conflicting findings. The issue appears to be similar to the case argued by Michael Rutter on the role of maternal deprivation. His research review showed that adverse effects of separation from mother on childhood adjustment were caused not so much by the separation itself, as by the quality of the substitute care-arrangements (Rutter, 1981). So in depression, loss of mother in childhood is not in itself a cause of vulnerability. It is only where a loss (by separation or death) is followed by a markedly poor quality of parental support in the substitute arrangements that it has such effects. This finding also means, of course, that 'lack of care' is a 'vulnerability' factor in depression among girls who have *not* lost a parent. In fact, most instances of lack of care will be in intact families where it is associated perhaps with a good deal of marital discord, with parental mental illness or with other marked social difficulties rather than parental loss. It is also possible that it may arise in an intact family home where there are no social difficulties and no lack of material resources, where an extreme of a *laissez-faire* parenting style is followed. But such instances, where the child has no sense of being loved and cared for, are likely to be exceptional.

Of course, extremely poor parenting, particularly when it is also associated with physical or sexual abuse, has long been the subject of considerable attention by primary health care and social services, and in recent years media attention has heightened public awareness of the problems faced. The prevalence of abuse and neglect is now generally understood to be considerable. Mitchell estimated that in 1975 six per 1,000 children were abused before their third birthday. A high proportion of these were taken into care. Ounsted and his colleagues (1982) point out that this is four times as high as the rate of Down's Syndrome (1.6 per 1,000 liveborn children). They argue that reducing bonding-failure between parent and child should be considered the fourth goal of perinatal medicine, the first three being the reduction of maternal mortality, infant mortality and infant morbidity.

However, reducing child neglect and abuse is an important role for a number of professionals other than paediatricians. If it is possible to predict which pregnant women or which newly delivered mothers are likely to have poor mother–child bonding then midwives as well as health visitors may have a preventive role. Once home with the first child and later children, health visitors, social workers and GPs may be able to pick up parenting problems at an early stage. The first issue, then, is how best can parenting problems be predicted or detected at an early stage. The second issue is whether or not, and what kind of, support can change the situation for the better and achieve lasting improvements. Descriptive details of two promising support services are given in this chapter, one a voluntary, one a statutory response. Many other interesting initiatives are mentioned. However, it is necessary to start with the issue of identification.

PREDICTION AND EARLY IDENTIFICATION OF PARENTING DIFFICULTIES, ABUSE AND NEGLECT

Some straightforward methods of predicting abuse have proved surprisingly effective. Ounsted and his colleagues (1982) report the results of a collaborative service set up in Oxford in 1978 between the maternity hospital social work department and the medical staff from the Park Hospital for Children. All midwives were simply encouraged to refer any 'patient who caused them concern, in particular in their interactions with their babies'. They were urged not to 'refrain from bringing up minor worries, however undefined'. The entire population of the maternity hospital was screened, and twice-weekly lunchtime meetings held between the consultant or his deputy, the senior social worker, and midwives. All worries were then freely and frankly discussed. In the first year, 5,356 mothers with liveborn infants were screened, of whom 109 were referred. This is a rate of 2 per cent, with ten the median number of referrals per month.

The reason for referral in every case was concern that the parent might not be able to cope with the new baby. There may have been several causes for concern, but usually one predominated. In 27 per cent the main worry was inability or unwillingness to care for the baby, where indifference, rejection or anger was evident; or where the mother was unable to adapt to having a sick or handicapped baby. Next most common (17 per cent) were diffuse social problems (poor housing, low income, combined with marital problems or chronic ill-health); a further 15 per cent of the women were referred because of their psychiatric history and concern that ill-health might recur. Another 14 per cent of the mothers were referred because of their strange or disturbed behaviour during their admission, and the midwife's observation that they were not responding appropriately to their babies; and 8 per cent because of recorded evidence of abuse of or bonding-failure to older children. The remainder were referred mainly because of ill-health, physical or mental handicap in the mother, or miscellaneous other concerns.

For 60 per cent of referrals, the only action taken by the service was to ensure that the family doctor and health visitor were fully informed of the midwife's worries, and alerted that considerable support on their part might be needed when the mother and child returned home. A telephone number at the hospital and assurance that help would be provided, should a crisis arise, was also given. Health visitors reported finding this alerting extremely helpful. (Although midwives usually do record their worries in writing, often such information is not relayed to other carers.)

One-third of the 109 women were seen by the consultant for a supportive and sympathetic discussion which it was hoped would help to boost the mother's confidence, but which would also offer a lifeline for future help if needed. Fourteen per cent were offered more extensive help, sometimes from a residential family unit.

At the follow-up one year later, concern was still felt about a quarter of the families. But weight gain, ill-health and home circumstances did not show unduly raised problems for the high-risk children compared to an unselected sample from the same hospital. An examination of referrals to social services or children's wards within the year, however, showed that seven of the 5,356 children screened, but not referred, by the service were later referred for neglect or abuse. One of the seven was seriously abused. A re-examination of the records of these seven showed that there had been worries about five of the mothers during their hospital stay, but these concerns had not been referred to the group, and there was therefore room for some improvement in the procedures.

Nevertheless, cases of serious abuse would appear to have been reduced by the service. Among babies born in the 18 months before the service began, six were referred for serious abuse (fractured skulls, limbs or shaken unconscious). During the first 18 months of the service, only one case of such serious abuse was referred (from over 7,000 births). The total numbers of referrals were similar, but most of those screened by the collaborative service were for minor injuries ('open warnings'), and probably represented an increased awareness of problems by GPs, and willingness to refer lesser problems to a service that had become well known to them. Ounsted concludes that as minor injuries and failure to thrive are known to precede abuse, the few cases missed by the maternity service are now likely to be picked up before serious abuse occurs, because of the increased awareness generated by the service. And most of the work done after referral at birth entailed making quite sure family doctors and their teams had been fully informed about what had come to light in the maternity hospital. The service cost the hospital no extra money (although there were small additional costs to primary care workers and family social workers), and while it may play only a small role in reducing bonding-failure it has clearly ensured that more care went to those who needed it.

This service shows that mothers likely to have parenting problems can often be identified by midwives in the few days after delivery. In fact, Ounsted reports that they have since extended the screening to pregnant women.

The quality of parenting, both of the new baby and older children, is also likely to be affected by postnatal depression. Postnatal depression can, to some extent, be predicted during pregnancy, and preparatory information and social support can then be set up as part of a preventive service (see, for example, Elliot *et al.*, 1988). Leverton and Elliot (1988) used a questionnaire with pregnant women attending for antenatal appointments to identify women considered vulnerable to postnatal depression by virtue of a less than satisfactory 'marital' relationship, or previous psychological problems, or a high score on a measure of anxiety. Twenty (40 per cent) of 50 women identified as 'more vulnerable' to postnatal depression were found to suffer from depression of caseness or borderline severity at some time in the first three months after childbirth, compared to 14 (16 per cent) of 90 women in the group considered to be less vulnerable, showing the questionnaire to have a reasonably good predictive validity. A third group, considered more vulnerable to postnatal depression, were offered monthly group meetings in groups of ten to 15 (led by the researcher or a health visitor) during pregnancy and the first few months after the birth. The group provided information, advice and support for the transition. Only 19 per cent of those 48 women had a depressive episode of borderline or caseness severity in the three months post-partum, suggesting that the service may have been responsible for halving the rate of depression during this period.

Health visitors are, of course, trained specifically in the promotion of health and prevention of ill-health in the community, and most of their work focuses on children under 5. They are registered nurses and usually qualified midwives who have completed a further course of training in health visiting, and should be expected to be able to spot emerging parenting difficulties at an early stage. Naturally, some will be better able to do so than others, but if health visitors are instructed to look for closely specified kinds of problems, there is evidence that they can reliably identify them. The Newpin befriending project, for instance, which is described later in this chapter, receives many of its referrals from health visitors. And a pilot evaluation of the scheme which described the life histories and current circumstances of the women involved showed that they were all character-ised by the experiences which research shows to be linked with vulnerability (Pound and Mills, 1985). For instance, ten of 11 referrals interviewed had been separated from one or both parents in childhood; eight had three or more changes of main caretaker in the early years; nine had been deserted by husbands or cohabitees during pregnancy or shortly after; and finance and housing problems were almost universal. Health visitors had simply been asked to refer to the project women with young children who seemed isolated and without good support at home, who were showing signs of depression, and whose problems had led to a poor parent–child relation-ship.

Further evidence that risk is predictable comes from a longitudinal study by Barnard and her colleagues (Barnard et al., 1985) in Seattle. They followed up 200 families, who were assessed during the mother's pregnancy, shortly after the birth, during the first year of the child's life, and at 2, 4 and 8 years. They showed that 'life change' (an assessment of recent events) during the two years before the birth, and other information collected at the time of the birth, were better predictors of later child outcomes than were measures of life change that the family experienced during the child's early years. They argue that low birth weight, low social status and/or high life change are 'all factors that warrant further monitoring in health-care systems', and indicate a potential need for support for the family.

These projects together suggest that it can be a relatively straightforward process to predict future difficulties and identify existing parenting pro-blems. Midwives and health visitors who are given the back-up of an efficient support service and specific guidelines about the problems it is designed to help can readily identify appropriate referrals. There is no evidence that a service which provides such specific criteria will be swamped with referrals, given that the midwives involved in the collaborative screening service in Oxford refer only 2 per cent of women screened (see above, p. 27).

If identification is possible, then what is the best kind of help to offer, and what is the evidence that it will be preventive?

OPTIMUM SUPPORT

Childhood quality of care is fundamentally about parent–child relationships in the home. But any one relationship within the family will be influenced by each of the others, particularly by the quality of the relationship between the parents (if a partner is present, of course), and between the partner and the children. Many other factors will influence individual family relationships – the personality of each family member, the amount of practical support available to the parents, the existence of any health problems, financial or housing difficulties, and so on. Hinde and Stevenson–Hinde (1988) give a taste of the complex ways in which relationships affect relationships within the family, and the consequences for the children. Given this complexity, most intervention strategies, and much of the discussion here, can be seen as a gross simplification of important issues, attending to only one part of the picture. However, changes which improve the parent–child relationship should also have effects on the mother's self-esteem, and possibly also on her other relationships. Similarly, intervention which attends first of all to the mother's self-esteem should also have effects on her close relationships, including those with her children. It would not be unreasonable to conclude, however, that one strategy alone may be insufficient to bring marked changes to all parts of the picture, and a combination of the approaches described in following sections may be preferable.

One particularly important approach involves a primary focus on the parent–child relationship itself, rather than the mental health or coping ability of either parent or child individually. Of course, a woman will be able to be more supportive of her children when not depressed, and the temperamentally easy child will be less likely to be scapegoated by a depressed and irritable parent (Rutter, 1966). But help for either partner should also consider their needs in relation to the other. Bronfenbrenner found this to be true even for seemingly straightforward educational programmes. He concluded from his evaluation of compensatory educational pre-school programmes for disadvantaged American children that the tutor must not only base the programme in the home, and tailor it to the circumstances found, but must also enlist the mother as primary educator. Supporting the parent in implementing an educational programme produced gains in child achievement levels which not only continued after the end of the programme, but also extended to younger siblings. By contrast, those pre-school programmes which were based outside the home, or which did not involve the mother as educator, had effects on the child which lasted only as long as the programme (Bronfenbrenner, 1975).

Bronfenbrenner argued that home-based and mother-mediated programmes had long-term benefits because the short-term gains in behaviour and attainment by the child were seen by the parent as a result of her own action, rather than that of the teacher. This in turn gave her a more positive view of her own capability for surmounting her other difficulties. Thus helping a parent to teach her child has beneficial effects for her view of the child and of herself. The rewards of bringing desired changes in her child will make her wish to continue such actions and therefore to show more interest in her child's development. And the extra responsiveness and interest from the mother will bring the child closer to the mother, and increase his motivation to attend to and learn from her. These sorts of changes are mutually reinforcing and therefore tend to last.

Further evidence that support for parents is most effective in improving the parent–child relationship when it is home-based comes from Olds and his colleagues, (1986a; b). Their randomised trial compared outcomes for four groups of women: 90 who had no extra services through the research project; 94 who were provided only with free transport to existing prenatal or well-child clinics; 100 who received an average of nine prenatal home visits (of one-and-a-quarter hours) from a nurse; and 116 for whom the nurse visited the home for a further two years. This last group were visited once a week for the first month after delivery, and thereafter at a diminishing frequency finishing at six-weekly intervals. The study was carried out in a semi-rural county in the Appalachian region of New York State well served by services, but with a community with some of the poorest economic conditions in the United States. The area had the highest rates of reported and confirmed cases of child abuse and neglect in the state, and high rates of infant mortality. The antenatal programme was intended to enhance the social support and health habits of the mother, and the length of gestation and birth weight of the child; the postnatal programme to prevent child abuse and neglect. Most (over 80 per cent) of the time during home visits was spent on education about foetal and infant development and health issues. The remaining time was spent discussing with the woman and her close friends and relatives (asked to participate in home visits) how they could help and what health and community services existed locally. A central aspect of the nurses' approach was to emphasise the *strengths* of the women and their families.

All the women were having their first child, and were either 18 years or less, single parents or of low socio-economic status. The careful analyses showed that antenatal home visits improved the women's use of community services, their informal social support, and their health habits. In particular, the women visited at home by nurses, compared with women randomly assigned to comparison groups, became aware of more community services, attended childbirth classes more frequently, made greater dietary improvements, reported more interest in the pregnancy by the father, were accompanied by a support person during labour more frequently, and had fewer kidney infections. Smokers, and women under 17 visited by nurses also had babies of greater birth weight and length of gestation than their counterparts in comparison groups (Olds *et al.*, 1986b).

The continued home visiting by nurses over the next two years revealed further impressive benefits. The poor, unmarried teenage mothers were expected to be at greatest risk of abusing or neglecting their children, and 19 per cent of such comparison group women, against 4 per cent of nurse-visited women, had done so at some time during the child's first two years of life. Observational data also showed a greater tendency of the former group to punish and restrict their children, while the latter provided a greater array of play materials. Further corroborative evidence came from social service records and emergency room records. Furthermore, the children of these highest-risk families visited by nurses made a greater gain in intellectual functioning during the intervention, of a magnitude comparable with those brought about by intensive early childhood educational programmes (Olds et al., 1986a). In follow-up data obtained after these reports, but contained in their research proposal for a replication, Olds also shows that this highest-risk subgroup (poor unmarried teenagers) had 75 per cent fewer subsequent pregnancies if they were in the nurse-visited group compared to their counterparts in the comparison group. They also returned to school more frequently. Post-teenage women in the nurse-visited group were also more likely to obtain jobs, to share the care of their baby with other family members and friends, and to be less dependent on welfare.

Although Britain has an impressive health visiting service already in existence, that provided by Olds and his colleagues involved considerably more intensive and frequent visiting than is routine in England. It was also a structured educational programme and concentrated on establishing rapport, identifying and reinforcing family strengths, and fostering both formal and informal community supports.

Other researchers have produced findings which are consistent with the conclusions of Olds' team about how support should be structured. Barnard and her colleagues (1987) compared two models of family support and found that the one which focused more on relationship building, increasing social networks, and where the health nurse treated the mother as the educator of her child was more effective. A didactic approach in which the nurse concentrated on giving information (on physical health and sources of service and so on) was less successful. They conclude that it is not enough to involve mothers in programmes aiming to improve the child's functioning if the mother's role is a passive one. Rather, the role of the parent must be emphasised as the primary influence, and the intervention must explicitly acknowledge her power in the relationship. Their experiences in evaluating such programmes also led them to conclude that help is often resisted initially, and support therefore needs to begin during pregnancy when it is possible to concentrate on building up a working relationship.

One reason why home-based services will be more effective than clinic-based services is of course that there will be many families who will not attend a clinic. Sheila Shinman's book *A chance for every child?* (1981)

confirms the now-widely-held view that the take-up of professional support services reflects a good level of self-esteem and coping skill. Her book describes research which shows that the reasons some families with young children do not make use of resources or services is often not so much to do with how far away they are, the cost of the bus fare, or the unfriendly, bossy or authoritarian personnel. Rather it is related more to characteristics of the families themselves. They are often highly alienated people: lonely, depressed or deeply suspicious, sometimes fearful of both services and service providers. They found that many families not using the professional services had difficulties in their relationships with their families, both at home and with other relatives and friends. Often, they also lacked a 'sense of control', instead seeing themselves as victims of a manipulative world in which their own actions make little difference to their fate. Eyken (1982) argues that what these families need, above all, is friendship, and through this friendship, an opportunity to extend their social contacts, before statutory services can hope to engage them. A lay person in their own community offering support through a voluntary befriending scheme will often have the time and credibility to become accepted by families who are distrustful of offers of help from professionals. A period of befriending, however, can help bring them to a point where they want, and are able, to take up statutory services (Eyken, 1982).

The evidence therefore suggests that optimal support will target the mother–child relationship; will be at least partly home-based; will start with a period of befriending or relationship building before any structured training or other intervention; and specific work with the child will be made the responsibility of the parent. In order to ensure that changes in child achievement or behaviour are automatically taken by the parent to be due to her own actions, the support must come from a professional or para-professional who relates to the woman on equal terms, or at least emphasises that it is the parent's influence which is paramount, or from a person from the same community who is seen by the woman to be an equal. Traditional helper–client roles must be avoided. To further enhance parental self-esteem, the support person must emphasise family strengths rather than focus on their negative attributes.

A BRIEF OUTLINE OF SOME INNOVATIVE PROJECTS AND SERVICES

Several programmes in Britain have set up experimental services with some of these qualities. For instance, Spencer and her colleagues (1986) have offered support for women during pregnancy modelled on the French *travailleuses familiales*, or family workers. They aim to provide social, practical and psychological support to women at increased risk of giving birth to a low birth weight infant. Risk was assessed from low social class, age under 20 years, single parent status and/or previous perinatal deaths, abortions, or low birth weight infants. Family workers were usually women who had already had a family and came from a broadly similar background to clients. They were not professionals, but were lay women retraining for paid employment and funded to take part in the family worker scheme through the government training board, the Manpower Services Commission. They were given a two-week induction course to the family support scheme, and they then offered 'common sense' advice and support to clients. This often began with helping to sort out financial benefit entitlements, housing problems and preparing the home for the baby. It might also have included practical help with older children, or with housework; trips together to the shops, to antenatal appointments; or discussions about diet, contraception or family problems. Some women simply wanted companionship. A key feature of the scheme, as perceived by clients as well as providers, was that family workers were seen as being 'at the same level' as clients, and empathised easily without interfering unduly or creating dependency. Family workers generally visited clients once or twice a week until about six weeks after the birth.

However, a very large proportion of pregnant women (nearly one in four in South Manchester) fall into this risk group, making even low-paid supporters an expensive service, and both the implementation and evaluation suffered due to financial difficulties.

An even cheaper alternative, befriending by volunteers, is a model which is spreading. Eyken (1982) describes and evaluates the befriending service Homestart, which now has numerous offshoots around the country. Although this service supports women who already have one or more children and have experienced difficulties, it can often involve giving support during second and subsequent pregnancies. Volunteers and clients are matched as far as possible by the co-ordinator as likely to get on well. Volunteers are women who live nearby, have children of their own, but are currently able to take on a befriending role toward another family.

A less formalised system of befriending could be organised quite easily by health visitors. They get to know client women well and are in an ideal position to foster friendships between women they feel would get on well together. A lonely, depressed mother could be introduced to a nearby woman with a child of the same age, perhaps by asking each if they are willing to give their telephone number to the other, or be contacted by her. A friend with whom to share trips to the park, shops and mother and toddler groups, and with whom to exchange information and anxieties would have obvious benefits to both parties, and would at the same time increase the social network of the isolated woman.

Other kinds of non-professional mutual aid have been established, but the emphasis in many is on help for the mother herself and on improving her living circumstances and social network, without any attention to parent-child relationships. The Scope project in Southampton, for instance, consists of group meetings where women discuss problems of mutual interest. They aim to reduce loneliness, increase parents' confidence, encourage the use of services and help to expand social networks. Homelink in Liverpool and the Tiverton Family Centre in North London focus more on community action to help disadvantaged families come together to work toward improving living conditions in their own neighbourhood or estate. There is tentative evidence that such groups do help to improve the mental health of the women involved. Preliminary results from an evaluation of Scope mother and toddler groups showed a greater decrease in scores of depression and an increase in self-esteem among 18 Scope users compared to 11 controls (Ingham, 1984).

Many health visitors have been active in getting various kinds of groups established, from mother and toddler groups in church halls and at local further education colleges, to small groups following Open University courses (on 'the first years of life') in family homes (see Palfreeman, 1982). There have also been innovative service developments where parents are actively involved in their management and administration. Pen Green Family Centre in Corby is run by parents, paid family workers and professionals. They aim to help local families with the most marked parenting difficulties, but successfully avoid any sense of stigma by also making the centre a community centre and offering a proportion of the nursery places to any local mothers wanting them (see Pugh, 1987). Families using the centre can simply 'drop in' to the family room and make use of the toy library, the bookshop, the book library and the coffee bar. Or they can stay for the relaxation and fitness class and discussion group, while fourth formers from the local school look after their children in the crèche. Other groups run at the centre include an Open University child care course, a 'Baby' group, and several closed groups focusing on issues such as child abuse, depression, family relationships or fatherless children. Parents can become involved in running the bookshop, library or crèche, or they may train as Family Friends to offer befriending to women referred to the centre but who are either unwilling or unable to attend.

The Pen Green centre has achieved a reputation for excellence, but although it has successfully involved parents to a considerable extent in its running, it is not a low-cost service. Probably because of its good reputation it has succeeded in attracting generous funding, receiving support from the education authority, social services, the health authority, Manpower Services Commission, Urban Aid and the Volunteer Programme. It employs 11 full-time and nine part-time staff, including seven family workers, two teachers, three nursery nurses, a social worker and a director.

Another way in which professional services could increase their preventive work would be for either midwives or health visitors to establish the pregnancy support groups described by Elliot and her colleagues (1988).

This experimental service was designed in such a way as to be a feasible component of routine statutory practices. Women met in groups of ten to 15 once a month only, for 11 months beginning at about the fourth month of pregnancy. Their aim was to prevent postnatal depression by offering education about the problems the women were likely to encounter and how they might cope, and about the emotional reactions they might experience. It was also hoped that the group would provide a sense of support and, indirectly, the possibility of forging lasting friendships with one or more of the other members. Very little practical support was available, or advice on coping with housing or financial difficulties.

The evaluation showed the service to be effective (see above, p. 29). However, the service seemed to be most appropriate for first-time mothers, while second-time mothers attended much less regularly, and more than half declined the offer of group attendance altogether. Second-time mothers were more concerned, very often, with the problems of the first child and his or her very demanding behaviour in response to the new arrival. It may be that while group meetings might be appropriate for first-time mothers, other models of support are more appropriate for the more vulnerable pregnant women with older children. To avoid problems of stigmatising users, and because the service can be provided fairly cheaply, the group meetings could perhaps be part of the service offered at the booking visit for antenatal care for all first-time mothers. Information collected at the booking visit could then be used to identify the more vulnerable women among them, and if these women did not turn up, extra time and effort could be given to this smaller group in order to encourage them to attend. This strategy would maximise the chance that the service will reach those who stand to benefit most (Elliot, personal communication).

An approach to helping parents of handicapped children is the American Portage scheme, offered, for instance, by St Gabriel's Family Centre in Brighton. This now-well-known system involves trained but voluntary home visitors (often parents of older handicapped children) visiting the family home to help parents specify individual skill difficulties in their child and work out a step-by-step approach to teaching the skill. Parent and visitor together decide on teaching targets and the frequency of visits, and the parent will get her child to demonstrate his progress at each meeting. Like the best of the pre-school support programmes, it is based on the assumption that parents are the best people to develop the young child's skills and the best place to do so is in their own home (see Pugh *et al.*, 1987).

Few of the new services are likely to reach women who are non-English-speaking, of different cultural backgrounds, and perhaps even unfamiliar with the most basic facilities of the British health care system. Organisations like Maternity Links in Bristol, which provides link workers, mainly to Asian women to improve the take-up of health care, are needed to make provision accessible to all. They help the women to understand what is available and why, provide tuition on antenatal and postnatal procedures, liaise with health workers, and generally support the women and advocate on their behalf. Hitherto the lack of utilisation of even standard antenatal care by a proportion of some ethnic minority groups had been reflected in markedly raised perinatal mortality rates as compared to the national average.

One training programme for health visitors which aims to improve the quality of support health visitors provide to families is the Child Development Programme based at Bristol University. This places primary emphasis on *how* the health visitor relates to client women. The training offers a structure to home visiting in which parents are helped to find their own solutions to their childrearing problems. It has now been taken up by 18 health authorities across the UK, mainly in areas of economic and social disadvantage. It is also operating in Dublin, where the programme has been modified. Here local mothers from the same community (usually disadvantaged communities) carry out the structured home visits after training by the public health nurses. This programme, and how it is run in one part of England are described in some detail below.

THE CHILD DEVELOPMENT PROGRAMME

The Child Development Programme (CDP) is essentially a training programme for health visitors to become more aware of the mental health and social problems of the families they see, to appreciate that the child is best helped by a mother who is coping well with her own life, and that the mother's self-esteem and competence are most likely to be improved by support which emphasises the importance of her own educational role with her child. Health visitors are encouraged to avoid any didactic, advice-giving approaches and to discuss childcare issues with the parent as one expert to another. They are also advised to take every opportunity to boost the mother's confidence in her ability to manage her own life. Any changes for the better on this interactive style might improve the health visitor's effectiveness with all her clients. However, there is also a structured interview which they can adopt and which is designed for use with two target groups. The first is women who have recently had their first child, whether or not they have good support or advantageous social circumstances. The second is women who have more than one pre-school child and who are experiencing parenting difficulties. Those health visitors using the programme with first-time mothers work exclusively with this group. The second group, who are colleagues of the first parent visitors, select a minimum of ten families from their caseload for whom they feel the approach might be particularly valuable. The project work is therefore taken on as part of their normal work.

Recruitment and training of staff

Sufficient numbers of the health visiting team and their managers must be interested in implementing the scheme. Training is provided by the organisers of the Child Development Programme and will last up to three years. The most intensive part of this training involves seven formal teaching sessions, and three accompanied visits each lasting a half-day, at five-week intervals. Teaching sessions cover issues around self-esteem, methods of service delivery and their effects on self-esteem and dependency, circumstances which may lead to family breakdown and circumstances which lead to children being taken into the care of the local authority. The co-ordinating nursing officer of the area is involved in all training sessions so that after one year he or she can take over the running of the programme, aided by one of the first parent visitors who is selected to become a trainer. After the first few formal meetings, a CDP tutor accompanies each health visitor on a visit to at least two families with their first child and afterwards discusses with the visitor their strategies and approaches. Training sessions then continue to alternate with accompanied visits.

Restructuring teamwork

Implementing the full Child Development Programme means that health visitors' caseloads in an area must be reorganised to some extent. Those working as first parent visitors need to be free to take *only* women having their first child and to be restricted to a caseload of approximately 100 such families a year. This number is lower than average and means that the caseloads of other health visitors must increase somewhat. However, given that women who have just had a first child often need longer and more frequent visits, the differences, in terms of time needed, tend to balance out as the other visitors lose their new parents. One disadvantage, of course, is that because working with first-time mothers is a satisfying and rewarding part of a health visitor's work, other visitors may resent the loss of this part of their job.

Other visitors, however, may opt to join the programme as family visitors, choosing ten of their families as likely to benefit from more intensive help. (A recent innovation has been to encourage a minority of family visitors to do programme visits full-time, on all families needing extra support.) These families would often be those with less organised or even chaotic lifestyles, obvious child management problems, and poor maternal self-esteem.

First parent visitors would mount the programme for a minimum of eight months with each new mother, and continue it for at least 16 months (or longer) if problems in coping were evident. After this time the family would be slotted back into the ordinary caseload of the team. In any area involved in the programme, all first-time parents receive programme visits, whatever their social and educational background. This helps to increase the acceptability of the programme.

The programme

The first parent visitor aims to visit mothers once or twice during the later stages of pregnancy and at ten days post-partum to build up a relationship and start the programme. Programme visits then follow at monthly intervals. The focus is on helping the mother to foster her child's language, social and cognitive development, and on encouraging her to look after her own and her child's health through eating a balanced diet. Visits to families with older children have the same structure, but give more attention to resolving any longstanding difficulties that have developed. The nutritional element of the programme became important quite early in the planning of the Child Development Programme, when it was found that many mothers and children had diets which were markedly deficient in essential minerals and vitamins, and over-dependent upon 'junk' food. An intensive dietary study in two of the projects' first four regions (Dublin and West Glamorgan) provided 'weighed intake data' on the daily diets of a number of children. This revealed that a significant minority of the population had a low standard of nutrition (Lee *et al.*, 1983, report findings on 67 infants aged three to 13 months). One frequent problem was the practice of feeding commercial rusks and weaning biscuits to babies and toddlers throughout the day, often accompanied by a large quantity of sugared tea or milk, which depresses the appetite for other foods. Such a diet becomes a more serious concern during the second and third years of life when neonatal reserves of micronutrients are exhausted. Deficits of dietary iron, vitamins A, C and D, and folate were observed.

In response to the findings of these dietary studies, the programme planners produced a wide range of easy-to-make recipes and menu ideas and cartoon leaflets about food and cooking for use during visits. It became a routine part of every visit to enquire about what the mother and the infant had eaten on the day prior to the visit.

On programme visits, a simple form is used to guide the discussion between parent and visitor, and to record agreed priorities. At each meeting they will agree on two or three activities which the parent and child will engage in (during the following few weeks) to help develop the infant's language, social or cognitive skills. The outcome of these efforts is discussed at the following meeting, and praised appropriately. The visitors will also ask about formal contacts with the health services for immunisations or health checks, for example, and the parent will be asked for his or her own view of the child's general health and welfare. Three of the cartoon leaflets will be given to the parent.

Over 170 cartoon sequences have been produced for the programme, on managing minor behaviour problems such as night waking, for instance, or nutrition, safety, teaching new skills, and so on. They have been found to provide a light-hearted means of discussing difficult issues and are produced on cheap coloured paper so as not to create the impression that they are in any way an authoritative judgement. Of course, the health visitor must be skilful in her handling of the discussions in order to avoid sounding patronising when she provides these leaflets or praises achievements.

Case examples

A first parent visitor

A first parent visitor, Susan, talked to me about her use of the programme and, with the prior agreement of the families concerned, allowed me to accompany her on her visits that morning. We went together to visit June.

June had just got up and was bottle feeding her baby in front of the television. Susan asked her what was new since her last visit. June explained that the baby could now sit up, make funny faces at her and no longer became upset if she left the room. They chatted briefly about June's mother, who was in poor health. Susan then asked about the activities they had planned at her last visit. June replied that the baby was still unable to roll from stomach to back, but enjoyed playing with containers and the 'peeking' games. Susan suggested that this might be why the baby was no longer distressed when her mother left the room. June could not think of any ideas that Susan could 'pass on that would be helpful to other folk'.

They then began to chat about food. June said she had made beefburgers last week, and Susan gave her a copy of the recipe she had promised to bring for meatballs. Susan also produced four other cartoon-style recipe sheets of dishes suitable for both adults and babies. June gave Susan two of her own food tips which Susan was clearly pleased to receive and wrote down. June described her diet and her daughter's diet of the previous day. Susan showed she was impressed: 'You're doing fine with her, aren't you?!'

Susan then asked about immunisations, vaccinations, clinic visits and health before they started to discuss the activities June might work on over the coming weeks. 'What could you try out that would help her on? What's she most interested in?' June replied that holding hands and walking about was what the baby most enjoyed at present. However, Susan did not respond to this suggestion. Instead she began to talk about shapes and sounds and suggested making sounds out of the baby's noises. June then put the baby in a 'walker' and the child then scuttled across the room. This was impressive for a 6- to 7-month-old child, but instead of expressing any pleasure in seeing this – which undoubtedly June was expecting her to do – Susan began to explain how walkers can be harmful. She said if used a great deal the tendons in the foot can stretch, and this prompted June to say that she would only use it occasionally. The suggested activities Susan wrote down for the coming weeks were primarily her own suggestions in relation to sounds. She added the walking idea, but with the comment that June should not expect too much too soon.

It was a disappointing demonstration of the theory. The mother had enthused about how her daughter enjoyed bouncing games on the bed and this would have been an ideal focus for discussion about how the game could be added to in order to develop cognitive, social or verbal skills.

Susan gave June some cartoon leaflets including one about potty training because June had asked for this at the last visit. They then chatted about June's husband and his chances of early release from the prison sentence he had begun shortly after the baby's birth. I asked June how she liked the programme and she said that she felt she had got to know Susan very well and could easily say things to her and ask her about things. And she enjoyed the cartoon material.

Susan had also arranged for me to visit a couple who had completed the programme. They lived in a council house on a new estate. Both were at home as the father, Mark, was currently unemployed. Sarah, the mother, was six months pregnant with their second child. The first child was just 10 months old. They were expecting me, and Susan left us while she visited neighbouring families. I asked Sarah to tell me about the visits from Susan.

She told me that the first visits had included weighing and measuring the new baby. Sarah had felt she got to know Susan very well. She seemed to rely on her advice and reassurance and looked forward to her visits. Sarah found the exchange of ideas 'from other Mums' via Susan to be very useful, as she had no friends with children with whom to exchange tips. I asked what she had done which she might otherwise not have done had she not been part of the programme.

'I bought books early on. And I started her on proper food earlier than I would have.'

Mark commented that she had said Sarah must do various activities. Sarah interrupted to correct him. 'She didn't say "must", she said "try this. . .". . . She also used to ask what I ate.'

Mark added that Sarah had been encouraged to buy fresh vegetables more often instead of tins, and to eat fruit.

Mark and Sarah were a confident and competent couple, with a good deal of support from nearby relatives. However, although many young families lived in the same street, they had not developed any friendships among them, and their own friends did not yet have any children. They therefore particularly appreciated discussions about childcare issues with Susan. It occurred to me that Sarah would have benefited greatly from contact with another mother and it seemed a gap in the programme that such social network building was not included.

My final visit of the morning with Susan was to a middle-class home on the outskirts of the town where I was introduced to Janet and her 3-month-old daughter. Janet was relaxed and controlled and listed numerous ideas for activities and first weaning foods for her baby. She had made her own soft toys and had already planned out what she was going to make for the baby next. She told me she enjoyed the programme and Susan's visits and liked the one-to-one attention. She said she would be less interested in group meetings with other mothers, despite the fact that she did not know any other mothers of young children. Susan obviously felt she was needed less by Janet than other mothers she visits, and stayed only half as long as she had in other homes that morning. By lunchtime she had done programme visits to four mothers.

A family visitor

After lunch I met Penny, a health visitor using the family programme. She took me with her to see a couple with two young sons, aged nearly 3 and 5 years. They had a small terraced inner-city home and the father was unemployed. They had found it difficult to manage child care and had little control over what the children did. Penny began by asking them what changes there had been since her last visit. The mother reported that the youngest boy had seven words, was much less 'clingy', was able to remember things better, and was becoming quite cheeky. He was still drinking a tremendous amount – often two pints of squash at breakfast, and his mother felt his behaviour may have improved since she stopped giving him orange-coloured drinks or lollies. The 5-year-old had been doing some drawing and had learnt to tie his laces, but had not done the jigsaw or scrapbook (which had been discussed at the previous programme visit).

They talked about their meals the day before, the children's physical health, and then Penny gave them a cartoon leaflet about sorting and comparing objects, cutting and matching shapes (entitled 'beginning maths'), and another focusing on beginning reading (with suggestions such as playing 'I Spy'). The mother also volunteered an idea to encourage colour labelling using coloured jellybabies. They discussed what the parents' priorities were for child development over the coming weeks. The parents decided they wanted to encourage the youngest child to do more walking, to focus on both of them getting themselves dressed, and to become firm and consistent in order to cure the eldest child of bullying behaviour with girls. The parents and Penny told me with some pride how the programme had

*helped them overcome a range of problems so far. Getting the boys into bed
at a reasonable time had been impossible and the parents had tended to wait
until the children literally fell asleep in front of the TV or on the floor. Now
they had developed bedtime routines including a hiding game, so that going
to bed had become fun, and took place at an appropriate time. They had
also succeeded in getting the children to eat more at mealtimes, and to chew
meat properly. The parents had also started to give the children routinely
their reasons for saying 'no', and generally felt much more able to cope.*

*I was impressed by the relationship between parents and health visitor
and the skilful way Penny helped to direct their problem solving without
ever appearing to be advising them. They were relaxed in each other's
company and chatted together like friends.*

*Penny then took me to meet Irene, who had agreed to talk to me about her
experience of the programme. Penny had specifically chosen Irene as an
example of a client with longstanding mental health and parenting problems.*

*Irene had three children aged 5 and 2, and 8 months. The first two
children were born prematurely at seven months' gestation, and had
remained slightly behind in their development. They lived with Irene's
boyfriend and father of her children in a small terraced council house. He
had been unemployed for some time. Irene had become depressed after the
birth of the first child but had gone back to work as soon as she was able. As
a single parent she had been able to secure a free nursery place. She had not
wanted or planned her second child and had rejected her at birth, wanting to
leave hospital without seeing her or telling any relatives she had even been
pregnant. She hoped to be able to go immediately back to work pretending
nothing had happened, and offer the baby for adoption. However, intervention by a social worker prevented her from carrying out her plan and after
seeing her child she took her home to 'face the music'. But she had
considerable problems in coping with her children, and the professionals in
contact with her became concerned about the adequacy of her parenting.
She was treated for recurrent depression, and regularly telephoned social
workers to ask for her children to be adopted, invariably changing her mind
at the last minute. During her third unplanned pregnancy she considered
abortion on several occasions. She received support from a social worker, a
health visitor and her GP and her children were provided with nursery
places. The eldest child spent most of the rest of his time at the home of an
aunt while her boyfriend did much of the caring for the second child.
Support workers witnessed the rejecting and stinging rebuffs she continued
to deliver to her children.*

*With her third child, however, her parenting improved to some extent.
Preventive obstetric care helped her pregnancy to go to term. She was still
moderately depressed after the birth and coping badly, but this time she was*

*infatuated with the baby. Penny decided to try the Child Development
Programme with her, specifically in relation to her third child, which they
had been doing for eight months prior to my visit.*

*When I met Irene she seemed cheerful and enthusiastic about the
programme. Penny left us together to chat while she went to visit a family
nearby. The baby was asleep in a carrycot in the corner of the room. The
eldest child came in from the street with a friend from time to time, but they
were told each time to 'buzz off'. Irene told me that she believed her older
children may not have had so many difficulties had she had the programme
when they were younger. She saw it as especially valuable for premature
babies who need 'bringing on quicker'. She gave me some examples of what
she had learnt. She went to the cupboard to get out all the cartoon leaflets
she'd been given and to which she clearly periodically referred. She showed
me the one on discipline. She said before, she used to 'just throw her [her 2-
year-old] in her cot and leave her there for ages'. . . or else 'shout and rave'
. . . when she was angry with her. Now she was trying not to get so angry, to
explain why she must not do such and such, and to find something else for
her to do. Irene had clearly found the programme of great benefit in terms
of helping her to occupy her older children. She was very impressed by how
one of Penny's suggestions had worked. 'I gave Jane some pans and some
spoons and things and she played with them for one-and-a-half hours!'.
'Before I might give them a sweet and just say "go away". Now I give them
something to do and I can organise my time. Before I'd be washing up and
before I'd get two plates washed the whole fridge'd be out on the floor. . .'
The house was 'always a tip' and she couldn't get anything done.*

*'I've learnt patience and discipline . . . I'm becoming like a nursery nurse
and they're learning like at nursery and they're qualified there . . . I do
nursery rhymes with Jane and the baby . . .'*

*However, the baby was the only one of her three children she had much
time for and she saw the project work as mostly for her. Irene boasted how
'forward' she was, saying sounds and nearly walking at just 8 months.
Already she was hoping to do reading and writing with her. But it also
appeared that the message was getting across quite subtly to change her
behaviour with her older children. She described how she had insisted the
eldest child allow her to wash his hair the day before, saying otherwise he
would be sent straight to bed, and the child had obliged. Previously, she
said, she would have let him 'get out of it if he made a fuss'.*

*Irene also felt that the programme had helped her to get over her
depression. She said she would still be 'a shambles and clawing the walls' if
she had not had ideas about how to occupy the children. She said she would
not have done any of the things suggested in the project on her own
initiative.*

*I asked her how Penny's health visiting had changed since they had been
doing the project together. Irene said, 'It used to be much more "how is the*

mum." There wasn't time for much chatting – it was just weighing the baby, food and diet. Now it's all about learning.'

Evaluation

Six health authorities were involved in the first phase of the project and its evaluation. Over 1,000 families were interviewed at home. The questionnaire used covered health, and educational, nutritional and developmental aspects of the child's home environment. The abilities and characteristics of the children were assessed, including language, social behaviour and cognitive development. In Dublin and West Glamorgan the diet of the children was also studied. Four hundred families conducted a 'weighed intake' assessment of their child's diet over a four-day period. In the North-West region, an assessment of maternal self-esteem was completed, and in the North-East, a child activity measure was used, and hair samples were collected in order to relate activity levels to trace elements.

Eighty-six health visitors were randomly allocated to the intervention or to the comparison group. From their caseloads of children aged between 27 months and 3 years, samples of 20 children were randomly selected. After training, intervention health visitors conducted up to 20 programme visits with their families during 1981 and 1982. Families of comparison group health visitors received conventional visits. Assessments were carried out at the beginning, middle and end of the intervention phase.

Unfortunately, research staff problems led to poor follow-up rates in two of the six areas. Data in the other four regions was completed on 355 intervention and 223 comparison families. Several indices showed benefits favouring the intervention group in terms of increased changes over the intervention period. Mothers in intervention group families more often praised their children for their achievements, talked about their achievements, and encouraged independent actions such as dressing. The language environment of intervention families improved more, and observational evidence confirmed their greater use of deliberate verbal strategies and turn-taking. More activities and materials were made available to intervention children, while ratings of parental enjoyment of interactions with their children, and of parental responsiveness to their children, also improved more for the intervention group over the evaluation period. The micronutrient content of the children's diet also improved more for intervention families, and both boys and girls showed a greater increase in height.

The areas which showed only limited benefits for intervention families were: changes to the emotional environment; forms of control used by parents; and the child's reading environment.

The evaluation data is relatively short-term, and further follow-ups will reveal how effective the programme has been in bringing about long-term changes. It seems likely that a greater insight into their children's educational and developmental needs and their own responsiveness to these will have effects which will endure, but this needs to be demonstrated. There is some evidence that the emphasis on the mother's crucial educational role could also bring improvements in physical health in that rates of hospitalisation of intervention group children were lower (Child Development Programme, 1987). A more recent evaluation paper (Barker and Anderson, 1988) provides more detail than earlier papers on the precise methods and content of the research assessments, and the complex analyses applied, from which it is somewhat difficult to judge the strength of the findings reported. The only data on the effects of the programme on child abuse is difficult to interpret. An annual rate of 0.62 injuries per 1,000 children per year was reported for the 7,000 children who had been through the programme, which is well under half the national average calculated by the National Society for the Prevention of Cruelty to Children (NSPCC). However, this must presumably be tempered by the instruction to health visitors recruiting the first 1,000 families (involved in the evaluation) to exclude those on child abuse registers.

Child Development Programme benefits: conclusion

This structured approach to health visiting has many features to recommend it and its emphasis on the interviewing and negotiating skills of the health visitor and on the educational role of the parent appears to contribute considerably to the effectiveness of their support, and to be valued by nurses and clients alike. The resource material in the form of cartoon leaflets was extremely valuable and helped health visitors to offer more positive support to mothers with difficulties.

A personal reaction to participating in programme visits was that there was insufficient emphasis either on the expression of affection and warmth toward the child, or on the social support of the mother. Given that first parent visitors would be in touch with up to 100 women in the same situation, I felt there was a wasted opportunity for putting lonely and isolated women in contact with each other. There might also have been some encouragement for mothers to find activities outside the home which both parent and child would enjoy, which would be educational for the child, and a chance to improve the social network of the mother.

After the visits with a first parent visitor, I was also concerned that the emphasis was perhaps too strongly biased toward cognitive skills. These visits typically take place over the first eight months of a child's life, a time when parents are preoccupied with the need to establish basic skills in the infant associated with eating, sleeping, sitting and crawling. The parent derives pride from getting the baby to sleep through the night; from weaning the infant and seeing them enjoy solid food; from getting their feeding routine to coincide with adult mealtimes; from seeing them achieve modest movement: reaching, sitting, crawling; and from seeing them laugh and play. Looking at books and focusing on sounds and language is more rewarding at a slightly later stage, when the infants are able to respond (by fetching books, turning the pages, copying animal sounds in stories). Pleasurable responses increase the mother's motivation to continue and the activity is mutually reinforcing. This is not often the case with infants under the age of 8 months old, although, perhaps, this opportunity provided by programme visits to encourage mothers to begin to introduce the child to books should not be missed.

One further observation of the scheme was that with the same training, one health visitor may nevertheless be able to employ the method far more successfully than another. The ease with which they adopt the approach is probably a reflection of how close it is to their own previous practice. This suggests that further courses of in-service training might be beneficial, or perhaps programme visitors might benefit from periodically accompanying a colleague to watch another person's use of the scheme.

Health visitors have reported that training has greatly improved their understanding of the difficulties faced by some of the mothers, and made them more sensitive to their needs. This improves job satisfaction, but at the same time makes the work more emotionally exhausting. Many would say they see it as 'real' health visiting, returning them more toward a preventive role instead of a sometimes rather medical one (Child Development Project, 1984).

BEFRIENDING MOTHERS: NEWPIN

Newpin offers friendship and support to isolated and depressed mothers with young children with the aim of enhancing their self-esteem, helping them to break destructive patterns in family relationships, and preventing child abuse and neglect. At the time of my visit there was one project only (based in South London), but it has been widely recognised as an exemplary scheme and has been successful in establishing four sister projects (also in south London), and launching itself as a national charity, planning to develop Newpins across the country. Four of the five Newpin centres are managed by women who began in Newpin by being referred to the project.

A new referral will be paired with another Newpin mother who has participated in the project for some time, with the hope that this friendship will enable the individual to begin to come to the Newpin centre on a regular basis. The centre offers a social meeting place to meet other Newpin women and children, with an adjacent crèche where their children can play under supervision. It also offers a structured educational programme covering issues concerning the self and child development, as well as a weekly programme of group psychotherapy.

The scheme thus offers much more than friendship or a social meeting place. It offers the opportunity to individuals to learn more about themselves and how they might make fundamental changes to the way they lead their lives. In fact, women are encouraged to join Newpin only if they are interested in making such changes. Through discussions with other women and through the educational and psychotherapeutic programmes, Newpin aims to help the women to confront and work through emotional as well as practical issues. They are expected to gain a greater insight into their problems, and into their habitual ways of dealing with them. The high level of mutual care and warmth, and the nurturing, family-like environment in the drop-in sitting room is also intended to enhance the woman's self-esteem and indirectly to enable her in turn to show more care and affection to her own children. It is very much a developmental or 'growing-up' model to help women gradually develop self-respect and 'grow' sufficiently to be better able to recognise and support the needs of their own children.

As many of the Newpin women are already depressed when referred to the project, it cannot strictly be described as a preventive service for them at this time. However, it can be viewed as preventive of future depressive illness if it enables the women to deal with future crises without getting severely depressed. It may serve a preventive function in this respect if it succeeds in creating close, confiding and supportive new relationships which endure, or if it facilitates positive action to improve existing close relationships, or if it enables the woman to act more positively to cope with or resolve long-term difficulties. These judgements are made on the basis of the demonstrated protective role of close relationships, and from the evidence that many severely threatening events arise out of long-term difficulties, and that such events and difficulties can provoke depression in vulnerable people. However, a second and perhaps greater preventive potential for such a project lies in the prospect for improved parenting of children. Should it succeed in changing neglectful, chaotic parenting into relationships offering warmth, attention and guidance for expected ways of behaving, then it may have long-term preventive significance for children. Improvements will have particular benefits to children whose home lives are so extremely neglectful that there is a real possibility that alternative parenting arrangements may need to be made.

Newpin was set up following meetings in 1980 between local medical and social work professionals who were concerned about the high rate of child abuse in the area. They concluded that a befriending project might help to reduce this, and set themselves up as Trustees. With the support of the district health authority they secured an office in Guy's Hospital and appointed a co-ordinator and an administrator in September 1981. In January 1982 the project moved into rooms on the upper floor of a large house belonging to the DHA in a side-street close to a shopping centre.

The co-ordinator (now the national director), Anne Jenkins, already had a large number of local contacts having been a health visitor in the area for several years previously. This enabled her to quickly build up referrals and potential befrienders. But she also came with a clear vision of the type of befriending service she would like to provide, which is reflected in the character of the project as it exists today.

Her approach to helping to prevent child abuse is that one must first 'care for the hurt child within the parent' (Jenkins, 1987). Many abusing parents will themselves have been abused in childhood, and Jenkins suggests that low self-esteem may be associated with a view of oneself as the bad child who to some extent caused their own abuse. They will hope for a much better relationship with their own children than their parents had with them. Misbehaviour by their children will, however, reinforce their view of their 'bad child self', further reducing their self-esteem. In order to achieve a good relationship with their children, they need to develop secure attachments of their own, and an improved self-esteem through feeling accepted and valued for themselves. This, in turn, enables them to become a supportive adult to their children. Newpin is founded on these beliefs.

How Newpin functions

Referrals

Between January 1982 and March 1987, 351 women with children under 5, were referred to the project. At first most referrals came from local health visitors, antenatal department staff, social workers, psychiatric unit staff, or a GP. But in later years many were also referred by existing members of Newpin, or referred themselves after hearing of the project.

The co-ordinator visits each woman in her own home, and describes to her what Newpin has to offer. It is made clear that participants are interested in positive self-change, and in achieving a greater understanding of their children, and only if the woman indicates that she is interested in this does the conversation turn to issues which involve a measure of disclosure about personal matters in home and family circumstances. This second part of the interview is essentially an assessment of how the woman's involvement in Newpin should best begin, and they may agree on a 'focus for change'. The specific change desired might be an improved relationship with child or partner, developing more self-confidence, trusting others more, or overcoming anxiety or depression.

Of course not all women choose to become involved. Some simply want a mother and toddler group and do not feel that they want or need to make changes to their ways of thinking or behaving. Others may find a job which satisfies their needs.

Joining Newpin

Most women joining Newpin prefer to start by taking up the offer of home visits from a befriender, another local mother chosen intuitively by the co-ordinator as likely to get on well with the new referral. The pair will be matched up within a week or two, unless no obvious befriender is immediately available, in which case it may take a little longer. The befriender will visit the woman at home by arrangement and they will agree between them how often to meet and how to spend this time. When they have got to know each other fairly well, the befriender will encourage her friend to go with her to the Newpin drop-in, although not all women will decide to do so.

The Newpin house in Southwark has sufficient space to allow women to meet in the 'drop-in' at the same time as others are meeting for group sessions. The drop-in is furnished as a sitting room and women arrive either singly or with a Newpin friend, invariably with their pre-school children. The children either stay with their mothers, or go to play in the crèche which occupies a large adjacent room with access down to an outdoor play area. Two crèche workers are there to supervise and play with the children. The arrangement is such that the children can wander back to see their mothers in the sitting room whenever they wish to do so.

The organised group meetings, which last one-and-a-half hours each are essentially of two types: educational sessions on child development, sudden infant death, postnatal depression, issues for women, starting a new life, and so on, and 'self-awareness' groups run by a trained group analyst. The course in 1987 consisted of one educational session and one self-awareness group each week for 20 weeks, and was seen as a training course to enable participants to become befrienders themselves and support new referrals to Newpin. The educational sessions were usually given by the co-ordinator, and/or by one of her local contacts in the health services. The psychotherapy sessions aimed to promote a greater depth of self-awareness, a toleration of others, and an appreciation of personal strengths, and offered a chance to come to terms with early experience of trauma and loss.

Once trained, a woman could take on the role of befriending a new referral and probably a series of new referrals. She would be supported in her befriending task through twice-weekly meetings at Newpin: the first a meeting with other supporters to discuss the difficulties and demands of the new role; the second a continuation of the group therapy. Supporters continued this high level of involvement for as long as they remained a part of Newpin.

Case histories

Maggie – a young woman who was befriended, trained and is now a befriender

Maggie was one of the crèche workers at Newpin. She also worked part-time in a local chainstore. She seemed confident and articulate. When I met her she had recently separated from her husband and was trying to support herself financially as far as possible. She lived with her two children, aged 5 and 2 years.

Maggie's involvement in Newpin began soon after the birth of her first child, when she was 21 years old. She had been anxious about the welfare of her baby throughout the pregnancy. (Her first pregnancy a few months earlier had spontaneously aborted at 13 weeks, and she had worried a great deal about the possible cause of this.) After the birth she did not want the baby near her more than necessary, and resented her demands. Both the midwife and the health visitor noticed this and she was referred to Newpin.

The Newpin co-ordinator visited her at home. Although Maggie felt she did not have any problems, she nevertheless took up the offer of a befriender. She had the impression she was going to be involved in doing some voluntary work. A short time later, Sandra, a mother of four sons, came to visit her. 'She was lovely – warm, chatted about her kids, and really laid back.' Maggie began to visit Sandra and go with her to Newpin on a regular basis. She told me that Sandra 'sustained' her, and she began to model herself on her.

Maggie told me how it was 'just a few weeks later that she suddenly realised how distant she had been with her child'. 'I went in to get her from her cot one morning and saw her smiling face . . . I had a powerful feeling of love and realised . . . I sat and cried.' From then on she felt less in need of Sandra's friendship, but says 'She doesn't realise how much she gave me – just seeing how she enjoyed her children and how unfussed she was about the mess they made.'

By the time her child was 6 months old, Maggie had begun the training course to become a befriender herself. She says, 'It gave me a buzz – to think Anne (the co-ordinator) valued me so much.' But her husband was not happy about the changes he saw in his wife, particularly her increasing assertiveness. Maggie, however, enjoyed the group training sessions, and felt the discussions about their childhoods showed the members had much in common. She started befriending a new referral immediately after training, but initially found it very difficult. She told me she wanted only to give practical help in the home and found she was unable to cope with being needed emotionally. This gradually improved, however, and over the following five years she befriended a total of 12 women for between one month and seven months. Her most recent friendship had been particularly successful. 'I've never had a friend like her, and I probably won't ever have another like her.' They see each other every day.

Asked what effect Newpin has had on her, Maggie answered that she has become more tolerant and self-confident. 'I'm much more likely to give people a chance now – I don't go on first appearances.' She has also gained a large number of good friends, including several other single parents (which she now is too), and they babysit for each other. She has had a second child, after another miscarriage, and this last successful pregnancy was a very positive experience. And this time she loved the baby 'from the word "go" '. However, her time at Newpin had also made her decide to separate from her husband, whom she now felt she had never really loved.

Maggie told me she still felt she needed Newpin. She was currently attending a weekly closed session for supporters with one of the paid staff, and a weekly self-awareness group for supporters with the therapist.

Carol, befriender

Carol had a son, Robert, aged 18 months, and was pregnant again when I met her. She had been involved in Newpin for almost a year and intended to remain so for some considerable time to come. Normally a shy person with little self-confidence, she had become isolated after giving up work during her first pregnancy. When her husband came home from work she felt she had nothing to talk to him about after spending all day in the house. She was timid to the extent that she would have found it impossible to have taken faulty goods back to a shop, or to have invited home for a cup of coffee any of the women she met at group meetings organised by her health visitor (despite wanting to do so). By the time Robert was 6 months old, she was feeling extremely lonely and miserable, and was not enjoying motherhood. Robert slept poorly and she found him exhausting and frustrating company. She did not go to any mother and toddler groups. 'I didn't like myself very much, so I didn't expect other people to like me.' However, when her health visitor told her about Newpin and the possibility of becoming a befriender, she was very attracted to the idea both of helping someone else and 'getting out of those four walls'.

The Newpin co-ordinator visited her at home, and shortly afterwards one of the Newpin mothers came to see her. Carol saw this contact simply as a friendly face to accompany her on her first visit to the drop-in, and this specific pairing did not continue. From then on, Carol went regularly with her son to the drop-in. She was able to enrol on a six-week introductory course at Newpin almost immediately, followed soon afterwards by a training course.

Carol told me that the course made her realise just how low she had been feeling at referral. Now that she was feeling well and happy and was enjoying being with her son she was able to see the contrast in herself. Part way through the course she met in the street one of the mothers she had been introduced to by the health visitor. 'I asked her then and there to come back for coffee and we've been good friends ever since.'

Carol told me that her confidence had grown considerably since she had joined Newpin. She could now use the telephone, she would be able to change a garment in a shop, and knew that through Newpin she always had friends who would help her out. Even if the Newpin house was closed she could go to one of the Newpin women at home to ask her to babysit, for example. Her son had also gained from Newpin. The crèche facilities were appreciated by both of them and he had gained new friends. 'At the end of an afternoon when we're both getting ratty and are at each other's throats because he's bored, we can just come down here.' She called in whenever she was feeling 'down', and said 'It's the sort of place where, if someone said "How do you feel?", you answer truthfully.'

Carol clearly felt very good about her role as befriender. She was currently with her third partner. The first friendship was shortlived, as Carol had found it difficult at first to be open about her own problems, and therefore empathise with her partner. The second lasted two to three months. Both of these women had gone on to do the training course to become befrienders themselves. The third woman, June, was her present 'friend'. Carol described this as the most successful pairing so far as it was more like a genuine friendship than the previous two. She had visited June at home once or twice a week for nearly three months before she could persuade her to come to the drop-in. Since then (four weeks previously), they had tended to meet once a week at Newpin and perhaps talk on the telephone in between times.

A few weeks later I met Carol again. Her pregnancy had miscarried and she was glad of her friendship with June who had been extremely supportive. The befriending had proved to have reciprocal benefits.

June

June and her husband currently had a good marriage. They had five children aged 12, 11, 3 and 2 years, and a baby of 9 months. Her husband was working as a self-employed builder. June had recently recovered from a prolonged postnatal depression with the help of Carol, who had been befriending her for four months.

June and her husband were married and had children very early, both eager to escape unhappy home lives. In June's case, her mother (to whom she was very close) had died when she was 15, and family life disintegrated. Her father coped badly, working long hours, drinking heavily, he was depressed and during the short periods he was at home he showed a violent temper. June was left to care for her 2-year-old sister, and both she and two of her four siblings left the family home within the year. June saw her only escape route as marriage, but because she was only 17 years old she knew her father would not allow her to marry unless she was pregnant. By the age of 19 she had two children. June said she had been in love with her boyfriend, but would not have married so early if her mother had not died.

The marriage was soon under strain. June discovered her husband in bed at home with a close friend of hers. She later discovered that the affair had not ended then, but continued. Her relationship with her husband became openly hostile and abusive, and June became more and more depressed. By the age of 23 she was addicted to valium (and remained so for four years). She also took slimming pills and began to starve herself and desperately wanted her husband to show concern for her.

Eventually June took the two children and went to stay with an aunt. Her husband attempted suicide. The crisis forced them to talk through their problems and brought them back together. They still had powerful feelings for each other and vowed to make a fresh start. June succeeded in giving up valium and became pregnant with their third child. She was mildly depressed after the birth of this child but otherwise was happy and coping well until the birth of her fifth child. Then she became markedly depressed, crying a great deal, and unable to cope with her older children at all. She was prescribed valium again, and her husband, though trying hard to be supportive, felt powerless to help her. She said she was desperate for help, and meeting Carol when the baby was 5 months old was a turning point.

June's health visitor had recommended a psychiatric referral. However, as June was against this, she put her in touch with Newpin instead. After the assessment interview, Carol had begun to visit her at home. It was many weeks before she was persuaded to attend the Newpin drop-in with her. When she did, she found it strange at first, but 'the atmosphere is so terrific that I've been once or twice a week ever since.'

June told me that she still felt low at times, but that she felt she was basically out of the depression. Of Newpin she said it had given her more confidence, that she was happier in herself, and that Carol had encouraged her to be less over-protective of her baby. She was quite obviously genuinely appreciative of the friendship with Carol, and felt it was a real rather than an artificial relationship. She was sure they would continue to meet if Newpin closed. She said Carol was the first real friend she had had since her mother died and her friend had an affair with her husband. She also described how she had changed the way she interprets events and people's comments, so that she does not now assume that people are making adverse judgements about her when their actions, comments, or glances are actually benign, and she gave me one or two examples. 'I'm much more likely now to look for other points of view instead of always thinking "it's me". I don't always see everyone as having a go.' She was trying to be more assertive in her difficult relationships with her husband's family, who were both intrusive and critical of her lifestyle. She needed to be able to answer criticism and to tell them not to keep coming over and, although she was getting better, she felt she still had some way to go. It seemed very much as though Carol was making use of her self-awareness training in the support she gave June in that she was drawing June's attention to her negative

*interpretations of events. June hoped to start a training course to become a
befriender herself in two or three months' time.*

Effectiveness

Newpin focuses on providing support for women with marked long-term
difficulties, poor self-esteem and poor or non-existent support in their
'natural' social networks. The objectives for its evaluation should therefore
be to see if it is successfully reaching its target group; then to see if it has
enhanced the quality and availability of support; thirdly whether this has
brought benefits for the mental health of the women; and finally if these are
reflected in improved parent–child relationships. Some light has been shed
on each of these issues by a pilot evaluation of Newpin in 1985 of 12 pairs of
women (befrienders and befriended) (Pound and Mills, 1985), and a
subsequent study of 40 Newpin women (Cox *et al.*, 1990).

Both studies showed that Newpin was being extremely successful in
reaching its target group. The results of the pilot study were summarised
earlier (p. 30).

In the main study, full data was obtained on 40 Newpin women, half
befrienders, half befriended, but who were not necessarily pairs. Sixteen (40
per cent) had experienced one major change of caretaker in their own
childhood, 11 (28 per cent of the Newpin sample) had been in care, 14 (35
per cent) had been physically or sexually abused. Furthermore, as many as
38 per cent had seen a psychiatrist for mental ill-health and nearly twice as
many (65 per cent) had seen either a GP or a psychiatrist for a mental health
problem (Cox *et al.*, 1990). Half the women had a discordant relationship
with their partner, and one in three had at least one child showing
significant emotional or behavioural problems. However, not all the
recruited women remained involved in the project for a long period. Almost
one-third either concluded their 'contract' or dropped out of the scheme
within two months. These tended to be women with less severe mental
health problems.

To assess improvements in social support, the pilot study asked the
women about close friendships. Almost all the 23 women reported having
made new friends including seven women who had no friends at all before
their involvement with Newpin. There were also fewer difficulties reported
in relationships with their family of origin at the interviews six months after
joining Newpin than at the interviews before entering the project. The larger
evaluation looked at improvements to social support in terms of the quality
of the 'marital' relationship. Sixty-two per cent were judged to have
improved the quality and stability of the relationship with their partner
(either gaining happy cohabitation or separating from a bad marriage). This
compares to 40 per cent of a sample of depressed women studied by the
same team in a separate study in the same area (see Cox *et al.*, 1990).

Both pilot and main studies also looked at improvements in depression over a six- to eight-month follow-up period. In the pilot study, 19 women were initially judged to be depressed, and all improved. One-third were judged to be recovered. In the main study, 25 (out of 40) were depressed initially and 52 per cent improved, 40 per cent were judged to be recovered. This is not very impressive as it is only marginally different from the rate of spontaneous improvement of depression among a sample of depressed women followed up over a similar period in a separate study in the same area (see Cox *et al.*, 1990). However, this study also examined the results separately for women who had a sustained uninterrupted involvement with Newpin and those who did not. This showed that the benefits were significantly greater for the women with continuous involvement, and these were more likely to be women who became involved in befriender training. Depression improved considerably more in the former group – 67 per cent judged to be recovered, and 77 per cent improved. Well-involved women showed significant improvements in their perception of themselves in comparison with those not so well involved, or in contrast groups. These were particularly noticeable in the areas of self-esteem and a sense of control over their own lives.

Finally, interviews showed that 70 per cent of the Newpin sample reported a reduction in child behavioural problems or reported that their children had remained without them. This was considerably better than the comparable figure in the sample of depressed women (51 per cent).

Of course half of the Newpin women will have received weekly psychotherapy and it would indeed be a costly service if this had not brought visible changes. However, many of the women, because of profound early deprivation, low current support or poor education would normally be judged unsuitable for conventional psychotherapy, yet reported substantial changes. They are a group whom professional services find extremely difficult to help but can be helped by this project, which, compared to support through statutory services, is a low-cost service. With the emphasis on psychological change and these promising early results of evaluation, it seems likely that the benefits of this project will be long term.

Costs

A Newpin project aims to support women who have considerable emotional, social and relationship problems for which many clients have sought support through statutory services. The cost of this (i.e. general practitioners, counsellors, out-patient support, etc.) must be born in mind when judging cost–benefit. Also the considerable cost of residential care, foster care, court action and social work time if family breakdown or child abuse leads to children being taken into care. No child has been returned to care after the parent joined Newpin. It seems reasonable to assume that some costs to statutory services are reduced by the presence of a Newpin scheme, although there is no clear evidence to demonstrate this.

The Newpin brochure (1991 edition) quotes the cost of running a Newpin centre (which would train 72 individuals and provide crèche facilities for their children) as £60,000 a year. Cost will include psychotherapy (three one-and-a-half-hour sessions per week in 1987). Psychotherapy groups consist of up to 20 individuals, but these individuals may attend a weekly supporters' group after the training sessions are concluded, and can remain in the supporters' group for as long as they wish – in some cases, several years. Other Newpin staffing costs include: a full-time co-ordinator and administrator, a playleader and sessional helpers, and occasional speakers for training courses. In addition there are the costs of the premises: the rent and telephone bills and travel expenses (of the co-ordinator and volunteers).

Not all the staff time is paid for by Newpin. All the crèche workers at the original project were supplied by voluntary organisations or from outside funding. Invited speakers are often professionals with goodwill toward the project who will not charge for their contribution. Furthermore, there is an imaginative use of community resources, other voluntary agencies, and government-funded training schemes. Toys are mostly donated by local mothers. A community scrap project which collects waste materials from manufacturers is used for paper and paint and such like. An educational trust paid for more expensive crèche items. Crèche workers have come on one-year placements from government-funded youth training schemes. Researchers involved in evaluating the project have helped in training without charge. Undoubtedly this ability of the project to attract hidden resources has contributed substantially to the quality and cost-effectiveness of the service.

CONCLUSION

The projects described in this chapter offer the hope that supportive services can help mothers who are more vulnerable to depression and those who are finding particular difficulty in their parenting role to become more self-confident and better able to control their lives. Some of their children should become less vulnerable to depression in adulthood if the quality of their parenting has been improved sufficiently. The important components of good practice include opportunities for women pregnant with their first child to meet and discuss common concerns, and for this support to continue for the first few months of parenthood; the encouragement of a healthy diet and the take-up of statutory services; an approach to health visiting and other support that is based on an equal partnership; and the linking of mothers of young children with existing community supports and with each other. It appears not to be a difficult matter to identify mothers, or even pregnant women, likely to experience problems in parenting. The judgements of midwives and health visitors are often perceptive.

Two approaches to offering greater help to this group have been described. The first focuses directly on the mother's expertise in assisting the child's cognitive, social and language development, and gains in self-esteem are expected to come from the woman seeing herself as successful in resolving her own problems and bringing improvements to her child's abilities and behaviour. The second focuses instead on the mother's self-esteem, her social support and her insight into her own behaviour through which improvements are expected to lead to improved parenting. Both approaches appear promising and neither carry prohibitive cost implications. In fact, these approaches help to ensure that the support that is provided to parents is effective with those who most need it.

Chapter 2

Adolescence to independence

This chapter is about supporting young people who have themselves already experienced significant adversity in their own parenting, and are about to take that important step into adulthood which comes with leaving the childhood home. Their circumstances, decisions and available support at this time will influence their vulnerability to depression and likelihood of facing other social and emotional difficulties for many years to come. If they simultaneously also step into parenthood, the potential for affecting adversely the vulnerability of the next generation as well as having major implications for their own lifestyle is there.

The ideal circumstances for leaving home and establishing independent living arrangements may be debatable, but must surely include a positive choice to do so, sufficient income (from work, education grants, state benefits or family), a network of friends, and close family or other ties to whom they can turn if they meet financial, social or emotional problems. It is also helpful if their opportunities for choice and independence have been gradually increased for some while prior to leaving home.

However, young people with a background of poor parenting are unlikely to be so fortunate. They may not have been able to exercise choice and take responsibility for themselves in a gradual way and at their own pace. They may be obliged to find independent accommodation before most parents would consider them mature or capable enough to do so, at 16, 17 or 18 years old, particularly if currently living in institutional care. They will probably also have less adequate sources of family support if they meet financial, housing or other social difficulties. Indeed they may have troublesome relationships with families which hinder rather than help their efforts to establish independence. All the evidence points to the extreme vulnerability of this group. Grosskurth (1984) documented the disturbingly high rate of homelessness among care leavers, Rutter and colleagues (1983) their high rate of pre-marital pregnancy and social difficulties, Harris *et al.* (1987) their high rate of depression. With a background of a 'lack of care' and current low support, they are clearly a high-risk group in terms of the research on the aetiology of depression.

Of course efforts on the part of those running community homes and those funding foster care arrangements to improve the quality of care will help to minimise the problems of the young people later. Successful, happy foster placements cannot be described as poor parenting experiences, and other experiences in care may well be the result of parental illness or social difficulties that have not damaged the parent–child relationship. If existing positive family ties can be maintained, and the alternative home circumstances be made stable, the experience need not be a damaging one. Unfortunately, this is too frequently not what happens. As Stein (1983) observed after listening to about 150 young people aged 16 to 19 interviewed as part of his two-year follow-up of those leaving the care of Wakefield Social Service in 1982:

> one is immediately struck by *the number of placements and movements* in care. For example John (who came into care at 3 and remained until he was 18): Foster parents – breakdown – assessment centre – large group home – foster parents – breakdown – assessment centre – large group home – another group home – working boys' hostel – lodging in an old people's home – lodgings – council flat. The experience of a significant number of young people leaving care at 18 is not dissimilar. For these young people their total social world (their family, substitute care, school, friends and neighbourhood) was frequently changing. Change was also mainly related to a crisis or breakdown situation.

It is easy to imagine how such an extremely adverse history may be linked to feelings of low self-worth, a sense of rejection, and of helplessness. When the circumstances under which the child was admitted into care, or moved from one home arrangement to another involved minimal preparation or warning, a feeling of powerlessness is particularly understandable. Many young people have complained that decisions were frequently taken about them without adequate explanation, let alone an enquiry as to their own preferences, and many years went by sometimes before they knew why things were happening as they were. Suggestions have been made about how the young person's sense of security, of self-esteem, of identity, and of understanding of the reasons behind his current circumstances can be improved while in care (e.g. Lupton, 1985). Many of these issues should be addressed by the Children Act (1989), which seeks to involve young people in decisions about their lives, with effect from October 1991. It is possible that the typical picture now is not as bleak as that painted by the young people interviewed by Stein.

Of course, despite their disadvantage, many young people leave care and do not experience marked social difficulties, or become pregnant unintentionally. They establish secure home lives and supportive adult relationships, remain free of depression and become good parents to their own children. How have they avoided or surmounted their early disadvantage?

In research by the Bedford College team (summarised in Brown, 1989) those young women who experienced lack of care but did not get pregnant unintentionally, or who coped well if they did, were those who had good coping skills and had not shown a 'helpless' personality trait. In Quinton and Rutter's research, they were the 'planners'. Although the pre-existing personality characteristics must be an important determinant of coping style, this research also indicated that experiences at school had an influence.

POSSIBILITIES FOR EARLY PREVENTIVE WORK BY SCHOOLS

The young women in this research who were leaving care and who showed planning skills were more likely than those brought up in care but not classified as 'planners', to have positive experiences at school (Quinton *et al.*, 1984). This was not necessarily examination success; it might have been an enjoyment of school work, a memory of good relationships with peers, or a clearly positive recall of at least three other aspects of school life (e.g. sport, extracurricular hobbies, opportunity to learn a musical instrument). Experiences at school were not, however, linked to planning skills among girls with more normal parenting experiences. In other words, it seemed that for young people without a relationship with a parent or parent figure from which they could derive a sense of their own self-worth, schooling could at times provide a substitute source of self-esteem.

This finding has implications for preventive work in school settings. Teachers responsible for the pastoral care of pupils will often be fully aware of those children living in unhappy and unstable home circumstances and without good parental support. They could make it a policy to go to extra trouble to engage these children in roles from which they might gain a sense of their own self-worth and self-efficacy. It seems unlikely that many will gain self-esteem from academic achievement – nearly all the 45 care leavers followed up by Stein and Carey (1986) left school at 16 without any formal qualification.

PREVENTIVE WORK AFTER SCHOOL-LEAVING AGE

Although in school settings it can sometimes be a straightforward matter to identify young people with markedly poor parental support, given that their teachers will have got to know them quite well over a period of time, it is not a simple matter once they have left school. For those aged 16 to 18 years, an alternative source of information about adverse parenting would be the social services registers of young people who have recently been 'at risk' or 'in care'. However, given that at least this smaller high-risk group are readily identifiable, there are at least two pointers for preventive work, and these are the focus of this chapter.

Children in care may either be at home 'on trial', in a residential institution, or in foster care. Their options at 16, 17 or 18 years are therefore either to remain in or to return to live in a difficult family home situation, to remain with foster parents (if that is possible), or to look for independent accommodation. They therefore need first and foremost a source of advice, information and support to help them establish the best possible home situation, to resolve difficulties in housing, paying bills and getting work, and to avoid unwanted pregnancies. That is, the sort of support the more fortunate youngster gets from his or her family. As mentioned earlier, support at this crucial time appears to reduce considerably the likelihood of unwanted pregnancy (Quinton et al., 1984), girls leaving institutional care to return to a discordant family environment being more likely to get pregnant at a young age than those who stay on in the institution, and these more than those who return to a harmonious family.

Another opportunity for preventive work is with those girls who have been in care and have become pregnant before they have either a stable relationship, secure home or income of their own. Their vulnerability is obvious, and is reflected in their high incidence of depression. In the survey by Harris and colleagues (Harris et al., 1987), of the nine women who had been in care and were depressed when interviewed, seven had had a pre-marital pregnancy. Pre-marital pregnancy was therefore almost invariably a link between institutional care and later depression. This must be at least partly explained by the sequence of events which so often follows. A decision to marry or to cohabit at this time is often made for negative reasons; that is, because of the unwanted pregnancy, or to escape from intolerable home conditions, or both (Quinton et al., 1984). This increases the chance that the relationship will be far from ideal. Often the partner will have had a similarly unstable home background and many problems of his own. He may not then be able to become the supportive partner and home provider so much needed. Moreover, not infrequently the girl will be without a spouse or partner with whom to share the parenting task.

Of course, some of these young women will cope remarkably well, despite their multiple disadvantages, even if they do become pregnant. Such women, as might be expected, are also at reduced risk of developing depression. Brown and colleagues (1986a) showed that those pregnant young women in their survey who decided to marry or live with the father for positive reasons (i.e. not just because they were pregnant), or who arranged adoption or termination of pregnancy (although this was not common among girls with a background of poor parenting), were less likely to become depressed. Those who became single parents or involved in a non-harmonious relationship were much more likely to become depressed. There seemed to be some link between these coping styles and the personality characteristic of 'helplessness'. Quinton et al. (1984) described girls who cohabited with a man for positive reasons (i.e. not because of an unwanted pregnancy or to escape an unhappy home), and who had known the man for at least six months before cohabitation, as 'planners'. Such 'planning' was in turn related to later social functioning and parenting behaviour. If help and support during pregnancy could help the young woman to make positive choices about her future, and to help her in carrying through those decisions, her vulnerability to depression might reasonably be expected to be reduced. If she was also able to establish her own effective support system, to gain self-esteem from how she was coping, and to improve her capacity to establish control over her life in the future, the benefits might last. Together with information, advice and accessible local family planning services, such support would make further unintended pregnancies less likely.

YOUNG PEOPLE LEAVING CARE: SOME STATISTICS

During the year ending 31 March 1987 over 30,000 people left care in England (DOH, 1990). Most will have been in care some three to five years, while a minority spend most of their childhood in care. Stein's research in Wakefield suggests that about 40 per cent leave care from a foster care placement, 31 per cent from 'home on trial', 13 per cent from community homes and 11 per cent from lodgings or other placements (see Stein, 1987). However, they had usually had at least one change of living arrangement prior to this. Three-quarters of the 45 young people followed up after leaving care in Wakefield had experienced three or more placements, and over 40 per cent had had five or more placements (Stein and Carey, 1986). Lupton (1985) describes the experiences of care leavers in Hampshire in 1981/82. Over one-third of the 600 leavers had been living in institutional homes immediately before officially leaving care, but more than three-quarters of leavers had been in an institutional placement at some stage prior to this.

Lupton (1985) described the characteristics of care leavers likely to have the most marked problems in establishing satisfactory independent home lives of their own. First, those whose lives prior to coming into care were particularly traumatic, who may for instance have largely lost contact with their family, friends and a familiar community. Second, a number of different placements increased the young person's sense of insecurity. Placement mobility was particularly common among those young people who entered care during or after their early teenage years. A long stay in institutional care reduced opportunities to develop any sense of self-reliance or independence. Finally, those leaving care at a very early age tended to have greater difficulties.

Although residential care is often intended to be a short-term measure to enable observation and assessment prior to arranging a foster placement, as many as 30 per cent of care leavers in Hampshire were found to have spent two years or more in community homes (Lupton, 1985). Furthermore, 18 per cent (109) of these 600 care leavers had lived in three or more different residential homes.

Experiences increasing vulnerability tend to go together. That is, young people who had had a particularly traumatic period prior to entering care were more likely to be disturbed and difficult to place successfully. Those who had several placements were more likely to have spent considerable periods of time in residential homes. And those in residential placements were particularly likely to leave care early – over 90 per cent of the 198 leavers from residential homes in Hampshire left within a year of their sixteenth birthday. As Lupton remarks,

> This is a little disturbing when we consider that not only is the break from care to independence more radical in their case than it is for those living at home or with foster parents, but that also they generally have less family/community resources available to them when they leave.
>
> (Lupton, 1985)

But what is the picture when young people leave care? Accommodation, employment, managing a low-level income, loneliness and lack of support are the most common difficulties. For the first two, the size of the problem depends to a large extent on local circumstances: the availability of good quality, cheap accommodation and of jobs, and the policy of the housing department. The quality of the preparation for independence given to youngsters whilst in care and the support provided afterwards is likely to influence their ability to manage.

There is no official information collected by government departments on what happens to young people leaving care, and this must be a cause for concern in itself. Available evidence suggests that the general picture is one of frequent movement, unsatisfactory accommodation, high unemployment and loss of contact with family and friends (Mulvey, 1977; Stein and Carey, 1986). Of course frequent moving is not unusual for young people first stepping out into independence; what is unusual about care leavers is how early they live independently, how ill-equipped they often are to do so, and how little choice they usually have in whether or not to do so. The moving and influential papers by Wolmar (1980) and Grosskurth (1984) have fortunately resulted in a much greater awareness of the difficulties of care leavers and the failure of local authorities to provide anything approaching good parental support at this time. Since these reports, preparation for leaving care strategies for 15- to 18-year-olds in institutional settings have proliferated (although provision is still patchy in both quantity and quality), and two national voluntary groups to push for more and better support for these young people (Naypic and First Key) have been established. Grosskurth notes that in 1983 less than one in 200 young people were living alone by the age of 18, yet two-thirds of care leavers were doing so. Many have questioned why this vulnerable group have been considered capable of unsupported independent living at this age. The evidence suggests that many do not succeed. The report produced in collaboration with the Department of the Environment *Single and homeless* found that one-third of the single homeless people under the age of 20 had previously been in care (Drake *et al.*, 1981).

OPTIMUM SUPPORT

Many of the schemes to prepare young people for leaving care which have been developed since 1984 have a mechanical air. In some, the regime of the children's home remains unaltered, with little or no opportunity generally for making decisions about one's own life, self-catering, choosing one's own clothes, or learning about household maintenance and repair. But at the age of 15 or 16 the young person may be offered the chance to move into a separate (semi-independence) unit, either attached to the children's home or nearby, where greater personal responsibility is possible. They may then move on to an 'independence unit', a hostel or bedsit where they have short-term tenure before moving yet again to open market accommodation.

Such a scheme means that as they mature and require less help to perform basic household tasks, they will be moved into different accommodation. Misdemeanours may mean a move backwards (from the semi-independence unit back into the main home, say), or loss of the opportunity to rent council accommodation. First Key argue that it is the level of support which needs to change, not the accommodation, and support should not come to an abrupt end when the young person moves into fully independent housing. Furthermore, because of the conflicts of the dual role of providing support to the young person and acting as rent officer, First Key suggest that accommodation management for leavers should be organised completely separately from support services.

The concept of 'floating support' advocated by First Key is described as follows:

> The new objective of support work would be to facilitate young people to develop their own informal and formal support networks. This should be based on free access to information about mainstream services as well as enabling contact with peers, family, professionals and colleagues rather than the support worker themselves becoming the mainstay of the network. A crucial area which may need more input to start the building of a network is developing self-confidence and work on self-image and identity.

> (First Key, 1986)

Fixed-term placements are not thought to help improve self-determination, and it is suggested that more information about the choices available, and the constraints upon those choices, is essential. First Key would also like to see rights to housing extended over a period of time so that the young person knows that if an arrangement with a friend or relative does not work out, they still have the option of a housing place (First Key, 1986). The duration and intensity of 'floating support' should be controlled substantially by the individual young person. There need not be a strong predetermined goal of quickly tapering off contact.

MINIMISING RISK: 1 – SUPPORT DURING THE TRANSITION TO INDEPENDENCE: BRADFORD AFTER-CARE TEAM

Early in 1984 Bradford Social Services became the first local authority to offer a planned support service for young people leaving care with the appointment of two specialist after-care workers. They based the service in a former children's home, with which many of the leavers had been familiar, offering a source of advice and information, and organised social meetings. Two evening groups were set up, providing a definite contact point where young people knew they could meet each other and the after-care workers informally. These soon evolved a clear structure: a meal prepared by the young people, a discussion group on topics chosen by themselves and recreational activities: TV, table tennis, darts. Several daytime groups were also organised, such as an 'unemployed' group and a 'mothers with babies' group.

The after-care workers also offered counselling both to young people still in care but preparing to move out on their own, and to those living independently but finding problems in coping with either the practical or emotional demands facing them. This was available any day by appointment, and often if the individual simply called into the office. Frequently a problem might be raised in conversation at a group meeting and then discussed by appointment the following day.

A third role for the team was to help to develop the full range of necessary services: to negotiate with the local authority, housing associations and private landlords in order to make available suitable long-term accommodation, to help plan programmes of preparation for leavers, and to plan supervised and supported housing schemes for those who needed it.

During the first year of the project 150 requests for direct help and general referrals were received, indicating that the resources required were greater than could be provided by two workers. Use of the service grew considerably, and after three years, referrals were being received at the rate of 143 within a three-month period. In 1987 the team had grown to two full-time senior social workers, one part-time social worker and a full-time ex-residential worker. The value of the service was recognised in other parts of the country, and a number of other authorities set up similar services, with one or two on a much larger scale than that at Bradford. Leicester, for instance, employed more after-care workers to support fewer care leavers.

Of the first 75 referrals to the Bradford after-care service, one-third were preparing to leave care, half had left care, the remainder were in other circumstances. The reasons given for contacting the service included accommodation problems (37 per cent), interest in a social group meeting (24 per cent), a need for individual counselling (15 per cent), or advice about finances, education or employment (Raine, 1985). In 1987 accommodation was still the single most important issue for which the help of the after-care team was sought (45 per cent of referrals). Financial advice and assistance were also needed by a large number (25 per cent), and others (13 per cent) wanted to make social contacts and to meet other young people with a similar background. The remainder of the new referrals were pregnant young women or young women with babies needing help (8 per cent), or young people needing individual support over a short period for other reasons (8 per cent). Many young people who had been referred in previous years also continued to use the service.

The after-care workers estimated that between 80 and 100 (that is, roughly one-third) of care leavers in Bradford were attempting to set up home independently each year. Those most likely to contact the after-care team were those with the fewest sources of support from their family, little support from their substitute carers (staff at the children's home or their foster family), and whose social worker was providing little help. Many young people heard of the service through friends, some through care workers or social workers. Inevitably, with such an *ad hoc* system, some of the care leavers would not have heard about the service at all. For this reason, the team have planned to prepare a quarterly information bulletin to send to all fifteen-and-a-half-year-olds registered as 'in care' in Bradford.

The take-up of the offer of after-care support obviously depended on more than knowledge of its existence. A care leaver was more likely to make contact if encouraged to do so by a social worker or residential worker, if they already knew someone who went to group meetings, and if particularly desperate for help. Some, inevitably, preferred not to have further contact with social services. Young people of mixed race were under-represented among the client group, and young men were slightly more likely to use the service than were young women. The existence of a specialist field social worker for Afro-Caribbean children in care may to some extent explain the low numbers of mixed race clients, but this low take up was not fully understood. Young men have been found to have fewer home making and self-care skills, and often to need more help than young women.

Aims of the service

One of the two social workers who set up the scheme in 1984, Shane Billington, described to me the objectives of the service as she saw them. She felt that it was important for young people in care to know that all official help did not end on their eighteenth birthday and that there was a place they could turn to for expert advice on the special problems they might encounter in their transition to independence. The aim of the team was to enable the young people to be better able to deal with the practical and emotional problems they had to face, and prevent or at least reduce the need for future social work support. At a more fundamental level they aimed to prevent the young people getting into arrears with their rent and bills (or recurrences of such), and prevent homelessness. They also aimed to improve their clients' self-esteem through the way they related to them at social group meetings. In their caring role they tried to provide what a good parent would. Birthdays (particularly their eighteenth) and Christmas were celebrated together and presents exchanged. If a close relative died, but the individual had a difficult relationship with the family, they might go with him to the funeral. They gave practical help when the young person moved house. The contact was open-ended so that a young person could feel able to keep in touch as long as they wanted. They also aimed to help them to forge links with the local community, to find local opportunities for further education, and to look for work. The young people were treated as responsible adults towards whom staff were accepting, honest and realistic.

A description of a group meeting

A small building adjacent to the after-care offices was used for group meetings. After-care workers emphasised that a meeting place for the young people which is separate from staff offices and is effectively their own territory is essential. One of the two groups which met each week was for young people who had not yet left care or had recently left care, the other was run as a drop-in for older leavers and those who had attended the first group for over six months. Most of those present on the evening of my visit had already left care. I had been invited, and was expected by the dozen teenagers who had already arrived by 6.00 p.m. Several of them had been preparing the evening meal which had been purchased earlier in the day by social workers from their after-care budget. The meal had become an important feature of the meeting both because it had been found that many young people had poor diets (because of poor self-care skills and lack of money) and because it was a means of helping them to learn to co-operate with each other and share – something they were not used to doing. Two or three other young people arrived as we sat down to eat and exchange news. Several group members co-operated in the clearing away and washing up.

Everyone then moved into the adjacent room furnished with chairs and floor cushions. As the TV was broken, the usual half-hour viewing of a pop programme was missed. A planned weekend away was the first topic for group discussion before I was formally introduced (by the social worker) and my interest in after-care described. Group members had at an earlier meeting already discussed my visit and agreed that for my benefit, their experiences of preparing to leave care would be their topic for discussion for that meeting. One or two chose not to participate and played table tennis in the next room.

Steve began by describing the supported housing project where he was currently living: 'Oakland Project houses five young people who've left care. We have a support worker who comes round weekly and we have house meetings where we get together in one person's flat and we discuss various problems – rent and all that. I've been there about three years and it's all right . . . we all get on O.K. I'll move on eventually, but I've been settled there a while. It's not as protected now as we were when we first went in – that's through our choice. You're better there living and doing all right, cos if the support wasn't there, you know what I mean – you wouldn't be living where you were – it's just due to the support that's been available – you know what I mean . . . ?'

Steve had had a good experience of foster care immediately prior to leaving care and now thinks of those foster parents as his family. They helped prepare him for independence by encouraging him to buy his own food from an allowance, and helped him to find his first independent home – a bedsit on a large unpopular council estate, and still keep in touch. However, most of his previous parenting had been extremely poor. He was taken into care at the age of 3 months and moved in and out of his mother's home and a range of other homes to such an extent that he now jokes, 'I just keep calling everyone I meet Dad or Mum! Are you my Mum [laughingly to imaginary person]? Didn't you care for me as a child?' Despite his jovial personality, he now clearly needs a great deal of support and was unable to cope with living alone in a bedsit. 'The walls started to close in on me and I started to feel trapped, and when you've just left care it's difficult . . .'

Julie seems a little more resilient. She lived with her mother until the age of 12 after which she spent two periods of time in an assessment centre, a year-and-a-half in a children's home and a final placement with foster parents. But in the foster home she had shared her bedroom with her sister and the daughter of the foster parents and was desperate to leave to get some privacy. She feels her foster parents helped to make her independent, but that their support ended as soon as she moved out into her own flat. Fortunately she had already made contact with After-Care, as she received no help at this time from her own social worker. 'It was me foster Mum who had to go out and put her own money down on this flat for me.' To begin with, she was delighted to have a flat of her own, although she found weekends alone difficult. As soon as she could, she found a new home, sharing with a girlfriend. However, she was forced to move again 18 months later when her friend had a baby and she now lives in temporary housing for homeless girls. Although she says that for a while in the shared flat she had good support from a social worker, she values the continuity and strong support of the after-care scheme. 'I got more from this group than I did from social services or my foster parents. I don't come up every week now –

but you can just say what you've been doing . . . I've generally managed with things, you know.'

By contrast, two others in the group were able to describe extremely good relationships with social workers from whom they had derived a great deal of support. One had the same social worker from the age of 7 for ten years and was still in regular contact, now visiting her and her new baby in her own home as she was no longer working.

Other group members describe very negative experiences of care in the final years. In particular, the threat of being turned out of their home if they did not behave well, and their own powerlessness in this respect, was sometimes made explicit. As one boy remarked: 'It's hard to get a thing out of anyone. I got out of foster parents when I was 16 – which takes a lot of doing. It was as though I had no choice in the matter. If I wanted to leave it was just tough luck – it was going to take at least six months. But if they wanted to throw me out – then I was gone the next night. They kept threatening me with things like "I could ring up Mr A and he'll come over and we'll have your stuff packed and ready and you'll be gone within the hour." ' Despite frequent arguments and his disappearance to friends' homes for a few days at a time he always had to return and was almost 17 when finally he was enabled to move out. 'You really have to go through it to get out – and yet it seemed as though anyone in the social services circle could ship you anywhere without a single moment's notice. That seems a real bad problem.' Two other boys agreed and described how they had both, in fact, been moved out of one home into another with virtually no advance warning.

The conversation brought out a good deal of anger and frustration about the experiences of group members while in care. One had been highly controlled, another had been obliged to do a great deal of housework and cooking in the foster home, while the children who were the foster parents' own children did nothing. Two others described how the independence training flat at their children's home was used punitively as a response to difficult behaviour, rather than in a planned and positive way. They were forced to move into it against their wishes. Others described how, because they had not 'got on' with the officer in charge of a home, they had been forced to leave long before they felt ready to live independently.

The social worker explained that the care available to older teenagers is now improving since a higher payment has been agreed for families willing to foster a child over the age of 14. This has attracted a 'better' type of family to come into the fostering service, and these families are much more likely to continue to offer some support to their foster children after the young person has reached the age and level of competence to make the family no longer eligible for payments for him. This has also meant that one or two of the least supportive families no longer need to be used.

It was clear that many of the group had met each other at some point in their care history – while in an emergency foster placement or an assessment centre. To give me an idea of how long they had spent in care, they each told me how old they were when first admitted to care. Three had been in care from being just a few months old. Three others came into care between the ages of 6 and 10. Three more were aged 12 or 13 years, while two were 15 and one was 16 years old.

The discussions had used up the hour and the meeting broke up and people gradually left the building in small groups. Most of those present would be back the following week. When each had first come to a meeting, their own social worker may have come with them for the first half-hour, and the after-care workers would aim to spend most of the rest of the evening with them to help to make them feel welcome, something group members themselves find difficult to do. Young people usually attend regularly for a few weeks, and may then lose contact for several months, attending again only when a particular problem occurs, or if they have some good news. Most have stayed in touch for between two and three years, and will be invited (by letter, if not currently attending) to come back to join their Christmas celebrations for at least three years.

Resources

The after-care scheme was run by a staff of four. Three of the four were qualified social workers. One of the four worked part-time. The scheme was funded under Section 27 of the Child Care Act which covered their salaries, expenses and provided a small budget of £6,000 (1988 figure). They currently had one 'half-way' house in which they could accommodate three young people, and one supported housing scheme for five young people in a housing association property. In the latter scheme, permanent tenancies were offered, with the agreement that when the individual wanted to settle with a partner or have children, they would move to other accommodation. Two more properties were currently being prepared as supported projects, housing a total of 11 more young people, and all the regular supportive visiting presently provided to the existing support project would need to cease by the time both new houses were occupied. A housing association had offered five more houses to enable the team to develop additional supported living schemes, but they were unable to take these on as they had insufficient numbers of staff to be able to provide the support, management and administration which would be needed. If they had additional resources, the team would also have liked to be able to offer emergency accommodation for the homeless, and temporary accommodation for those needing a short escape from difficult living arrangements.

Client interviews

Angela, aged 17, and her daughter, aged 5 months

Angela left the children's home where she had lived for nine years when she was 16, shortly before the home was scheduled to close. The closure was regretted by Angela, who had been happy in the home and now had no possibility of return visits to see the place and the people she had grown to love. However, although the staff had moved on to other homes, several had kept in touch – her key worker had visited her every week. Angela also regularly went to see one of the other ex-staff in her new place of work nearby. And she had a large network of friends and relatives. One of her friends from the home now lived in a nearby block of flats, and her six sisters and two brothers also lived in the area. Four of her siblings had lived in the same children's home as herself and during their early years in care they had been able to return to their mother's home at weekends. It had been planned that all children would return home when their mother was able to cope with them, but the date was put back several times because of their mother's own health problems and road accident injuries. When Angela was 11, her mother died.

Currently, Angela was living in a pleasant two-bedroom council flat on the sixth floor of a block on a large estate, with her boyfriend and their 5-month-old daughter. She had met her boyfriend when she was 14 years old while truanting from school to visit a nearby city. The staff at the children's home had tried to discourage the relationship, but as she was determined to keep seeing him the social worker had eventually helped to find them this council flat. After-Care had assisted in getting their names on to housing association and council lists for a house, and she was hopeful they would move within six months. Their baby had not been planned.

Angela had attended school fairly well, but left without sitting any examinations. Both she and her boyfriend had worked in a paint tin factory but currently both were unemployed. Angela was the youngest of her siblings and the two eldest girls, aged 29 and 30, seemed to have taken on a parental role toward her. But she felt she had quite a close relationship with all her family. Recently, she had been spending a great deal of time with an older sister following a tragic family event. Her sister's husband had been stabbed by his brother in a fight at their mother's home, and had died. Angela's sisters were taking it in turns to stay with their widowed sister to help look after the children and prevent her carrying out her threatened suicide.

I asked Angela how she knew of After-Care, and she told me that one of the staff from the children's home had gone to work in an intermediate treatment service in the same building that After-Care was based in, and had told her about it. Angela had in fact already heard about it through friends, but had chosen not to get involved, as she didn't feel she needed it. However, when her social worker ceased contact when she moved into her flat, she felt she still needed social work advice and contacted After-Care. For instance, when she wanted to see if they could get a house, and when they ran into debt when their post office giros didn't arrive, she wanted advice from a social worker. After-Care had helped her with both problems. They had also helped her to get a clothing grant at Christmas and obtained a lump sum to pay off her electricity and rent arrears. They had secured grants for her for baby equipment, a fire guard and safety gate and helped her generally to sort out her finances. By keeping the young couple out of debt, and helping them to manage their income more efficiently, After-Care had prevented their financial difficulties from getting out of hand.

Angela realised that these sorts of debts could only be paid off for them once, and that she would now have to cope, but knew that she could obtain advice whenever she needed it from After-Care. She had attended an occasional group meeting at After-Care, but now she had a baby, the After-Care worker came to visit her at home. She was invited to the After-Care Christmas party and was touched to find she even received a Christmas present. She felt she would need to stay in contact for a while, particularly since there were many changes in the DSS payment schemes planned for April. She had had a long battle getting the correct payments originally, which had caused her to get into debt, and was worried she may have further problems when the system was changed.

My impression from meeting Angela was that despite the traumatic experiences of her past and the extremely disturbing recent event, she was probably one of After-Care's clients who least needed them. She appeared to have a good relationship with her boyfriend and she had her own highly valued social support network. She needed practical help only to enable her to sort out her financial and housing problems, and had her social worker continued to provide this it would have been enough. However, several clients of After-Care are similar – people whose social workers had discontinued support.

Peter, aged 20

Peter had lived in a children's home for six years, from the age of 10. He returned to live with his mother for two years when he reached the age of 16, and then went into the Army. After six months he left the Army and went back to his mother's house for a couple of weeks before he was offered the one-bedroom council flat he had lived in for the past two years.

Peter met me at the entrance to the low-rise block on the outskirts of Bradford. His ground-floor flat was badly designed and in a strikingly poor state of repair. Black damp areas were showing through new layers of paint, a broken window was covered in polythene. Offcuts of wood burned in the open fireplace, the only form of heating in the flat. A year previously while his brother was staying in the flat there had been a fire in his sitting room causing the loss of the new furniture and part of the floor. Peter repainted the flat and purchased replacement second-hand furnishings. Not all the problems were linked to the fire: windows let the water in, pipes in the kitchen leaked, and a layer of water lay under the linoleum in there. Despite its disrepair, Peter says he would probably stay there if the council would agree to do improvements to it.

Peter had a good preparation for leaving care. He lived for two years with six others in a 'semi-independence' unit – a house a short distance from the main children's home. A member of staff lived in, but they did their own catering and cleaning and had a considerable amount of freedom. 'Once we were in there, I think it were the best time I had, ever.' Currently, Peter was unemployed. Following his six months in the Army, he had a four-month temporary job in a garage, three months in a mill (which he'd found too boring), and a few part-time odd jobs. Now he chased any job he saw advertised at the job centre, and had recently applied to the Inland Revenue. He wanted to work full-time, but had also considered doing part-time classes in draughtsmanship or design. He had missed most of his examinations at school, but passed those he sat, and excelled in art.

He saw his three brothers and his parents (both now remarried) regularly, often several times a week. He also had a good friend called Chris, whom he saw once a week or more. Chris's brother was currently staying with Peter as he was on bail for theft and needed to give a secure address to the court. Peter was always willing to help out friends and relatives, frequently incurring expense which he could not afford. Giving his youngest brother use of the flat while he was away working had left him with an electricity bill of £200. As he was unable to pay this, his supply had been cut off. Some weeks later, when he told staff at After-Care about his situation, they obtained a lump sum to add to the amount he had saved in order to get him straight. Currently he was out of debt, and he had small electricity bills which he could afford. Recently, After-Care helped him out of a difficult situation again, when he and his friends ran out of money and food over the Christmas period.

He had heard about After-Care just over a year previously. An ex-residential worker (Dave) went with him to introduce him to After-Care staff. He was asked to join the Wednesday group, and because Dave had taken him there personally, he felt obliged to 'give it a go'. Through these meetings he met John, who was running the Wednesday group, and 'had a laugh' with him. He saw John as a friend in whom he could confide and whom he could drop in to see at any time. He had been particularly helpful when Peter had gone through a painful separation from his girlfriend. After their initial separation, she had discovered she was pregnant, and for a while they renewed the friendship, planning and saving for the baby. However, the couple did not get on well and soon split up again, 'and she started being silly and wearing tight clothes and I was certain she was doing everything she could to lose it'. He was obsessed with the worry she would miscarrry, and when she did 'I was really peeved . . . it were about the only time I would have wanted to do meself in – cos I were that peeved . . . ' He got very upset if he saw his girlfriend afterwards. 'I just used to look at her and think – "you cow!" She didn't seem to care . . . ' John was very supportive and helped him to take his mind off it. 'When me mind were off it I were normal . . . I could have a laugh . . . but when I thought about it it really wound me up. It doesn't bother me so much now, unless someone brings a kid in at After-Care . . . He [John] didn't give me advice or tell me what to do – he'd just listen. But things aren't that bad now. They're getting better. Things are good really, apart from not having a job.'

Peter is clearly someone who would benefit from continued support. His trusting, easy-going and generous nature is likely to mean he continues to be used by friends and to get into debt on other people's behalf. In less than two years of independence he has had his flat gutted by fire, his electricity supply cut off, suffered a major loss (the child he might have had), run out of money, and accommodated at least three friends or relatives for varying periods of time. His own support network is clearly ineffective and he is emotionally vulnerable. After-Care has played a major role in helping him cope.

Sonya, aged 19

Sonya moved into After-Care's first supported housing project when she was 17. She had a bedsit on the top floor, but when the warden recently moved out she asked for and received his large one-bedroom flat on the first floor. It had central heating, large, pleasantly furnished rooms, and overlooked a communal garden.

Sonya's support worker from After-Care (Eileen) visited each Tuesday, and she and the tenants met in each flat in turn to discuss any problems 'and have a laugh'. The tenants of the house regularly called in to visit each other. Sonya also had a good friend whom she saw about three times a week, and she spent a day with her mother once every few weeks. They 'get on O.K.'. But her mother had given her no support in setting up home on her own or moving house. Her own social worker no longer visited, and her contact with After-Care had declined from two to four times a week when she first moved into her bedsit to one to two times a week.

Sonya told me that she was first taken into care at the age of 11 months, to a children's home in Birmingham. Her father had more or less abandoned his family and her mother was unable to cope alone in a bedsit with her two children. Sonya was fostered by her mother's parents until her grandfather died, after which her grandmother could no longer cope. She was taken back into a children's home at the age of 8, and back to her mother when she was 9. By then her mother had remarried and had three more children. This worked well for a while, and Sonya was very fond of her stepfather. However, her mother and stepfather divorced when she was 13, which Sonya was unable to understand, and for which she held her mother to blame. Sonya started to truant from school and to run away from home. When she was 15 she walked into a police station and told them she did not want to go back home. One of her brothers was already in care as he had attempted to set fire to the family home on three separate occasions.

Sonya was fostered for two weeks before going to an assessment centre, where she stayed for six months. After three months she felt settled and did not want to move again, but she was placed next in a children's home for ten boys and ten girls. She stayed almost a year and 'sort of liked it'. She renewed contact with her mother while there, but then broke it again soon afterwards. The staff at the home discussed independence with her and she spent a few months in a semi-independence flat in the home. When she told staff she wanted to leave the home and have a flat of her own, they tried hard to dissuade her, wanting her to stay on in the home for at least another year. However, as she was determined to leave, they agreed to help her to flat-hunt. Her name was on a waiting list for a housing association flat and for a council flat, but she thought it would take too long.

Her £300 leaving care grant was spent on bedding, pots and pans, an iron, and so on. A few months after moving in to her first bedsit she found herself a maisonette and moved. Several friends moved in with her but the arrangement was not successful. When the others moved out she was both lonely and unable to pay the rent. Soon afterwards she was offered a flat in the house where she lives now, through After-Care.

Sonya had been fortunate in making contact with After-Care almost as soon as she left the children's home. While in the first bedsit, she had met two other young people living in the same block who had also been in care. They were involved in After-Care and took her down there with them the first week after she moved in. One of these boys 'was like a brother'.

As she was not receiving any housing benefit, workers at After-Care first helped her to claim this. She had found 'a little job' for £30 a week, and as her rent was £15, she received a rent rebate of £7. But Sonya felt she still had too little money to survive on, and gave up the job. She took another job outside Bradford at a mill where her mother worked. But the journey made it a long day – leaving home at 6.45 a.m., returning at 6 p.m., and Sonya could not sustain it. She began to lose weight after a period with a good deal of overtime, and could not cope. She became ill and gave up the job and had been unemployed since (almost a year). She now lived 'on the dole' of £62.90 fortnightly, and her rent was paid.

Q Do you still go to After-Care to sort out your bills?

A Well I'd try to sort it out meself first. But if I really did get stuck I'd go across for help. I can't depend on them all me life.

Q And you would also talk to them if you got upset about something?

A *Yeah - if me and me Mum had had another row, or if someone were hassling me, you know, just stuff like that . . . I could ring up and ask someone to come over if I were right upset - or just turn up. When I were at [the flats] . . . I'd be up there a few times a week! I were on the gas [butane gas] - and I wanted to get off it - but I did and I didn't . . . People say it's not addictive but I'd say it were . . . it were just like an escape cos I used to go on these real downers and get really depressed and that and think - oh I want a tin of gas - cos you forgot your problems then . . .*

Q *Did you ever feel suicidal? [Sonya showed me her wrists] Goodness - you have! How many times?*

A *About three. I never got taken to hospital for me wrists cos I always quitted on that one - you know, I'd get so far and think 'gulp!' . . . but the tablets - I were in Manchester then and I took 24 paracetamol and a quarter-bottle of rum and were found collapsed on t'road. But I were out the same night - cos they just pump you all out. That's when I were still at home. I slashed me wrists once while at home and once while at the maisonette.*

Q *Do you get depressed now?*

A *Not really. If I do I just go out for a walk or see somebody - I don't think about committing suicide anymore. And I won't take gas anymore - I won't even buy gas in the 'ouse. And I don't drink hardly.*

Q *What do you think has stopped you getting depressed?*

A *I don't know - I've just mixed in with a load of new people and I've got lots of people I can just go and visit and talk to, you know?*

Q *So if you're feeling down now - who would you go and see?*

A *It depends what kind of downer I'm on. If it's a really bad one I'll give Eileen a ring, or she'll see and say 'Come on - what's up' . . . she can tell when I'm down, I don't know why . . . It were After-Care that brought me out of me shell like that, cos at first I wouldn't talk to anybody - I'd just let it all build up and that's when I'd feel suicidal and that.*

Q *How did they bring you out of your shell? By talking one-to-one or in groups?*

A *Sometimes they talk to you in groups. Sometimes one-to-one. But they wouldn't say 'Come on what's up with you' - they'd just talk friendly and eventually you just bring it all out yourself. Before then I couldn't trust anybody. But Eileen has been really good to me - and she's always there when I need her.*

Q *Can you talk in the group meeting now?*

A *About some things yeah. But some things I'd rather keep to meself or just me and Eileen or me and me friend Sue. Sue and me know each other inside out. She's helped me through a lot of rough patches [she's been a friend for two years].*

Q *Do you expect to keep in contact with After-Care?*

A *Yeah - I'll just pop up when I want to. I don't go so often now. I've got to make a break. They're not going to be there all me life and I've been going two years . . . it's mostly 16 to 21 but you can still pop up afterwards. She'll be down on Monday – we're going to get my housing benefit sorted out . . . They kept losing all me forms and at one point me arrears went up to over £300 cos housing benefit weren't paying it.*

Q Has After-Care made you feel any differently about your childhood problems?

A I don't hate me Mum as much as I used to. I used to really hate her. But now I can see things from her point of view as well.

Q Is that because of people at After-Care – or do you think it might be just because you're older?

A I think it's through talking to people at After-Care – cos I understand it all better now. At first I were pretty selfish – I just thought of meself.

Q Do you ever discuss your plans for the future with anyone at After-Care to try to give your own kids a better life than you had?

A I don't think so. I discuss it with Sue. I want kids as soon as possible. I'd love to be pregnant now. But I don't want to get married. My boyfriend wants kids an' all and there'd be no stopping him seeing the kid – but I don't think I want to live with him. I don't want to give this place up. My real dad kept walking out, and when me stepdad left we nearly all had to go in care – so it's better if you don't have someone at the beginning. Otherwise if we split up – how's it going to affect the kids? I'll have someone there – but if they start relying on the father when they're older and then he leaves – that's no good for the kids, is it?

Q Do you think you'd be able to cope without anyone?

A Yeah – I think it'll be hard . . . I haven't taken any precautions since I was 16 – so I don't know if I'm able . . .

I asked her how she planned to support the baby. She gave me a range of equally unrealistic options. Also she does not seem to have appreciated that she will not be allowed to remain in her present flat if she has a child.

Problems encountered in running the after-care scheme

One of the major difficulties the after-care scheme had endeavoured to overcome was the lack of priority given by the council in housing the young people leaving its care. After four years the council had agreed to review the 'pointing' of this group so that they received greater priority. Until recently they had faced long waits for a council house, and the flats offered were often the difficult-to-let properties for single people in poor districts, on large unpopular estates or in poor condition. Ideally, these young people needed to be offered a flat within three months of their application so that they were able to do some realistic forward planning, but this did not happen. If anything the housing situation had worsened, because the housing stock was not increasing but there were an increasing number of high-priority groups. The policy of finding community rather than hospital accommodation for more mentally handicapped, infirm and mentally ill people had increased the numbers of their rivals.

The social workers in After-Care had built up a good relationship with many housing departments and housing associations which helped them in many individual applications, but a 'who-you-know system' is no substitute for a positive policy. One obstacle to such a policy was that After-Care were not able to support all young people leaving care and wanting council accommodation, and those without support were more likely to become a liability to the housing department. After-Care's inability to support all care leavers in their own homes was not simply attributable to staffing level; some young people did not want any further contact with social workers.

The supported housing scheme had proved extremely valuable, but one early assumption about its operation had had to be revised. It had been thought that an older person in one of the flats was needed as a 'liaison tenant', someone who had also been in care but could have a supportive and supervisory role to the others. However, this arrangement had been discontinued: it had proved an impossible role as the other tenants felt he was 'spying' on them and were unsure whether he was checking up on their behaviour or offering support.

Another difficulty was that although young people leaving care who are under 18 should still be supported by their own social workers, many social workers effectively handed over all responsibility to After-Care if the young person was offered a place in their housing scheme. Yet those offered such places (like Sonya, p.76), were those who needed a great deal of help – help which to a large extent their own social workers should continue to provide. If it falls instead to After-Care workers this limits the number of supported housing schemes they can set up.

Another early assumption which proved to be misplaced was that older leavers would be able to help support new leavers. As it turned out, their help was often inappropriate – they might, for instance, take a 15-year-old to the local pub. They were not free enough of their own problems to be able to provide valuable counselling, and it was too much responsibility for a group of people who were still needing some support themselves. Furthermore, it created a hierarchy within After-Care in which older leavers identified more with staff than with other leavers.

It had also been thought that once After-Care had existed for more than a year, and had made contact with all the residential homes and responsible social workers, the availability of their service would become common knowledge. However, it had been found that as staff in children's homes change frequently, After-Care needed to continue to publicise themselves.

One further change had been made. Initially After-Care workers had aimed to offer support of a parental nature. But they had found that if they become too close and too much like parent figures to individual leavers they could create dependency rather than foster independence. The line between being where they were needed but not offering too much was a fine one.

Evaluation

No attempt to evaluate this service has been made. However, within the terms of this book, there is circumstantial evidence to suggest that it is effective in preventing psychiatric disorder. The client group are known to be those care leavers who by and large have the least satisfactory support network. They also have a parenting history associated with a raised risk of adult depression, social difficulty, and problems of parenting when they have children themselves. The service has offered a stable and secure source of support to which care leavers feel able to return when they encounter difficulties, as the client interviews and group discussion confirmed. There are many instances where After-Care staff have averted homelessness and have been the only effective source of support to enable young people to cope with a range of other practical and emotional crises they have encountered. What would have happened to Peter and Sonya without their assistance? Interviews with these two young people also indicated improvements in their confidence and self-esteem attributable to contact with After-Care. And the continued group attendance of many of the young people, and their long-term contact with the service, indicate that they value it. For such a vulnerable group, the kind of support provided by After-Care could be argued to be the very *least* which should be available.

That this service, although a pioneering one, is still to some extent insufficient is indicated by their inability to make contact with and offer support to all young people leaving care, by the very low take-up of their service by children of mixed race (of whom there are many in Bradford), and by the low level of supported accommodation they are yet able to offer. Many leavers must still cope with living alone, albeit with After-Care support, which is neither normal for nor desired by their age group. Of course some of those not in contact with After-Care will have been supported by efficient and caring residential and field workers. Unfortunately it was unclear how many young people there were who needed help but were not receiving any. More co-ordination, clearer policies and guidelines, and a contracted basis for shared work with other social workers would seem necessary, and possible *within* the existing resources (see After-Care Team, 1987).

The After-Care team devoted almost all their effort toward basic goals like housing, financial competence and building social networks. In these areas they had made considerable achievements. Their relatively long experience of specialising in support for this age group also meant that After-Care workers gained detailed knowledge about all potential sources of accommodation and the available state benefits, and built up a close relationship with housing associations and the local council. This meant that they could often secure accommodation which would otherwise not have been offered to these individuals. However, there was little evidence as to whether they might be succeeding in other areas such as getting young people to further their education or vocational training. A disturbingly high number of the care leavers seemed to be unemployed. Moreover there was nothing to suggest that After-Care workers had had any influence on the policies of individual children's homes to improve either their preparation for leaving care schemes or the opportunities for young people to stay on in the homes or to return to them when housing difficulties arose.

Young people who have spent some time in care are quite evidently a group who need support from statutory services which is flexible enough to last until they have established independent lives, a support network, and have learnt how to manage a home, work and finances. While they may continue to have difficulties, most, with help, will learn how to 'get by'. This is the role After-Care fulfils. Without it, more young people would be homeless, lonely, without basic commodities like electricity or gas, depressed, or suicidal. If statutory services have deemed the natural parental support unsatisfactory, and have taken parenting responsibilities away from parents and on to the local authorities, surely those authorities should provide the support a good parent would offer at this important transition?

MINIMISING RISK: 2 – SUPPORT DURING AND AFTER PREGNANCY

Although teenage girls are frequently as capable, loving and efficient mothers as women several years their senior, statistics show that on average they will have many more disadvantages. Early disadvantage, early motherhood and later social and emotional difficulties seem to be highly associated with each other. For instance, Birch's longitudinal study of 122 pregnant schoolgirls in an inner London borough (Birch, 1986) revealed that 40 per cent of families were already known to social service agencies before their daughter's pregnancy, and 20 per cent of the girls had been in care.

Young people and motherhood: some statistics

About one newborn child in ten in England and Wales has a mother who is not yet 20 years old. The total was 60,754 in 1980, and an estimated 36,000 teenagers that year had pregnancies that were terminated or resulted in a stillbirth (Wells, 1983).

Wells examines these statistics in the light of data from two major British studies, one based on a cohort of more than 1,000 teenage mothers from the

1970 British Births Survey (Taylor *et al.*, 1983), the other an in-depth examination of the circumstances of 92 teenagers presenting at booking clinics in Bristol in 1980 (see Wells, 1983). Follow up of the former group show that children born to teenage mothers face a raised chance of experiencing a wide range of physical and educational problems. Infant mortality during their first year of life is 50 per cent higher than for children of mothers of all age groups combined, and at birth babies born to teenage mothers are considerably lighter than those born to older women, more likely to be born pre-term or post-mature, and more likely to suffer foetal distress during labour. During their pre-school years, they are more likely to need hospital treatment even if disparities in social and biological factors are allowed for. At school, compared to children born to older mothers, they have poorer performance scores in vocabulary, motor co-ordination and cognitive ability, shorter stature, and a raised rate of bad behaviour.

These differences are thought to reflect the effects on the child's experience of the disadvantages associated with teenage childbearing (Wadsworth *et al.*, 1984). Teenage mothers frequently have unsatisfactory support from parents and partners, few material resources, and their opportunities for taking up employment or further education are restricted. 'Available evidence [suggests] . . . that motherhood serves to inhibit any potential that might otherwise exist for escaping from the difficulties and disadvantages already confronting many teenagers at the time they become pregnant'. (Wells, 1983). For instance, teenage mothers among the British Births Cohort were found to be less educated than women of their age not having children, and this situation did not change over five years – that is – there was little chance that they would catch up on their education or, for that matter, improve their social and economic circumstances over time. The five-year follow-up also found a raised rate of depression among these young mothers (Wells, 1983).

While about one in four teenage pregnancies are planned and wanted, and other pregnancies are unintended but not necessarily unwanted, the Bristol Bookings Survey showed that at least one in three of those pregnancies which successfully went to term were to single women who were distressed by their unintended pregnancy.

So why do they carry it to term? Experience of supporting and educating pregnant schoolgirls over a 13-year period led Hudson and Dawson (1987) of the Bristol Unit for Schoolgirl Mothers to put forward the following reasons. First is denial of the pregnancy – the belief that 'it can't happen to me' – coupled with a history of erratic menstrual periods during adolescence, which often means the girl is unaware of her pregnancy until an advanced stage, too late for termination to be an option. Second is the fear of telling anyone and therefore discussing practical responses. Often too the girls dare not face the fact themselves and therefore put off the trip to have a pregnancy test for many weeks.

The much reduced social stigma attached to single parenthood and illegitimate birth must also be a factor. This reduced stigma has also affected the proportion of girls having babies who decide against marrying the father. Even those who wish to continue the relationship with the father and had planned and wanted the pregnancy increasingly now choose to do so out of wedlock. And many fewer girls with unintended and unwanted pregnancies feel pressured to get married 'for the sake of the baby', to a partner who might otherwise not have been chosen. In 1984, 62 per cent of births to teenagers in England and Wales were illegitimate compared with 23 per cent 20 years earlier (Brook Advisory Centres, 1986).

If all abortions (approximately 36,000) and at least two-thirds of births (40,000) to teenagers represent unwanted or at least unplanned conceptions, these estimates indicate that effective use of contraception would have had the possibility of preventing about 76,000 unwanted teenage pregnancies in 1980. Research by the Bristol team (see Wells, 1983) indicated that some of these young women make no use of contraception at all, but a significant group will have been regular users of contraception, but for one reason or another had given up their chosen method (perhaps finding problems with it), and failed to replace it with another, without specifically wanting to become pregnant.

Nevertheless, the indications are that teenagers are much more effective in preventing unwanted pregnancies now than they were 20 years ago. Compared with 20 years ago, more people are sexually active in their teens and more begin sex at a younger age (Brook Advisory Centres, 1986). However, the teenage conception rate (births plus abortions) has been falling since the early 1970s (from 82 per 1,000 women aged 15 to 19 in 1970, to 60 in 1984; see Brook Advisory Centres, 1986). Of course, improvements in the efficiency of known methods of contraception must be partly responsible but the easy availability of these to teenagers is of considerable importance, as cross-country comparisons have shown. Other countries where the same methods are obtainable have not achieved as great an improvement (e.g. the United States) and others have achieved more (Sweden and the Netherlands) apparently due to *accessibility* of family planning services (Jones *et al.*, 1985). Free contraceptive services, wide acceptability among the medical profession for the contraceptive pill as the most appropriate method for adolescents, sex education, and a link between schools and contraceptive clinic services for adolescents all appear to be related to rates of unintended pregnancy (Jones *et al.*, 1985).

For girls who have already conceived an unwanted pregnancy, it is not too late for education, advice about contraception, and counselling to have a preventive effect. Indeed, teenage mothers more frequently than older mothers go on to conceive several more unwanted pregnancies within a short interval (see Osofsky *et al.*, 1973). How can the risk of further unwanted pregnancies be reduced, and the disadvantages of early motherhood be minimised? Young people without support from their family or from the father of the child, and who have had poor parenting experiences themselves will be most in need of assistance from external sources. They will need more than advice on contraception in order to cope with the difficulties of single parenthood and to reduce their high risk of depression. Often, they need a good deal of nurturing themselves. One possible way forward is described below.

ST MICHAEL'S HOSTELS, SOUTH LONDON

The Fellowship of St Michael and All Angels was founded at the turn of the century with the aim of helping unmarried mothers and their babies (Pettigrew, 1987). Until the end of the 1960s it ran various homes for educated girls from the professional classes. As society's values changed and the stigma of single parenthood diminished, the needs of this client group diminished. St Michael's have since focused instead on young unsupported mothers coming from deprived backgrounds, and older single mothers, two-parent families and occasionally single fathers with special problems such as mental illness, learning difficulties, or a history of drug or alcohol abuse.

At present St Michael's run three hostels for these groups in South London, and a fourth hostel is planned to open in 1991. They aim to help mothers to improve their home making and child care skills, to gain confidence in their own ability, to be fully prepared for independence, and hence prevent the need for their own children to be taken into care. The hostels provide pleasant, comfortable surroundings to enable the families to feel 'at home', but also to give a clear message to them that the staff and the organisation value them as individuals – they are 'special'. This is felt to be an important characteristic of the projects because of the low sense of self-worth of the client groups. A professional social worker lives in each hostel and has a high degree of autonomy in the running of the house. But as a small voluntary organisation the staff provide each other with a close and strong support network and develop committed personal relationships with the mothers with whom they work.

The hostel which I visited works entirely with adolescent mothers. Most of the referrals to whom they offer accommodation are between 16 and 18 years old, and have been brought up in care or in insecure, unstable families. They usually arrive shortly after giving birth and are, prior to referral, homeless. They stay at St Michael's for about 18 months. Eight young women and their babies can be accommodated, and between 1972 and 1987, over 80 mothers spent some time there.

The hostel itself is a large rambling Victorian house set well back from the road and with a long garden at the rear, with a swing. It contains eight bedsitting rooms on the first and second floors, each with its own small kitchen. There is one bathroom on the top floor, two on the middle floor. On the ground floor is a communal sitting room and kitchen and a 'sleeping-in'-room/office for staff. There is also a playroom and a laundry room. The remaining rooms on the ground floor are made into a two-bedroom self-contained flat for the residential social worker and her husband, which also occasionally serves as a meeting room.

Each bedsitting room is fully furnished but the young women must purchase their own furniture for the baby, and luxury items such as a television. As they will need these items when they leave the hostel, it is thought prudent for them to acquire them as soon as they arrive. The cot and cot-bedding are often bought with the maternity grant payable by the DSS after the baby's birth. The rooms also have gas fires, and both gas and electricity are metered for the young woman to pay herself. The women claim DSS benefits, which include income support, and their rent is paid by Housing Benefit.

Referral and selection of pregnant girls

St Michael's advertise their residential support service in social services offices in the area, and social workers refer women to the project. The residential worker at the hostel for teenage mothers sometimes receives several telephone enquiries a day; written referrals averaged at seven each week in mid-1987. Those social workers who have kept in touch about the possibility of a place will be told when one becomes vacant, others will be assumed to have found a place elsewhere. The girls referred will also have been invited to the house to see around and meet the staff and the other young women. The place will be offered after a selection meeting of the residential social worker, assistant director and a St Michael's Fellowship committee member. A choice is made on the basis of age (16 to 18 years), vulnerability, poor childhood parenting experience. As there will frequently be several who meet these criteria, the residential worker will recommend the young woman she and her team feel would fit in best with the existing group, and who appears most enthusiastic about moving to the hostel. The girls offer each other a great deal of support, and each new young mother needs to be able to live with the others to get something from their friendship, and to be able in her turn to give support to the others.

Unsuccessful applicants to St Michael's can only pursue the small number of other mother and baby units in London (about which St Michael's staff will advise them), or seek some other housing option. About four out of five applicants must be turned away, despite being suitable candidates. This is an under-estimate of demand, as many social workers do not put in written applications to St Michael's when a verbal contact has indicated the extent of current competition for places.

Living at St Michael's

During 1989 and 1990 the regime of the house became more structured than it had been when I visited. Mothers living in the hostel are now expected to stay in the house during the mornings, and this time is spent caring for the baby, having key worker sessions, meeting with their own social worker, or doing their household chores. After 1 p.m., they may come and go as they please, their friends and boyfriends can visit, but overnight stays are not permitted. The mothers are expected to establish a routine for their baby, with regular sleeping and eating patterns, and to keep their room clean and tidy. They may babysit for each other, but must not leave the baby with the staff. The team aim to help them understand and accept the physical, emotional and developmental needs of their children and to become good parents. For the most part, this is done in an informal, unstructured way as part of daily living, and great care is taken not to undermine the mother's already fragile self-confidence. Because they are in a residential setting, staff rapidly become aware of specific skills a mother lacks, and they look for naturally occurring opportunities to teach them.

However, as the young women at the hostel have usually come from a background of poor parenting, sexual abuse or neglect, they are often so lacking in self-esteem that they have little capacity to offer emotional support to their child. It is recognised by staff that they must be helped to overcome their own difficulties before they can be fully effective in helping them to develop their parenting skills. Many of the young women believe that motherhood and independence are going to be easy and then find that they are not. Some will say that they have been looking after younger siblings or cousins for years, yet are clearly unaware of the most simple dangers to avoid in the care of their baby.

Furthermore, workers here, as well as other experienced workers in the field, have noted the frequency with which young women with such disadvantaged home backgrounds establish impoverished relationships with men, and often with men whose childhood was also characterised by deprivation or neglect. Abuse and abandonment of the women by their partners is something both parties may be used to and is what they expect.

The presence of a social worker and her partner in the hostel provides an alternative model of a relationship, and there are obvious advantages to this residential arrangement. It was pointed out, for instance, that some women calling in to the flat were astonished if they saw the social worker's husband cooking, ironing or cleaning. The previous residential social worker had lived in the flat with her husband and two children, so that at that time there were the additional advantages to the young women of witnessing at first hand the way in which the social worker and her partner related to their own children.

One of the many important issues for discussion at St Michael's is contraception. Despite regular encouragement to consider this matter, it has been found that some of the women fail to protect themselves adequately from further unwanted pregnancies. One of the difficulties appears to be the attitude, common among the partners, that the ability to father children is a measure of their masculinity. Partly, too, the women are sometimes willing to give their boyfriend whatever he asks of them, including a baby. Some of the young men, still in their teens, had already fathered several children. Some women, of course, wanted to have more children, but did not necessarily assume they needed either a home or a stable partner first. In fact, only a few of the mothers who live at the hostel move on to live with the father of their child, and very rarely do any of them marry – nor do they wish to.

Many of these mothers will have missed a fair amount of education. Occasionally one of the young women will have a poor level of literacy and numeracy and may even need help to memorise methods of making up baby food or milk, or how to sterilise equipment, in order to avoid the need to rely on written instructions on the packets. After a short time at St Michael's, when any difficulties of adjusting to motherhood and other specific problems have been identified, one of the staff will spend an hour or two each day planning with the mother what she needs to do. Frequently an individual contract is drawn up with personal targets, restrictions or routines. For a child considered at risk of accidental injury, one of the many items the contract may include is a weekly visit to the clinic. For a girl who lives in a chaotic and dirty room, failing to keep rubbish in an enclosed bin or wash dishes or baby bottles between use, the contract may include a daily routine of housework every morning straight after breakfast.

Josie

Josie, aged 21, has a son, Remi, who is 9 months old. They are black. They arrived at St Michael's six months ago and are leaving again in two or three weeks' time, as housing has been found for them. This accommodation has become available a bit too soon and neither Josie nor the staff feel she's quite ready to leave. As the flat needs quite a bit of work done, they're hoping to delay the move by a week or two more.

Josie told me about her home life. Her parents had lived together for only a short while. When her father left her mother, her mother had not been able to cope and so had given up her daughter to local authority care. Josie was 18 months old. She was then fostered to a couple who also later split up. The foster mother left the family home when Josie was about 4 years old. Josie went with the foster father to live with his mother (her foster Gran). When her foster father remarried he left Josie with her foster Gran in Kent, where she lived until leaving home at the age of 20. Her foster Gran is now 76 years old and she and Josie did not get on with each other at all well.

After she left school, Josie did factory work in the area and paid rent to her foster Gran. They argued a good deal, but Josie was able to continue living there. However, after a while Josie decided to move out and find a flat with her friend. The two girls found work and temporary accommodation in Sussex, then moved to London to stay with new friends they had met. Josie met a young Dutchman and she and her friend moved in to live with him and his friends in a squat. After a while difficulties in the household developed, including use of drugs and a police raid, and everyone left.

Shortly afterwards, Josie found out she was pregnant by the Dutch boy. It was too late for an abortion and she was no longer in contact with him. She traced the father and went to see him when the baby was 3 months old. 'But we still don't wanna know, the pair of us.' 'I don't really mind about boys now, blokes, and I don't go out much.'

Q *Did you want to have the baby?*

A *No I didn't.*

A *How come you didn't realise until you were four and a half months pregnant? What happened?*

A *Well, when I moved in with him, I went on the pill. I realised I was sort of mucking the pill up. I didn't take it every day. So I went back to the doctor's and said is it all right if I have some other contraception, and he gave me a sheet about it and said, 'Read this and go away and think about it and come back and we'll have a chat about it.' And I said, 'Well I'm not going to do it am I?' That's when I must have got pregnant.*

Q *You mean you didn't carry on taking the pill?*

A *Well I did, but I was really bodging it up then. I'm terrible – I don't like taking tablets – even though they're really little . . . I didn't think I was pregnant though . . . I thought I had an ulcer or something. I was sort of missing, but sort of bleeding as well . . . I thought I was bunged up, or had bunged-up tubes – you know, like some people have . . . When I went to the doctor's he said, 'What do you think it is?' and I said 'I think it's an ulcer, he said 'Have you had a lot of worry?' He said, 'It's one of those things – you've either had a lot of worry or you're pregnant.' I said, 'I don't think I've been worried' . . . so he gave me a test . . . and I was pregnant!*

Q *What did you think when you found out?*

A *Oh – well – I said 'No – you must be wrong' – I didn't believe it. He said, 'What are you going to do?' I said, 'Can I have an abortion?' He said it was too late. So I just carried on pretending I wasn't pregnant. I didn't think about it at all. I worked as well and didn't tell them at work. But I had to leave when I was seven months.*

Q *Where were you living then?*

A *Deptford. I was living with my mate and her friend but they didn't want me to live there with a baby. They were worried about if it was found out, cos it was a council flat that was sublet to them.*

Q So how did you hear about this place?

A I went down to the homeless families place and said, 'I'm having a baby in a few months' time, and I might not keep it – but then again I might change my mind. What should I do? So I filled out some forms . . . I can't remember what the woman said. But I still stayed in Deptford and then I went to hospital to have Remi. I stayed in two weeks cos I knew I couldn't go back to Deptford with my baby and I had nowhere to live, and then my other mate put me up in Kent. You see what happened was I'd been put in bed and breakfast first and I couldn't cope – I had no fridge, no money, no support of a family and that, my foster Gran didn't want to know. So I phoned my social worker and said, 'Can you take Remi, I can't cope.'

Q You mean, you wanted him adopted?

A Yeah. And she said to me, 'Well why don't you put him into temporary care?' Cos I didn't know about that so I said 'What's that', and she told me, and if I changed my mind I could have him back. So Remi went to stay with this lady in London and my mate put me up in Kent. Then I started to miss him, and I realised that I did want him back, but I didn't want to go into a bed and breakfast and be in the same position again. So they said about mother and baby units . . . and she said she'd see what she could do.

Q Do you get much help now in getting used to looking after Remi?

A I think I learnt that off the other girls here, and health visitors, and I went to the clinic and asked, and read it off the back of packets and things. And books, Sarah lent me books. All the staff might have mentioned it as well.

Q What do you think you get out of being here that you wouldn't get if you weren't here?

A I think you'd be very lonely if you was on your own. You feel more secure here with other young people around you. And the staff talk to you if you feel down. If I wasn't here I'd probably be in a bed and breakfast.

Q Do you think you've changed at all since coming here?

A I know I've changed since having a baby. I find it very lonely, and I feel a bit bitter and I feel old.

Josie has started studying part-time at a nearby college since coming to St Michael's leaving Remi in the college crèche. She has ambitions to join a full-time Access course and gain qualifications in order to study at a polytechnic or university. She is without a boyfriend currently, but keeps up contact with two older friends with whom she worked in Kent, who both also now live in London.

Q Have you made any new friends here that you will keep in touch with when you move out?

A Well I have, but they're not the sort of friends I'd go out with. My two mates, we're all very similar with similar outlooks on life and we're very close and really get on and that. I do get on with the girls in the home, but they're not so similar. They're younger, and still crying over boys, and I think I'm over that. And they are all great lovers of kids and always talking about them . . . I find it very hard to adapt to this kind of life. Before I was free and always off different places. Next thing I'm sitting here without me mates. I can do all the things, but I remember the other years sometimes and get really upset. I know I've got to get on with it. I've had an offer of a flat – but it's a bit of a mix-up cos I wasn't supposed to move yet – I'm not ready for that . . . It's a house like this converted into flats, so I won't have to go on a council estate. But it needs a lot of work.

Q Are you in touch with your foster father or anyone who can help you get settled in?

A No. I see my foster Nan. I go over there sometimes.

Josie's main interests were her girlfriends and going to college. She was not interested in looking for a boyfriend, and did not want to have any more children. She was obviously very anxious at the prospect of living alone. 'I'm frightened of going in to my own flat, cos it's going to be just me and Remi. The best thing here is I'm surrounded by people. And I don't get bored. It's happened to me before. When I moved out to the squat. I was on my own a lot and I got depressed. I went to the doctor's but he wouldn't give me no tablets. And when I first left school I was very depressed. Just being at my Nan's and not seeing all the friends I used to have. The doctor's said I should get out more. I didn't want to leave the house. I saw my best mates, but you don't see them every day do you?'

'It's nice here being able to talk to the other girls and knowing they've felt the same way – like when you sometimes can't stand the child . . . '

Emma

Emma, aged 17, has a son, Robert, aged 11 months. They arrived at St Michael's nine months ago and will be leaving again in three months' time when the hostel is due to close for repairs and refurbishments.

Emma has a complicated family history, as she explained to me. She has three natural siblings, one of whom lives with her mother, another is in a children's home and she has lost contact with the third. Her mother has remarried and had four more children, her father has one illegitimate child. He now lives with a woman just three years older than Emma who has two very young children of her own and is pregnant again by Emma's father. Emma was living with her father and stepmother most recently and up to the birth of her child. However, she was obliged through a court order to leave when her father was convicted for sexual abuse of his eldest child. She was in any event finding life with a depressed and suicidal 21-year-old stepmother, her two toddlers and a young cousin she was caring for too much to cope with.

Emma was housed for three weeks in a children's home shortly after the birth of her child, before coming to live at the hostel. Although a highly inappropriate setting for a young mother, the children's home was, at least, familiar to her as two of her siblings had lived there. She has fallen out with the father of her child and for the past three months has been seeing a man who is much older than herself. However, Robert's father is keen to re-establish his relationship with Emma and to see their child and frequently calls at the hostel to try to see them.

I talked with Emma in the communal sitting room in the presence of one of the residential workers, Bridget, with whom Emma has established a good relationship.

Q What did you think of this place when you first came?

A It was all right. It was different cos I'd never been used to being on my own. But I soon got over the loneliness.

Q Did you want the baby?

A I did, yeah, I've always wanted a baby, but not at such an early age. I fell when I was on the pill, and I've never believed in giving a child up – abortion or adoption.

Bridget: Emma's a really good Mum actually. The baby's really happy.

Q Are you planning to have any more?

A Not yet. I don't want no more until he's at least 5. Let him get into school first.

Q So what are you doing about contraception until then?

A I've got a contraception jab.

Bridget: It's called a depo injection – progesterone.

We discussed her plans for housing and education. Like all girls accepted at the hostel, she has a guarantee of a flat from her local council. She has plans to take up her education again when she moves out, but has not looked into the practicalities of doing so and in her home area it sounds unlikely to be possible. Emma had missed much of her final year at school through exclusion because of her pregnancy, receiving some education instead at a community school. However, the baby was born shortly after her sixteenth birthday so there was no opportunity to take examinations. She has been encouraged to take up classes at the local college while at the hostel, but attends only very sporadically.

Bridget explained that as the hostel must close temporarily in three months' time, both she and Sarah will be free to do a good deal of resettlement work. Those girls who need most support can be visited almost daily for the first few weeks to help them sort out the practicalities of independent living and benefit entitlements. Emma is also getting some support from an aunt and uncle.

Emma quite clearly has a powerful bond with Robert and was very loving *towards him. During our discussions he played happily and she kept a close eye on him to ensure he didn't hurt himself in his efforts to walk around the furniture. She also has ambitions to become a registered childminder eventually. However, from conversations later with staff, I learnt that despite Emma's claims to have gained experience in child care at the home of her stepmother, she displays minimal ability to look after either herself or her child. She left dirty washing to accumulate in bags, and put rubbish in an open pile in her room. Even when provided with a bin she allowed it to overflow, and her room rapidly became pungent and a danger to her son. Feeding bottles were not sterilised, and often not even washed, and they grew mould. She was unable to stand up for herself in sexual relationships and had needed a great deal of support to prevent her boyfriend moving into her room. She also managed badly with money, tending to spend it all on the day she received it.*

She had required a great deal of help to learn to be self-sufficient and independent, but had made considerable progress, especially in her ability to manage her daily home making and child care tasks and in being more assertive in her relationships with men. However, she was likely to need continuing social work support, and would probably continue to live in fairly squalid conditions. But with help, and if she separates from her current manfriend who is a concern to her social workers, she will probably be able to look after her children adequately. In fact, I heard two weeks later that she had re-established her relationship with Robert's father. The staff at St Michael's feel that girls like Emma are those for whom their support can achieve the greatest change.

Moving on

Most of the young women who live in St Michael's are offered accommodation afterwards in the same area. One of the conditions of acceptance at the hostel is a guarantee from the authority funding their place that housing will be offered to the girl when she is ready to leave. As most referrals are taken from the local and neighbouring boroughs, many girls find they live quite near friends from St Michael's when they move out, and can meet up. A recent development at St Michael's is the establishment of a full-time resettlement post to help in the transitional period. This worker will be able to accompany the young women in their search for nursery places, to help iron out any problems with DSS or Housing Benefit, to go with them as a friend on their first visit to local mother and baby groups and so on. She will also ensure the young mother knows of and makes contact with any other appropriate community support networks, from incest survivors' groups to the toy library. In addition, the young women may return at any time to see friends still living at the hostel, and the staff.

Resources and costs

At the time of my visit in 1987, the hostel was staffed by a residential social worker (qualified) and two other workers experienced in working in residential settings. By 1990 the staffing had doubled. Changes in local authority finances have meant that the type of preventive work offered by a unit such as this one is a luxury they can no longer afford. Hence the client group of the hostel has gradually shifted toward young people with more severe problems. The fee charged to local authorities (social services department) for social work support in 1990/91 was £350 per mother per week. This included a contribution toward replacement furniture and fittings. The young mothers themselves receive £52.60 per week if aged 16 or 17 years, £60.50 if 18 years or more, plus a separate payment of £55 per week Housing Benefit to cover St Michael's rent (1990/91).

Although it is sometimes cheaper and considerably better if young mothers are housed in such hostels, the alternative is accommodation in bed and breakfast hotels and this would have been funded by the housing department instead of social services. Although recent legislation may change this, it may be one reason why more such projects have not developed so far.

Because the client group of the hostel visited were young women expected to be able to cope with motherhood, albeit with considerable support at various stages, they were able and indeed encouraged to lead independent lives. Other hostels run by St Michael's, for women about whom there is much greater doubt that they could become 'good-enough' parents, and whose children were often considered to be 'at risk' (perhaps through drug misuse by the parent, or severe mental illness), provide much more intensive support and therefore have higher social work charges. For mothers about whom there is a marked concern, there are no personal catering facilities or sitting rooms and they live communal lives where they can be supervised and supported in all their activities with their children.

Almost all mother and baby hostels are provided by the voluntary sector. Some which cater for more competent mothers are run with less social work support. Variations on the theme include one which provides three independent flats with an adjacent office which is staffed just a few hours each day where mothers can seek help and advice. Another provides bedsits with their own cooking facilities with daytime but no night-time support. Others have staff who sleep-in in turn, but do not have a resident worker. The degree of supervision needed depends on the problems of the target client group. The staff of St Michael's believe that only if night cover is provided should a hostel accept high-risk women, that is, women with problems other than their single parenthood.

However, most mother and baby units offer accommodation for a much shorter time – often six weeks before and six weeks after the birth, and do not provide the same kind of support and preparation for independence that is available at St Michael's. This is an unusual service.

There is not nearly enough provision to meet demand, either for the 16- to 18-year-old client group served by the hostel I visited, or those served by two other St Michael's hostels (older women perhaps with marked mental health and social difficulties and often several older children already in care). St Michael's are opening a new hostel in 1991 for the adolescent group but each new house takes several years of planning, preparation and negotiation with housing associations. Their existing adolescent hostel cost £90,000 a year to run (1987/88 prices) of which St Michael's contributes 5 per cent from voluntary funds. This is presently being sold to a housing association which will renovate and upgrade the facilities with a grant from the Housing Corporation. St Michael's will continue to run the project while the Housing Association own the property within the terms of a management agreement.

Evaluation

A follow-up study of all the girls leaving the hostel between 1973 and 1988 was commissioned by St Michael's Fellowship shortly after my visit there (Clark, 1991). Eighty-four young women had stayed at the hostel and moved on during this 15-year period. Seventy of these women were traced, and 50 (with 110 children between them) were interviewed during 1989. The women interviewed ranged in age from 18 to 39 years, their children from 2 weeks to 18 years.

Of the 110 children, eight children (of six mothers – as they included two sets of twins) were not cared for by their mother, but by their fathers (four) or local authority foster parents (four). Five of these six mothers had not been coping adequately, while one of the six was judged 'unfit' in her standards of parenting. Of the remaining 102 children, 15 per cent had been fostered at some time in the past but were back in the care of their mother. A total of 19 per cent had some record of concern which had led to their becoming 'wards of court' or being considered 'at risk'. Five children had experienced some form of abuse and had been on the 'at risk' register, but after counselling and support for the parent over a period, they had remained in their parent's care. These figures compare favourably with the findings from a follow-up of 80 girls leaving care by Quinton and Rutter (1983). In their study the children of 18 per cent of the women had been taken into care (compared to 12 per cent in Clark's study), and one-third had experienced some form of transient or permanent breakdown with at least one of their children (compared to 15 per cent in Clark's study). Eighteen of the children of the St Michael's mothers had reached their teens, and none had yet become parents.

All but three of the women interviewed by Clark (1991) gave positive views about their time at St Michael's. (Although more of those not interviewed are likely to have had criticisms.) It was often described as the place where they had learnt to cope with a baby, to manage money, to be independent. For many of them it was the first time they had had a room of their own. The criticisms received were mainly connected with differences of personality between themselves and other residents rather than of the hostel or its regime.

Sixty per cent of the young women were receiving income support, the remainder working, studying, or supported by a partner. They appeared to be coping reasonably well, in a financial sense: over half (56 per cent) having no debts; the remainder either repaying money to the social fund (28 per cent), or with some arrears on rent, catalogues, hire purchase agreements (16 per cent). One in five reported having received treatment for depression from their GP at some time.

I gained additional insight into the experiences of these young women from the records of a sub-sample. Choosing a date exactly three years prior to my visit and looking up the records available on the girls resident on that day, I asked staff what had happened to each of them, their babies, and subsequent children. Nine girls were living there, as the downstairs flat now used as a communal sitting room was also occupied. Records showed that they stayed at the hostel, for between five months and 35 months. (Two stayed for under a year, three for between 12 and 18 months, four for two years or more.)

Altogether, the nine residents of three years ago had ten children between them on arrival, and three years on had borne seven more. One of the nine women had not been able to take on the responsibility of motherhood and, after discussions with staff at St Michael's about the possibility of giving her child up for adoption, had abruptly left one night, leaving the baby with one of the other mothers. The father's family have since adopted the child. None of the other 16 children have been taken into care.

All the young women are now living in good accommodation, either council or housing association: five largely supported by the DSS. Three women (two of whom were single parents with just one child each) work full-time to support themselves, one other works with her boyfriend and his mother in their own shop on the coast. Two of the nine women live in a stable relationship with the father of their children; two others live as single parents with no contact with the father of their child; four have maintained a relationship with the father of their children (or the latest child), but live alone with their children and receive only minimal support from him. One is unknown.

Most of the young women had neither planned nor wanted their first child. Two of them, however, had wanted to be pregnant and one of these has gone on, intentionally, to have two more children (with the same father). Four women have not had any more children, while four have had another child, two of whom, it is understood, were planned and wanted. It would seem that these young women have coped well in terms of planning subsequent pregnancies and preventing further unwanted pregnancies over the past three years.

With the formidable difficulties such as these young women have experienced, it is evident that they and their children have a raised risk of mental and physical health problems; that they need organised and continuous support to help them minimise their social difficulties at this crucial point in their lives; and that the future health and welfare of their children may be considerably helped by doing so. It cannot be claimed that such support will, on its own, ensure that these vulnerable young people will become model parents. But their children should, at least, have more supportive home lives than their mothers had, and a more settled infancy than they would have had without their short stay at St Michael's. That this sort of help is unusual, and even in South London is offered to less than one in five similar referrals should, I believe, be a cause of concern.

RELATED ISSUES: EDUCATION

A small proportion of teenage pregnancies are conceived before the age of 15 (1,281 babies were born to girls aged 15 or less in 1980; a further 4,304 babies were born to 16-year-old girls; OPCS figures cited by Wells, 1983). Those girls carrying their child to term (just under half of conceptions) are excluded from school. As the law obliges everyone to be educated until they are 16, other options must be offered. The most usual option is home tuition, but in some areas a better service is available. In Bristol, the Unit for Schoolgirl Mothers has been educating and supporting girls for over 14 years. As well as basic and relevant examination qualifications, such a unit offers antenatal and postnatal care, support and guidance for the young mothers and their babies, and the opportunity for thoughtful discussions about their present circumstances and needs, their own and their children's upbringing, and their future prospects (Hudson and Dawson, 1987).

The Arbour project in Liverpool is similar. There in a converted two-bedroom flat above a shop, six or seven girls attend each weekday for a year. They benefit from a sense of being 'all in the same boat', and the pregnant girls get used to seeing the babies of those who have already given birth. (A handful of other such units exist in England.) Girls who attend are invariably enthusiastic about the unit and return to see staff and friends at weekly open days for long after their statutory year is completed. Most gain more qualifications than they would have done in school (Sharpe, 1987a and 1987b).

When a programme combines intensive medical, educational, social *and* psychological support for disadvantaged pregnant teenagers, and young mothers, impressive benefits have been demonstrated. Osofsky and his colleagues (1973) describe a service based in a disused school building in New York State for pregnant girls aged between 10 and 20. In the first five-and-a-half years of its existence, 490 girls were enrolled and 450 delivered within the programme. Compared to national figures for the same age group, the prematurity rate of the babies and their small-for-dates rate were considerably reduced, and perinatal mortalities were reduced to below the number that would be expected for a privileged middle-class adult population. Educationally, many under-achieving students responded with two or three years of skill from one year of instruction. Between 1968 and 1971 91 girls received high school diplomas and 40 per cent of all the girls have chosen to pursue some form of post-high-school education. Only 59 per cent of the first 325 girls followed up had become pregnant again within four years and invariably only once, and together with other figures this indicates a marked reduction in expected numbers of repeat pregnancies.

This is further evidence that it is possible and effective to mount preventive programmes for adolescents.

SUMMARY

This chapter illustrates the extreme vulnerability of many young people leaving local authority care to set up independent home lives. The disturbing but not untypical case histories provide us with considerable insight into the problems they face and the very few resources they have to fall back on. They illustrate too how valuable a role has been played by the agencies providing each of the two preventive services described.

Chapter 3

Supporting people through crises

Most of us know only too well, from our own experiences or from those of someone close to us, that extremely unpleasant events or continuing social or emotional difficulties can take us to the brink of mental illness. Whether these extremes of emotion become sufficiently marked or prolonged enough to be considered an illness, how long the 'illness' lasts, and how the symptoms are manifested depends on a range of factors. The importance of certain childhood and adolescent experiences which affect our self-esteem, our social situation and our resources for coping in adulthood have been considered in preceding chapters. The key issues in the present circumstances of the individual which affect risk of depression relate to qualitative aspects of the event or problem itself, particularly its significance to the individual's long-term aspirations, and existing resources (social and psychological) for coping with it.

For instance, we know that events perceived to carry a profound and long-term threat of loss or disappointment commonly precede depressive disorders (Paykel, 1979; Dohrenwend & Dohrenwend (Eds), 1974; Brown and Harris, 1978). And it appears that events which have more of a quality of danger, or threaten to bring a *future* loss, are more likely to be followed by a disorder with anxiety or phobic elements (Finlay-Jones and Brown, 1983). Life events and stresses have also been found to affect the course of schizophrenia, and to play a role in the development of physical disorders such as heart disease, multiple sclerosis and gastrointestinal disorder (Neilson *et al.*, 1989; Grant *et al.*, 1989; Creed, 1981; Craig and Brown, 1984). And here, too, there are some suggestions that particular qualities of event are linked to particular types of disorder (goal frustration and stomach ulcers, for instance), but such links remain speculative. At the same time, of course, it must also be remembered that most people cope with all sorts of problems and events without *any* serious adverse mental or physical effects most of the time.

Factors which are inextricably linked together in determining likelihood of psychiatric disorder are the context in which the event arises (affecting its meaning and significance to the individual); the availability and perceived adequacy of social support; and the coping responses and the psychological resources of the individual. There may be organic and genetic factors contributing to a specific vulnerability to a particular disorder (something is known about these for disorders like schizophrenia, and physical conditions like coronary heart disease, for instance). And there will be social and psychological factors in childhood and adolescence which will contribute to the individual's current social and psychological resources for coping. But given that psychiatric disorder tends to occur in the context of a stressful experience – could something be done at this time to prevent it?

In an earlier review, it was argued that the primary health care team have a key role in identifying vulnerability and helping individuals to find support in dealing with their difficulties (Newton, 1988). It was suggested there that there were two points at which intervention might be appropriate. The first was before a predictable event occurred (during the 'event-producing situation'). Knowledge about the individual and their current circumstances might mean that adverse events are predictable (poverty, physical frailty, trying to conceive a child after several miscarriages, receiving a test for HIV infection, for instance). Counselling or practical support may play a preventive role at this stage. Following an event – in the preceding examples – a final rent demand that cannot be paid, a worsening of disability to the stage where self-sufficiency is no longer possible, a further miscarriage, a positive HIV test, the individual will become distressed. At this stage, the support they receive and the meaning and significance they attribute to the event will affect how distressed they become. Those with poor support and those who see the event as having catastrophic consequences are those most vulnerable to depression, and this was suggested as the second opportunity for preventive work. If the distress and the difficulty itself are coped with well, psychiatric disorder can be prevented.

The *meaning* of an event to an individual is critical in terms of likelihood of causing depression. A fourth miscarriage to a 25-year-old woman who is enjoying her job and is in no great hurry to start a family will have a different significance than to the 40-year-old woman who has been trying to start a family for a number of years and had taken two years to conceive her last pregnancy. This particular example has a meaning at two levels: first, whether the miscarriage is interpreted as a loss of the possibility of ever becoming a mother (or having more children); second, how important it is to the individual to become a mother (or have more children). The latter aspect is particularly important in terms of risk of depression, as recent research has confirmed (Brown and Harris, 1989).

Psychological coping strategies to reappraise meaning are a common approach to coping with events which we are unable to change, as Pearlin and Schooler (1978) have demonstrated. Many events also require a behavioural response, of course, and in the earlier example above of a final rent demand, this will obviously be more important.

The availability of support from someone close to the individual, and the perceived adequacy of this support, will affect the individual's ability to cope. In particular, the close other must provide the support expected of them (by the individual) at the time of the crisis, otherwise their presence is more likely to increase the individual's vulnerability to depression (Brown *et al.*, 1990). And the individual's level of self-esteem will also play a role (Brown *et al.*, 1990). These are the main issues affecting risk of depression: the meaning of the event to the individual, and their *resources* (material, psychological and social) for coping with it. These considerations enable decisions to be made about who might benefit from external sources of support, and what form this support should take. If expensive professional help, say counselling, was to be provided, it would be advantageous, in cost-benefit terms, if it could be directed toward those who really needed it. For those with good resources available within their personal networks of friends, counselling would afford little further protection from depression, although, of course, it may well be greatly valued by the individual.

It is often the family doctor who is the first professional contacted by someone feeling unable to cope with the problems they are faced with. In fact, it is commonly estimated that at least a quarter of all consultations with GPs are in connection with problems which are fundamentally psychosocial in origin. Is it possible for general practitioners to spot those most vulnerable to psychiatric disorder, and what can they provide that will make a difference? It is suggested in this chapter that there are ways in which general practices can use their own, their neighbourhood's, and other existing resources to improve the preventive potential of their service.

The starting point must be some insight or further enquiry into how much of a problem a situation is perceived to be, how vulnerable the person is, and the extent and quality of existing support. One obvious difficulty in gaining this information is that many people with social and emotional problems do not present them as such to the doctor. They may instead describe their sleeplessness, backache, obscure pains or other physical problem. It needs skill and perceptiveness to uncover underlying psychiatric problems. A good deal goes unrecognised and has been termed the 'hidden psychiatric morbidity' of general practice (Goldberg and Huxley, 1980). But some of these 'undetected' cases may, in fact, be suspected cases by doctors who feel they would not be able to offer an effective solution, and fear the lengthy and distressing interview which may follow should they ask the leading question. Given their severe time constraints it would not be surprising if a lack of confidence in handling psychiatric problems was reflected in a low level of detection. The purpose of the following sections is to suggest that in fact the doctor can, without too much difficulty, offer something of real assistance to such patients and thereby encourage them to ask those leading questions.

Identifying people coping (or not coping) with difficult circumstances in a general practice setting will inevitably mean that those vulnerable to depression will usually already have a number of psychiatric symptoms. Sometimes they may have been quite seriously depressed for a considerable time. However, the GP may see them at any stage – before a predictable event; just after the event (where prodromal signs are present); some time after the event, when a person has recently become acutely depressed; or when the individual has been depressed for some time. Help at any point will be valuable and although at later stages additional treatment consider-ations will apply, the kind of support described here which might be preventive to those not yet depressed may also help those already depressed to recover.

Three issues will be discussed: first, the opportunity in the general practice consultation for identifying those vulnerable to psychiatric disorder, in the prodromal stages or already depressed; second, how best the patient might be helped; and third, whether suitable resources can be made available.

DETECTING PSYCHIATRIC SYMPTOMS IN GENERAL PRACTICE

Most of the research on the detection of psychiatric disorder in general practice has focused on the consultation with the doctor (rather than on nurse contacts). Because of this, and because of their central role in determining what is made available at the practice, what formal links are made between the practice and local organisations and other professionals, and their opportunities for screening for disorder large numbers of their client group, the following discussions on identifying need also focus on the general practitioner. The roles of the health visitor, district nurse, and (with the advent of health promotion clinics) the practice nurse in detecting psychiatric difficulties are also of great importance, and some aspects of their work in relation to prevention have been considered in Chapter 1.

Research on how doctors conduct their interviews with patients, and how this affects the accuracy of their diagnosis, and their success in 'getting to the root' of the problems presented has shown that a number of factors are influential. These include personal characteristics of the patient: his or her educational level, marital status, age, symptoms, gender, frequency of surgery consultations and previous psychiatric history (Goldberg and Huxley, 1980; Hoeper et al., 1984). For instance, better educated people and men are less likely than less well educated people and women to be thought to have psychiatric problems. (Yet once a psychiatric problem is diagnosed, more of the better educated and male cases than less well educated and female cases are referred to psychiatrists! Goldberg and Huxley, 1980.) Perhaps related to, but more important than any of these individual characteristics, however, is how the patient describes his problems. A large proportion of patients whose underlying problem is a psychosocial difficulty at home or at work will present their difficulties purely as a physical problem of some kind. The physical problems described (their 'ticket for admission') will of course be present, and the patient may or may not recognise that they are associated with the psychiatric symptoms. On average, doctors fail to detect the underlying psychiatric problems in at least one-third of such cases (Goldberg and Blackwell, 1970).

The characteristics of the doctor which will determine how well they discriminate the physical/psychosocial mixed pathology from the purely physical are: the way in which they interview their patients, their academic ability and their personality (Goldberg and Huxley, 1980). Interviewers who are outgoing, assertive and accessible do better (Lesser, 1985). Those with greater knowledge about psychiatric disorder, and how it is likely to be presented in general practice, can differentiate more easily those patients who present with emotional disorder from those with physical disorders (Lesser, 1985). In terms of interviewing style, ten aspects of the doctor's behaviour are important. The doctor should make eye contact with the patient at the beginning of the interview; refrain from reading notes while history-taking; start with open questions and keep closed questions for the end of a sequence of questions; clarify the presenting complaint; use directive questions for physical complaints; have an empathic style; be sensitive to verbal, and to non-verbal cues; ask a limited number of questions about the patient's past history; and be able to deal with over-talkativeness (Goldberg and Huxley, 1980).

All these aspects of the doctor's behaviour can be improved with training. Lesser (1981) suggests that newly qualified doctors and some more experienced GPs often feel more comfortable if they stick to formal diagnostic history-taking rather than follow the cues the patient provides, and that they may have difficulty confronting patients about subjects raised. He argues that the interviewing time available to the GP is often not used as effectively as it might be. Important cues missed by the doctor, perhaps in the first sentence ('. . . and it's really getting me down . . .', '. . . and I've been getting into a real state about it') may lead to a wasteful final ten minutes of a 15-minute interview where the doctor is trying to conclude the meeting, the patient is continuing to talk, and the doctor repeats his or her advice several times over. If after the first five minutes the doctor had gone back to the opening remarks, 'You mentioned that it's been getting you down . . .' and if perhaps he had asked other open questions such as, 'Have you thought that it might be something else?', the interview may have uncovered the concern which motivated the patient to consult the doctor. It also means that the reassurance offered will be more effective. If, for instance, the answer to the second question was 'Oh yes, my father died very young from heart trouble and I've wondered if this . . . is connected with the same sort of problem', it would render a reassurance that he does not have anything to worry about much more meaningful.

Lesser (1981) describes a group training programme which he developed to teach doctors a problem-oriented approach to interviewing. Doctors are reported to have found it to be easily acquired, to work well with their patients, and even to help them in their own relationships with their colleagues and family. It is a significant departure from traditional medical history-taking and is an approach which is oriented toward the patient rather than the illness and which holds the patient accountable.

Essentially the approach begins with a careful exploration of the reason the patient has come to see the doctor (i.e. assuming the reason given may not be the real reason). It involves problem-sensing (picking up verbal and non-verbal cues, e.g. tenseness, inability to make eye contact); problem detection (questioning to decode these cues – e.g. interrupt to clarify affect-laden statements like 'I haven't felt like doing much lately') followed by a concise description of the problem. To aid the description, examples of the events are sought, the behaviour which needs changing identified, and its antecedents or controlling influences listed, as well as its consequences. The assessment of the problem may include physical examination or mental status examination; whether the patient has the insight and the capacity for change; and whether the doctor can provide treatment or needs to refer to other health professionals. Intervention and treatment follow.

This sort of detailed exploration of problems presented is essential even if the basic problem is quickly identified as a relationship problem that the doctor would normally refer on to other agencies or attached counselling services. Referral to a psychologist or marriage guidance counsellor attached to the practice, for instance, may well fail if the doctor and patient have not first discussed the problem fully and together determined that the irritability, stomach cramps and weight loss are unlikely to clear up unless the marital conflict is eased. If the problem is jointly reformulated and the necessary changes identified, then the patient will have realistic expectations from counselling and appreciate the need for it. Otherwise, as some of the case histories in the next section show, patients are often angry at their referral, see it as a waste of time, or have unrealistic expectations of what the sessions should achieve. In other words, not only is it necessary for the *doctor* to detect and diagnose a problem accurately, and to know what treatment options are appropriate, but an intermediate step is also essential – one which involves bringing the patient to the same conclusions about the problem. This must incorporate a negotiated agreement about the most appropriate course of action.

Of course, the doctor must have understood correctly what, primarily, has motivated the patient to seek help, and what the patient's own beliefs about his illness are. It is not uncommon, when such understanding has not been reached, for patients to find, after discussing the consultation later with a relative or friend, that the advice does not accord with their understanding of these matters, and to decide not to follow the recommended course of action. This issue of health beliefs is discussed further by Tuckett (1985).

If the doctor finds that the problem is one which needs several further counselling sessions, they may decide either to do this themselves, or refer the patient to other services. Lesser (1985) also describes a problem-oriented approach to counselling, which is suitable for most psychosocial difficulties and which the GP could employ (although it would need consultation longer than the seven or eight minutes commonly available). Training courses for GPs based on Lesser's model have now been successfully mounted in Manchester and London (see Gask *et al.*, 1987; 1988). Real consultations of the trainees are videotaped or audiotaped and subsequently discussed by a group, examining the interview for verbal and non-verbal cues, and considering how the interviewer's responses could have been improved. The courses consist of 18 two-hour weekly group sessions and are appropriate for GP trainees, for established GPs and for GP trainers. Those running the courses have reported finding the method as effective, more wide-ranging and less costly than the one-to-one video-feedback teaching found to be successful in improving interviewing skills developed by David Goldberg and colleagues (1980a; b). The style of interviewing taught is considered to be suitable for three types of consultation: patients presenting with overt psychiatric illness where management is unclear (non-specific anxiety, depression which has not responded to previous treatments); patients in whom specific problems have been identified, such as marital difficulties, family conflict, alcohol or drug abuse; and patients in whom a covert psychiatric illness is suspected (with chronic pain, multiple symptoms and frequent consulting, pain not typical of known illness, or whose non-verbal cues indicate that the problem is not simply the physical one presented). Gask and her colleagues' evaluation of their group training courses showed that both established GPs and GP trainees improved their interviewing style and the trainees showed a marked improvement in their ability to identify psychiatric illness accurately (Gask *et al.*, 1987; 1988). Their management style also showed some improvement in that they gave more advice which was pertinent to the psychosocial problems and less non-specific advice (such as suggesting rest).

WHAT SORT OF HELP IS NEEDED BY PATIENTS DEALING WITH CRISIS?

In this section, four potential sources of help are outlined which may prove valuable to people experiencing difficulty in coping with stresses of one kind or another. Some existing examples are briefly described, supplemented by a small number of case histories, and evaluative data is included where available. The suggestions are counselling, information, befriending and crisis intervention.

Counselling

Research studies on how people cope with crises have indicated that, at least for loss events, the opportunity to ventilate anxieties, sadness, anger or despair seems to have some generalisable benefit (Silver and Wortman, 1980). Parkes (1981) and Raphael (1977) showed how bereavement counselling reduced a range of symptoms associated with stress. Parkes' study showed that the benefits were much more marked for bereaved relatives known to be at high risk of becoming depressed due to their poor resources (a particularly traumatic bereavement, family seen as unsupportive, a previous ambivalent relationship with the deceased, the presence of other social stresses and so on). He also showed that counselling did not have to be by a medical or social work professional in order to be effective, and that volunteers could become as skilled as professionals with a little training and support after a few months of experience.

In fact there are a large number of voluntary bereavement counselling services already in existence, including the well-known national group CRUSE. In London, the Bereavement Projects Group which meets under the auspices of the London Voluntary Services Council represents 25 counselling services in the Greater London area. Some groups are community-based, others run from hospices. For example, one group, set up in September 1984, is based in the Royal London Hospital, a large general teaching hospital in the East End. In this service, there are about 20 counsellors working at any time, and they meet every two weeks in groups of four for supervision and support. Many have full-time jobs in caring professions (often nursing). They tend to be young (in their twenties), female and white. They are unpaid, except for travel expenses, and must be prepared to spend up to 60 hours on a training course before taking on any cases. They are also asked to give a minimum of one year's commitment, and the co-ordinator has found no shortage of volunteers willing to become counsellors and make this commitment. They were trained by a specialist social worker in her spare time, with occasional input from the co-ordinator, and from a consultant psychiatrist. There were 226 referrals to the service in the first two years, primarily referred by GPs, social workers, and occasionally from nursing staff on the wards. Clients were usually offered between four and six weekly one-hour sessions, followed by three more sessions at three-month intervals until the first anniversary of the bereavement. After this, the counsellor would often leave the client with her telephone number in case the client felt in need of further meetings.

There is also a long established history of voluntary counselling for people facing relationship problems and considering separation. And the services of organisations such as Relate are in such demand that in many parts of the country they operate a waiting list. Many clients of Relate have been experiencing major difficulties in their relationship with their partner for some time, and are already becoming quite seriously depressed or anxious, or drinking heavily. A good deal of the support is therefore over a long period of many months, and sometimes years. Clients are asked to donate as much as they can afford toward the cost of the counselling.

Many family doctors fully appreciate that patients with such tragic or difficult circumstances would benefit as much as or more from counselling than they would from the prescriptions often given out for minor tranquillisers, anti-depressants and sleeping pills. Two responses have developed. Some doctors have managed to forge working links with existing voluntary counselling services such as Relate, whereby either a counsellor from the voluntary organisation is based at the practice one or more sessions each week, or they agree a referral mechanism to the voluntary group. A second strategy is for group practices to establish some form of counselling service of their own – either a lay counsellor, a psychologist, community psychiatric nurse or social worker, or their own special counsell-ing sessions of GPs, and some examples of these kinds of arrangements are described below. That is not to say that a good deal could not be achieved by GPs themselves within their current consulting schedules. Indeed Balint and Norell (1976) and Lesser (1981) have described how this can be achieved. However, many patients require more time than their doctor can offer.

Links with existing voluntary agencies

In July 1983 there were already 120 Relate counsellors working in general practice surgeries around the country (Toynbee, 1983). Many more arrange-ments of this kind have been established since. For example, in one North London health centre, Christine Manzi, a Relate counsellor spends one morning each week counselling patients referred to her by any of the nine doctors. Some of the doctors referred more patients to her than others, and she had found that the more patients they referred to her, the more appropriate their subsequent referrals became. That is, they had a more accurate view of the kind of difficulty she was most able to help with. Those doctors who very rarely referred anyone to her tended to refer patients with longstanding and intractable problems whom she often felt she could do little to help. In her first 12 months at the practice, 43 patients were referred to her (33 on their own, ten with a partner), usually with marital problems.

She found that compared to clients she counselled through Relate's own offices, the clients she saw at the practice were much more likely to be at an early stage of difficulty, more likely to be socially disadvantaged, and were often people who would not think of referring themselves for marriage guidance. They were seen for an average of only four weekly one-hour sessions after which they were advised to try out some of the coping strategies discussed, and return either to the GP or the counsellor if the situation did not improve. By contrast, the more longstanding problems seen through Relate might receive counselling support for months, or even years.

The counsellor explained to me that she saw people with a range of emotional problems linked to relationship difficulties. As well as problems between sexual partners, examples included severe loss of confidence and inability to return to work after bereavement; difficulties between mother and child; difficulties between the individual and (say) their mother-in-law; mounting resentment and anxiety from caring for a dependent elderly relative; and severe loneliness. Clients had not always welcomed their referral for counselling. Three of the 43 people seen in the first year were angry about the referral and did not want to discuss their difficulties with the counsellor at all, and six others failed to return for a second meeting, either because they found it unhelpful, or because they could not attend a series of appointments during work hours.

As NHS clients do not expect to be asked for payment toward treatment, and as they have not usually specifically sought counselling, it was not found to be acceptable to ask for any financial contribution from clients toward counselling sessions in general practice.

Existing voluntary counselling organisations can become involved with local family practitioners without having to locate the facility in the practice itself. The Family Welfare Association is a voluntary social work agency which operates primarily in London and which also provides counselling for relationship difficulties. In Kensington, West London, a working link was forged between the FWA and a local practice of three GPs. The agency operated from an ordinary house near the practice. In deciding whether a patient should be referred, and before offering the possibility of such counselling to a patient, the GP would usually discuss the matter with the FWA co-ordinator. The GPs would keep informed of progress through a weekly meeting with the co-ordinator. This meeting would also help both parties feel less professionally isolated, and increase the GP's awareness of other support networks in existence locally.

In Islington, one-third of all referrals to the local FWA originate from one health centre (150 in 1980/81). The remainder came through recommendations from families, friends, health visitors, social workers, other voluntary agencies, and other GPs. The client group were all ages, but predominantly 25 to 44 years old and suffering from depression, anxiety, isolation, grief, or relationship difficulties. This particular service offered a range of support groups (a stroke sufferer's relatives' support group, a mothers' support group, a group for parents of physically handicapped children) as well as one-to-one counselling.

Establishing a practice's own counselling service through professional attachment schemes

Three different professional groups in particular have begun to take referrals for counselling in general practice through a formal attachment scheme: psychologists, community psychiatric nurses and social workers. Although there is bound to be a considerable overlap in the kinds of problems they will see and can help, they obviously also have a somewhat different expertise. Hence, the former two will more often see patients who might otherwise have been referred for out-patient treatment, may help people with long-term mental health problems avoid rehospitalisation, and offer behavioural management advice for anxiety-related conditions. Social workers will often see more of the kinds of relationship problems which might also be referred to Relate or the FWA, and they are inevitably seen as troubleshooters for a range of social difficulties.

Some general practices fully exploit the opportunities for outside support of these kinds for their patients. Dr Reginald Yorke's practice in Maghull, Lancashire, for instance, has an attached social worker (part-time on joint funding), a lay counsellor (one day a week) and an attached psychologist who is based in the practice one half-day each week. While the lay counsellor (a psychology lecturer at a nearby college, trained in counselling) offers bereavement counselling and support for other loss experiences, the psychologist tends to see patients who already have a number of psychiatric symptoms, or who have a history of recurrent disorder. For instance, when I visited the practice, she was seeing a middle-aged man (Mr A) every two weeks who had a history of recurrent severe depression, acute anxiety, attempted suicide, epilepsy and domestic violence.

Mr A's long history of severe mental health problems included extreme mood swings, in which he sometimes became excessively angry or jealous, at which times he became threatening to his wife or a danger to himself. He had frequently been admitted to hospital for treatment, sometimes as often as three times in 12 months. He was keen to break this pattern, and together with his GP, the psychologist, and his supportive new wife, he was trying to prevent the need for further in-patient treatment. The psychologist was teaching him ways to control his anger, and trying to help him gain more insight into his behaviour, and the links between his current difficulties and his disturbed family background. She was also regularly reviewing his medication, which previously had built up from his numerous periods of treatment, so that at one stage he was taking an unnecessarily large range (anxiolytic, anti-depressant, anti-convulsant, and major tranquillisers). The support was proving effective, and although his regular depressive episodes were not prevented, the early intervention enabled him to avoid the depths of distress which had previously resulted in hospitalisation. He had managed to find voluntary work as a driver, and he was extremely

appreciative of the time devoted to him by the psychologist and the GP. He told them that he felt he was taken seriously, that he was valued and that he was not blamed.

The kinds of problems helped by counselling are diverse, as other case histories show. Two much less extreme examples illustrate better the potential preventive role of the counsellor through putting clients in touch with voluntary community support.

A young mother who felt she was 'falling to pieces', and who was worried about the damaging influence she might be having on her children, was referred by her GP to the attached psychologist. She had recently had a second child, who was handicapped by Down's Syndrome, and although she had initially coped well with the child, she had recently become a regular attender at the surgery for chest pains, stomach pains and sickness. The apparent absence of a physical cause led to her referral to the psychologist who discussed with her the difficulties of looking after a handicapped baby. However, by the third session, the discussions revealed that in fact this difficulty was not the prime cause of her distress; rather, it was reawakening unresolved feelings of grief about an earlier pregnancy and events surrounding this. Some years before she had had a violent lover who had regularly beaten her, and during one of his several prison sentences, the young woman's mother persuaded her to terminate the pregnancy she had conceived by him. Their relationship continued when he was out of prison until, following her hospitalisation for injuries inflicted by him, her family intervened to discourage further contact. Some time later she had met the man by whom she currently had two children, but whom she chose not to live with.

The psychologist provided the opportunity for her to talk through her problems, and aimed to help her to relearn trust, and to commit herself to her current partner whom she loved, but whose requests for marriage she had so far refused. She also put the young woman in touch with a woman from a voluntary group for parents of handicapped children, and she in turn arranged a liaison with another young mother in a similar position with whom she could arrange for exchange babysitting. After a few weeks, no additional support or treatment from the practice was needed.

Another referral to the psychologist was a woman who was almost blind and suffered recurrent bouts of depression.

This woman had experienced many problems in coping with her children (one of whom was hyperactive), and these difficulties reached crisis point when their resentment toward her blindness became marked because it meant they were unable to go swimming. The woman's mother-in-law reinforced this criticism. Furthermore her husband had lost his driving licence and a police case was pending. After brief counselling, the home situation was defused by an offer from a local Good Neighbours voluntary scheme (again, mobilised by the psychologist) to take the children swimming and provide other kinds of practical support.

The clinical psychologist works closely with the GPs, but also meets every few weeks with the lay counsellor to decide which of the new referrals would be most appropriately treated by each of them.

A large practice in North London arranged to have a community psychiatric nurse based in the practice almost full-time (see Feinmann, 1985). He saw patients with problems stemming from obesity, psychosexual difficulty, eating disorder, phobias and other anxiety states, psychotic symptoms, and addiction to minor tranquillisers. However, the nurse concerned also had a strong personal interest in prevention, and counselled people coping with personal crisis such as divorce, redundancy, unwanted pregnancy or bereavement.

The practice found the attachment had several beneficial effects for them (Feinmann, 1985). The quantity of prescriptions for psychotropics, sedatives, hypnotics and anti-depressants fell; hospital referrals were reduced; and doctors reported that they had begun to sit together more often after surgery and discuss problems with each other. The CPN also started to train the GPs in counselling and shared consultations with them so that he could gradually withdraw from the practice and work instead in another practice.

There are many consultations during which worrying social and relationship problems come to light for which the general practitioner may want to secure social work advice or support. Clearly an efficient mechanism for mobilising support is essential, and there has been some enthusiasm for attachment schemes. However, there are many problems to be overcome in achieving a successful liaison of this kind and attachments sometimes fail. Marshall and Hargreaves (1979), writing at a time when such schemes were particularly popular, advised that difficulties that arose were largely due to the very different approaches to problem solving of medical workers and social workers. The former are trained to 'diagnose, treat and cure' and may expect social workers to have the same approach to social problems. The social work approach is rather different, however, and a poor understanding of this can lead to frustrations in their dealings with one another.

Nevertheless, many practices do now have an attached social worker and are finding it helpful. There is evidence to demonstrate the benefits of their combined management for patients who have been depressed, anxious or phobic for a year or more, but unfortunately not for preventing disorder. The evidence that any type of counselling in general practice is effective is summarised below.

Is counselling effective?

Considerable interest in the role of counsellors in the general practice setting, and in the effectiveness of deploying them in this way has been reflected in the number of evaluative reports. The findings have been mixed, and this to some extent reflects the difficulties of evaluating this kind of service. Martin and Martin (1985) studied the effects that a Relate counsellor joining their practice team had on the numbers of prescriptions for psychotropic medication and anti-depressants and on consultation rates, and found disappointing results. However, they were not comparing counselled patients with a group of patients with comparable difficulties. Nor were they able to examine what might have happened to those consulted without this support. A more useful comparison, by Waydenfeld and Waydenfeld (1980), was of prescriptions and consultation rates for patients across nine practices in the six months preceding their referral to a practice (Relate) counsellor and the six-month period after counselling was terminated. This showed surgery consultations of these patients reducing by 31 per cent, prescriptions for psychotropic drugs by 30 per cent and for other medication by 48 per cent.

However, the difficulty in judging the beneficial effects of counselling from before-and-after comparisons of improvements in mental state, reduction in consultation rates, and reduced reliance on medication is that results will not necessarily indicate changes brought about by the counsellor. The natural history of most psychological disorders is one of crisis followed by remission (Freeman and Button, 1984). Earll and Kincey (1982), for instance, showed that early advantages for patients randomly selected (from referrals) for counselling by a psychologist, compared to referrals not counselled, diminished over a seven-month follow-up period. It appears that the main benefit of counselling is that patients will resolve their difficulties more rapidly. People with similar problems but not offered counselling will be coping as well as those counselled after 12 months. But those offered a course of counselling (up to ten sessions, but probably taking up an average of four) show greater improvements 14, 22 and 34 weeks after referral (Robson et al., 1984). Robson and colleagues' carefully controlled trial involving 429 referrals also showed considerable savings in prescription costs throughout the 12 month period.

Evaluation of social work counselling in the general practice setting has shown little benefit for the majority of referrals with a new acute depressive illness (e.g. Corney and Briscoe, 1977). However, for referrals with longstanding mental health problems which have recently markedly worsened (often allied to current relationship difficulties), there is some indication that a referral to a social work counsellor is helpful (Corney and Briscoe, 1977).

Whether or not measurable benefits are agreed, the inclusion of a counsellor in the practice team is seen as beneficial, by patients, doctors and counsellors. Waydenfeld and Waydenfeld (1980) found that the Relate counsellors in the nine practices reported appreciating the back-up support of the doctors (particularly for a potential suicide). They like sharing the responsibility of difficult cases, the reduced sense of professional isolation, the control over their own waiting list, feedback about the patient after counselling ended, and dealing with pre-selected well-motivated clients who came from a trusted personal recommendation with a fairly realistic view of what counselling could achieve. Doctors valued the availability of the counsellor's advice even if referral was not needed, enjoyed referring to a personally known counsellor, found counselling improved their subsequent communication with the patient and lessened the pressure to prescribe. But they did not feel it reduced their workload, partly because they became more personally involved with patients and needed regular discussions with the counsellor (Waydenfeld and Waydenfeld, 1980).

Patients also preferred to receive counselling within the practice setting rather than elsewhere. They appreciated the doctors' increased readiness to recognise an emotional background to somatic symptoms, and the continuity of care.

Occasionally a practice nurse may have the aptitude and interest to be able to take on this work as well as her other duties, with as little as one year of training, and one London practice has followed this course (Stone, R., personal communication). However, for many nurses, counselling skills which commonly require listening and refraining from giving advice may be at odds with their clinical training where immediate judgements and specific advice are regularly essential.

An advantage to primary health care providers in liaising with voluntary organisations, such as Relate and the FWA, apart from their low cost, is their considerable experience and expertise. Relate counsellors, for instance, receive a basic two-year training, followed by weekly supervision, group meetings and tutorials, and many individuals take up a range of other training opportunities that arise, being highly motivated toward their work. Their training is essentially psychotherapeutic in nature and the emphasis is on enabling clients to see their own way to resolve their difficulties. However, voluntary organisations have limited resources, both financial and personnel, and are likely to need some form of financial recompense. In particular, those counsellors who regularly work hours that approach those of a full-time job usually expect to be paid accordingly.

Information

Of course many people primarily want information, advice and reassurance when they go to see their GP – information about what is wrong with them, what they can do to rid themselves of the problem, or how they may control it, and to know that it *is* controllable. It is unlikely that they will always be able to obtain all the information they require during a consultation. It may be difficult to talk about some of the issues underlying a particular physical problem; other physical problems may be causing great anxiety, and this may not be made clear; and some treatments required may also give rise to considerable worry. Some of these anxieties may be due to an inadequate explanation of a disorder and its treatment by the doctor, other worries may not have been revealed during the short discussion time. Some will be trivial, but others will not be. Some lack of information or misunderstandings will of course also relate to psychiatric difficulties, their own, or those of a relative in their care. There is a useful role, supplementary to one-to-one advice, that written or audiovisual information can play. It is known that, for instance, the more a person understands about a problem the better, usually, they are able to deal with it. In the non-medical sphere research has shown that frightening events that can be prepared for can be made less distressing by anticipation and mental 'rehearsal' (Epstein, 1983). The more we can prepare for medical procedures the less anxiety and often the less pain we experience (Peterson and Brownlee-Duffeck, 1984; Johnson, 1984). And it is the sense of control that we gain (e.g. knowing that it helps to exercise as soon as possible after a particular operation, or to follow a particular diet afterwards, for instance) that is most valuable, rather than knowledge of details of the procedure (Johnson, 1984). This realisation has long been put into practice in antenatal care in preparing women for childbirth.

In a small number of pioneering health centres around the country, a waiting room health library has been set up, the first reported being in Leeds in 1981 (Varnavides *et al.*, 1984). In this practice the library is run by a qualified librarian who works as a part-time receptionist at the practice. Books, audiotapes, videotapes and two tape recorders were gradually acquired for loan, and the library was administered much like a public library. Audiotapes were found to be popular, particularly relaxation tapes, and over 700 loans of books or tapes were made in the first year. Most books were borrowed on specific complaints; otherwise fitness and diet, infant and child care, pregnancy and mental health were the most popular categories (for example, a book called *Self-help for your nerves* was particularly popular). Two-thirds of the books were chosen while the patient was in the waiting room for some other reason; nearly 15 per cent resulted from patients coming to the library specifically to look for a book; 14 per cent were borrowed following a specific recommendation by the GP or a friend. In addition to loans, books were read by people waiting for their appointment.

The library was used more by women than by men, but otherwise by a cross-section of the patient group, including people who rarely or never used a public library (one-third of borrowers), and people who had left school without qualifications (one-third of borrowers). Anticipated drawbacks to the practitioners such as feeling threatened by increasing questioning from more knowledgeable patients, or patients becoming more anxious by studying books about problems they did not in fact have, did not materialise as justified fears. The main problems were practical ones – missing books, paying for new books. About 5 per cent of the stock was lost each year, other books needed replacing through wear and tear, and old books needed replacing by up-to-date ones.

Paying for a library can be done by registering it as a charity to which patients and local fundraisers can contribute (see Siddy, 1986). Drug companies can also contribute as the charity is a separate entity administered by trustees, and ethical codes of conduct barring doctors from receiving money from drug companies are avoided. Gifts to and profits from the charity are exempt from tax, so long as all monies are spent on the library.

A practice library was also set up in Dr Reginald Yorke's five-GP practice in Merseyside in 1984, as a memorial to a young partner who had recently died. A memorial fund raised over £3,600 of which just under half was spent immediately on stocking the library. The remainder was invested to buy new and replace missing books. The bookshelves in the waiting area (overlooked by reception staff) were accessible to anyone waiting there, and increasingly staff at the centre referred patients to specific books (infertility and coping with arthritis were two recent examples).

Of course there are also a great number of information leaflets produced, those on specific disorders or complaints usually by a voluntary group for sufferers of that condition, or by health education groups. They will often offer contact addresses, telephone numbers and advice through the organisation, as well as information about the problem, through which the individual may be able to obtain considerable support. The health centre is arguably the most appropriate place from which such information could be obtainable, particularly concerning local community and voluntary support networks. There are excellent leaflets produced by MIND – about schizophrenia, major tranquillisers, minor tranquillisers, lithium, depression, anxiety, mental handicap, and bereavement, for example. They explain what the terms mean, what is known about the condition or the drug, what to expect, how to get help, what to do if you are a friend, and so on. Similarly, other groups produce equally professional information: about drug dependence and drug abuse (by the Standing Conference on Drug Abuse); on 'Coping with a confused elderly person at home' (Alzheimer's Disease Society); and relevant information by the Association for Postnatal Illness, CRUSE (a bereavement support service), the National Society for Epilepsy (e.g. 'Epilepsy and work', 'Diagnosis and management'), MENCAP, and Relaxation for Living (who also produce audiotapes), to name but a few. It would not be a difficult matter for practices to make these available, although as yet there have been few services offered to which a cost is attached for the patient.

Finally, one other possible source of information which might be utilised in waiting areas are videotapes. The Kentish Town Health Centre in London experimented with waiting room videos, showing four ten-minute programmes obtained through the Health Education Authority (Koperski, 1989). The waiting area was partitioned into two by a heavy curtain so that patients could choose whether or not to watch. During the experimental sessions 161 patients attended, of whom just over half chose to watch the programmes. Four out of five of the patients interviewed gave positive views on the project, whether *or not* they chose to watch, and very few were clearly negative. Over half of those watching could recall specific facts from the programmes when asked. Videos have been in use successfully for some time in some accident and emergency waiting areas, and antenatal clinics. Comments have been favourable and at the very least, they help to pass the time (and reduce complaints about waiting times). But they may also prove to have health benefits. Subjects could include coping with a range of physical, mental or social problems, preventive health advice and information; and the addition of specific local information may be possible – local self-help groups, local sources of advice and information and facilities available at the practice. Videos of specific relevance to specific clinics could also be used (e.g. antenatal, health promotion, diabetes). Undoubtedly there will be an increasing range of resources of these kinds becoming available with the recent interest in preventive health care.

Befriending

Apart from advice, information and counselling, most people coping with distressing events or long-term difficulties need emotional and practical support. Most important, in this respect, will be their spouse or partner, or a close friend. Their support can prevent a depressed mood from developing into a depression of clinical proportions. However, where there is no such close relationship, or where close friends live some distance away and are in contact infrequently, or where the partner or friend does not for other reasons offer support through the difficult times, then other support may sometimes play a role in prevention. Also, for the person who has been depressed for some time, a new friendship offering new opportunities for social activities or support with current problems may be the kind of event which will mark the beginning of their recovery. The kind of support frequently suggested as having particular value is that of someone who is coping with the same event or difficulty. For instance, the lonely mother suffering from postnatal depression may be helped most in the first instance by a loving supportive husband, but the key to helping her have the confidence to take her new baby out of the house, to the shops, on a bus, and lead a normal life, may be the friendship of another new mother who lives nearby and can do these things with her, as the case history below illustrates. Similarly, the case history described earlier of the mother of a

Down's Syndrome baby indicated that she benefited greatly from the friendship and babysitting help offered by another mother of a handicapped child. Many other examples could easily be found.

The primary care team is in the ideal position to mobilise this kind of help. Although the case history below of a woman introduced to me through a general practitioner in South London does not illustrate a disorder that was prevented, it is described because it shows how befriending helped a seriously depressed woman to recover, and because the support and friendship provided may well be preventive in the difficult times ahead when she has her second child. For other women at an earlier time – perhaps during pregnancy, this simple act of putting an isolated young woman in touch with a potential friend might prove to have greater preventive effect.

Tracey is 26, her husband John 25. They live on the sixth floor of a tower block on a large council estate. They have one bedroom only, a sitting room and a small kitchen. They have a son, Jack, now 5 months old, and Tracey is three months pregnant. She says they will not be considered for rehousing in a two- or three-bedroom flat until the eldest child is 2. They are new to the area, having both recently left the Navy after Tracey became pregnant. Tracey was lonely and the local design of the housing could only exacerbate her problems. The two lifts up to the flats are long and narrow so that it will be impossible for her to have a double 'buggy' when she has two infants.

Tracey told me that a few days after the birth of her first child, she became weepy and depressed. The two- to three-hourly feeds day and night exhausted her and she became less and less able to cope. Her husband was extremely supportive and took over much of the child care and as her depression worsened he was unable to return to work. After four weeks she had lost all interest in the baby, had become rude and difficult with relatives who offered help, and yet was unable to see that she was behaving in an unusual way. One night she reached crisis point, feeling sick, shaking, hyperventilating, crying for help, and she needed urgent psychiatric treatment. However, she refused in-patient care and her treatment was managed at home by her GP and a CPN.

As she recovered, her health visitor was able to resume contact and established a good relationship with her. She introduced her to a young woman of the same age who was a single parent of a child just two months older than Jack, and who lived in the adjacent tower block. The health visitor asked Tracey if she would like to be put in touch with her and then gave the other woman Tracey's telephone number. Tracey says this friend 'is a double of me'. 'She's just a little more headstrong, which is not surprising as she's had to fight for everything for herself (DSS and stuff). She's terrific. And when I'm bad she'll play with Jack as well as her own kid.' At first she always came to Tracey, but recently the contact is reversed too. Before, Tracey was too nervous to try to feed or change her baby anywhere other than in her own home, but her friend has given her the confidence to get out. Tracey told me that she would never have gone anywhere with her baby, she was too scared about getting in and out of shop doors and so on. Now it's just like any other everyday thing – 'I don't think twice. We've been all over together – Woolwich on the train even!' Tracey sees her friend almost every day.

Tracey says she feels terrific now, and has no anxiety 'about what I'd do if he was sick. Before I couldn't watch TV or anything and leave him asleep in the other room – I'd be too worried he might be sick. I couldn't go to the shops without him – but if I took him, John would have to come too. I had no confidence in myself.'

The value of this relationship was undoubtedly as great as it was because they became 'true' friends. They genuinely liked each other, wanted to spend time together, were able to share their parenting experiences and help each other with child care. Other types of befriending, where less reciprocity is possible, may have less impact but can sometimes prove quite valuable, and some health centres have experimented with volunteer schemes in collaboration with a local voluntary services co-ordinator. However, volunteers often find it difficult to provide intensive long-term support to particular individuals and are best used for befriending people with a short-term difficulty, or in a less personal capacity, perhaps offering transport or other practical help to ease particular problems.

Crisis intervention

There are some people, often well known to their GPs and social services teams alike, whose multiple problems seem to become entrenched, and disastrous relationships combined with longstanding social or health problems defy easy solution. When they then experience some new or related crisis, they have few resources to help them cope. Treating either the social or the health or emotional problem separately is unlikely to achieve great improvement in their situation or reduce their vulnerability, and a period of intensive support to consider their problem in context may be what is needed.

The Crisis Service in Tower Hamlets, East London works in this way. It is directed more toward psychosocial crises than are many other crisis teams who deal more often with relapses of psychiatric illnesses previously treated in hospital. Like other teams, however, there are a psychiatrist, a CPN and social workers who work together and who aim to respond rapidly to crises (within 24 hours), to 'stay with' the crisis and to help the person to acquire good coping responses. They assume that the unit of care is not just the individual, but also the family or friends he or she is intimately involved with from day to day. They avoid labelling disturbed behaviour as mental illness unless this is clearly in the best interests of a particular family member. And the initial asessments are normally carried out in the family home with all family members involved in or affected by the crisis.

Crisis intervention theory is based on the writings of Gerald Caplan who describes crises as short-lived emotional upsets (usually about six weeks) which occur when an individual, 'faced with an obstacle to important life goals, finds that it is for the time being insurmountable through the use of customary problem solving methods' (Caplan, 1964). During crises, people are particularly vulnerable to psychiatric disorder, but are also receptive to outside help. If a crisis is resolved in such a way as to reduce the tension and distress without removing the problem (using denial or by turning to alcohol or tranquillisers, say) the person's vulnerability to future crisis may increase. And if such solutions fail and the problem cannot be avoided, symptoms of a specific psychiatric disorder may emerge. If, however, an adaptive response mobilises new coping solutions, redefines the problem and leads to a successful resolution of the situation, the individual becomes stronger, *better* equipped to deal with future crises. Crisis intervention teams aim to achieve this third outcome.

The Tower Hamlets Crisis Service grew out of a request (in 1974) from social workers for meetings with psychiatric service personnel to discuss mental health issues they encountered. Dr Colin Murray Parkes, with experience of preventive psychiatry and crisis services in America, joined Tower Hamlets shortly afterwards and helped to establish a pilot collaborative project offering crisis support. After two years, joint funding was awarded to pay for offices and the salary of an administrator. A qualified nurse who was also a Relate counsellor, and who was attached to the CPN service, worked with a rota of social workers from the team and psychiatrists from the hospital to man the service. In 1985 the district health authority took over funding and by 1988 the service was well established with a consultant psychiatrist, a CPN, an administrator and a part-time assistant administrator. Social workers from the area teams worked with them and additional time was given to the service by junior doctors and a senior registrar from a nearby psychiatric hospital. All workers involved in the service received training in crisis theory and practice.

The administrator plays a crucial role in a service of this kind. They must make the first check that a referral is appropriate, then pass it to team members who will decide which two of them (a combination of social worker, CPN or psychiatrist) should visit. They must then trace all other professionals who may have some involvement with the client (their GP, social worker, probation officer, say) and invite them to attend a case conference. If they find that a large number of other agencies are involved with a client, they may try to organise a meeting between them *before* any visit is made to the client. Each case will then be discussed in a case conference every six weeks for the three to six months of their support. This is mainly in order that the two team members involved with the case can be offered support and supervision by more senior colleagues. This is crucial when so many referrals are on the brink of suicide or serious mental illness.

The fact that two people turn up at the family home very rapidly in response to, say, a demand that an individual be taken into hospital because of his worrying and very disturbed behaviour can often make the family more willing to stick with a problem until the best solution can be achieved. Problems that involve whole families are those particularly appropriate for the help a crisis team can provide. Relationship difficulties are often at the heart of psychiatric problems, and work with whole families offers the opportunities to tackle such underlying issues.

For instance, Mrs Knight, referred to the crisis service with her husband by the emergency clinic at the psychiatric hospital, had for ten years suffered from anorexia nervosa. She did not consider the disorder to be her main problem, although her husband obviously did.

They had a turbulent relationship, Mr Knight being an insecure but dominant husband who had used violent means to reinforce his control over his wife. He was excessively concerned with the appearance both of his wife and his home. She had at one time been very overweight, but soon after the birth of their son, Mrs Knight developed anorexia, becoming so ill that she required several months of in-patient care. She continued to be extremely thin, which greatly concerned her husband.

Their marital problems were longstanding but when her son was 10 years old Mrs Knight finally decided to move out, taking her son with her to a women's refuge. Mr Knight responded by locking himself in his flat, telling neighbours and other visitors that he would cut his wrists if his wife did not return, which she felt obliged to do.

A social worker and student CPN from the crisis service visited the home and received a friendly welcome from Mrs Knight, though not from her husband. However, their presence enabled the couple to discuss Mrs Knight's anorexia civilly for perhaps the first time in years, and at the second visit, Mr Knight was much more amenable, and both acknowledged that the intervention was proving helpful. The team meeting soon afterwards confirmed the decision of the case workers not to fall into the trap of identifying the anorexia as the problem by treating it. As Mrs Knight had successfully controlled it for ten years there was no urgent need for treatment. The visits were to continue and the team suggested that a teacher from the son's school be involved at the next meeting so that they could ascertain how the problems were affecting him.

This case perhaps best illustrates how a crisis point in a longstanding psychiatric/marital problem provides the opportunity for supportive intervention. Previously it would have been impossible to gain Mr Knight's co-operation in discussions toward resolving a problem that he saw as pertaining only to his wife.

A large proportion of the clients seen by the crisis team have a combination of psychiatric symptoms, marital problems, and/or problems with young children and social difficulties. Of course it is not always possible to involve both partners in the intervention, and sometimes the support of the crisis team will enable one partner in an unhappy relationship to arrange to separate. While this may be a positive outcome, it may also bring a new set of problems. Consider the following example.

Mrs Kane was referred to the crisis service from an abortion clinic. She was 19 weeks pregnant. The doctor who saw her felt she did not really want the termination that she was requesting and that she appeared to be depressed. In addition, Mrs Kane seemed to have no friends other than those at work.

A CPN and social worker from the crisis service visited her the next day, less than 48 hours after Mrs Kane's consultation at the abortion clinic. She was a 31-year-old woman from Guyana who had lived in England since childhood. Her parents were dead and her sister lived in another part of England. She had married a much older man, also from Guyana, two years previously. He already had an 18-year-old daughter and did not want any more children. Mrs Kane described the marriage as unhappy, and her husband as a bully who would not allow her to use items of furniture that were his and whose cruelty had once included cutting her arms with a knife.

By the second visit the case workers had established with Mrs Kane that she did not want to terminate the pregnancy, and that although in a depressed mood, she was not clinically depressed. They arranged support for her over her pregnancy with the help of antenatal staff. They also sought legal advice on her behalf about her tenancy rights to the flat should her husband leave and after six weeks of supportive discussions the case was closed. Mrs Kane refused to involve her husband in any work with the crisis service.

Eight months later Mrs Kane re-contacted the crisis service. She had recently returned to work after maternity leave. She was separated from her husband and had been granted the tenancy of the flat but was finding it extremely difficult to cope with single parenthood. The CPN who had been involved with Mrs Kane at the first referral visited her again. She seemed to be worried about the dampness of the house for the baby, and the difficulties of getting her daughter to a nursery and herself to work on time some distance away. During the next few visits, however, Mrs Kane's mental health was clearly worsening. She was distressed, unhappy, feeling unable to cope with her child and expressing suicidal thoughts. She was also about to be made redundant from her job as a hospital ward orderly. The baby was cared for but Mrs Kane's distress and tearfulness were reducing the attention she received. Her behaviour toward the baby was somewhat rigid and inflexible, and she seemed unable to find sensible solutions to her many practical difficulties. For instance, the baby's cot was damp and covered in mildew. She was therefore sleeping with her mother, which was obviously unsatisfactory as she had fallen onto the floor several times. Although distressed about this Mrs Kane was unable to take the necessary steps either to claim money from social services for a new cot or to convert anything else into a safe bed.

The team felt Mrs Kane needed psychiatric assessment, which in turn led to a prescription for anti-depressants. A social work member of the team also arranged money for a replacement cot, and representations were made to the estate officer about the decoration and insulation of the flat. Support was continued for several more weeks and Mrs Kane rapidly improved. She secured a place at a local adult education college on a community work course and after two more months of monitoring where she continued to cope well, the case was closed.

Cost-effectiveness

The preventive benefits of a service of this kind are difficult to measure, given that it focuses more on psychosocial crises than psychiatric relapses. Numbers of people admitted for in-patient treatment might be an appropriate outcome measure if the service was primarily mobilised for people with a history of recurrent major mental illness in order to prevent hospital admission (as many crisis services aim to do). This service, however, aims to prevent first as well as recurrent admissions, and a wide range of pathology which would not be seen in psychiatric hospitals even without their intervention. This does not mean, of course, that it is not preventing serious mental health problems (or mobilising early treatment), but rather that many problems of this kind currently exist untreated in the community. Mental illnesses treated by traditional psychiatric services represent only the tip (if, by and large, the most severe end) of the mental illness iceberg.

A recent evaluation of the Tower Hamlets Crisis Service has focused instead on an evaluative description of case note data and interviews with clients and referrers (Parkes, 1988). An 18-month period of operation of the service (from January 1984) was studied, and interviews conducted with 107 clients and 82 referrers using the service during this time.

The largest number of referrers were general practitioners (referring 38 per cent of clients), followed by social workers (23 per cent), psychiatrists (17 per cent) and health visitors (12 per cent). Those referring people to the crisis team felt they dealt with a good deal of family crisis themselves, but needed additional support when there was also a threat of violence, psychosis or suicide (GPs) or family separation (social workers). The crisis service was seen to have a number of advantages (by referrers), over 11 other types of service in the area which offered various kinds of support for families, namely the domiciliary visiting service, their rapid response to referral, frequent visiting, multi-disiciplinary involvement, and use of a social worker and psychiatrist in the team.

Not surprisingly, given the clear priority given by the service administration to the care of family crisis, the client group was found to be biased toward younger, female clients with partners and jobs. This contrasts with the profile of long-term sufferers of mental illnesses in the borough who tended to be older, male, solitary and unemployed. In fact it was found that for people with existing psychiatric symptoms relatively uncomplicated by other issues, referrers tended to refer people directly to psychiatric wards. It was also found that the client group did not represent the ethnic groupings of the community. People from Bangladesh seemed neither to come through to the crisis service nor hospital services as a representative proportion of clients, suggesting that existing services were not acceptable to this community.

Two out of three clients said they felt things had been better since the end of crisis support, and most of those who had experienced further difficulties had contained them in the family. Asked what they thought would have happened without the service, one in four said they might have committed suicide, and nearly as many said they would have had a 'nervous breakdown'. Others said families would have separated or violence occurred. Referrers too felt risk of further crises and of psychiatric admission had been reduced by the service in almost half of the clients, and risk of mental illness reduced in 39 per cent. Case note data showed that of 160 specific client problems whose outcome was recorded, 36 per cent were considered to be fully resolved, 36 per cent partially resolved and 29 per cent unresolved.

The average family received an estimated 10.8 telephone contacts, 23 hours of team members' time, plus other administrative and secretarial time, at a total cost of £390 per family (1984 prices). There were not great variations around this. Viewed in terms of hospital bed prices it is relatively inexpensive, with a total cost in 1984 of £45,630, or a little over the cost of maintaining two hospital beds for one year. For this cost they supported 117 families.

The separate referral mechanisms for the hospital services and the crisis service do not seem to be ideal in that almost certainly some people likely to benefit from crisis support will not be referred for their consideration. If greater liaison in the referral mechanism was established it might improve efficiency and cost–benefit, and it may also help some people to avoid acquiring a psychiatric label.

However, the potential financial benefit of this service should not only be assessed against costs or savings to psychiatry. If the predictions of the families about what might have happened without crisis support were correct, the effects need also to be assessed against the cost associated with suicides, broken homes, child abuse, criminal proceedings and imprisonment. Its effectiveness in these areas, either in financial or personal terms, is difficult to demonstrate, and evaluation to date has not succeeded in doing so. But it is obviously the view of the service staff, their clients and the referrers that benefits of these kinds are being achieved.

ACCESS TO RESOURCES

A range of support which can be sought by GPs for their patients when endeavouring to help them to cope with crises have been described: counselling, information, friendship, crisis intervention. If the GP can accurately determine the underlying source of difficulty, has discussed with the patient and perhaps with other members of the patient's family what kind of help is needed, how can such help be found?

The first priority is a good knowledge of the demographic, social and health characteristics of the community served, and its health-related resources and services.

Good counselling services may already exist. The practice needs to know if there is a Family Welfare Association, Relate or similar voluntary counselling service of repute operating nearby and, if so, open discussions with them about the possibility of establishing some sort of liaison. Alternatively, they might have discussions with the area social services director about the possibility of having an attached social worker. Similar discussions could be held with local psychology and psychiatric nursing services to ascertain where the best prospects for professional collaboration lie, and whether that collaboration would best involve a practice-based counselling service or a stronger working link with counselling services elsewhere. If unable to obtain the kind of practice-based counselling wanted, they might consider whether the practice nurse had the personality and interest to want to undertake a training course in counselling, and whether she could combine counselling work, when trained, with her nursing duties. One final possiblity would be to advertise locally for a trained counsellor to come and work on a voluntary basis (or for a sessional fee reimbursable at 70 per cent from the family health service authority) at the practice.

A good supply of information leaflets or a well stocked library of up-to-date health texts would require a certain amount of research, initially, by someone in the practice. There are several directories of self-help groups which should say if groups supply information (e.g. Gillie *et al.*, 1982; Help for Health project at Southampton General Hospital; and *Someone to talk to* (Tod *et al.*, 1985)). The existing libraries in health centres could be approached to supply a list of their stock as a starting point for books and tapes, but the list would need checking, of course, so that books ordered were indeed among the best or most up-to-date currently available. The library at the Royal College of General Practitioners may be able to help, as should the Health Education Authority. Leading publishers of popular medical books might be approached for a list of relevant titles and summaries of contents. The local library may give assistance.

Information about local voluntary services could best be gained first of all by some detective work to find out what exists nearby. The local library may help, and many areas also have in post a voluntary services co-ordinator. Good Practices in Mental Health, a London-based charity, have commissioned numerous local studies of geographical areas to describe available 'good practice'. Many areas have already produced directories of local projects about which local health education units may be able to offer advice. Family doctors may not, however, wish either to advertise or recommend services about which they know very little, including their quality and professionalism. A strategy could be devised to enable the practice team to become more familiar with organisers of local voluntary and community groups. As practice managers are often charged with arranging team meetings, it might also be made their responsibility to arrange for a key figure from a local voluntary group to attend during the first ten minutes of the meeting to describe their service. By the end of a two-year period of regular team meetings, practice team members would have gained considerable knowledge about the range and quality of services which they might sometimes wish to recommend to patients (MENCAP, Gingerbread, CRUSE, etc.) and of services they could perhaps call upon on their patients' behalf (Good Neighbours schemes, for instance).

Only a relatively small number of crisis intervention services exist, but those which do will be more heavily used as a resource by the GPs who know most about them. Many crisis services would welcome a much greater involvement of GPs, perhaps as occasional members of visiting teams, certainly as participants in case conferences on their patients.

A practice example

Some health centres have for many years offered an impressive range of information and support and have the mechanisms in place to keep staff well informed themselves about local activites. The James Wigg Practice in Kentish Town Health Centre, North London, for instance, have two lunchtime team meetings every week. One of these is open to a large number of colleagues and there is often an invited visitor. Many local voluntary groups have been represented over the years: Parent and Co.; MENCAP; the Stillbirth and Neonatal Trust, the Law Centre, the Citizens Advice Bureau. They give a short presentation and answer questions. All the team may attend, and the receptionists usually send one representative.

The health centre also offers itself as a resource for the local community.

There is a crèche where parents can leave their children not only for the time they are with a doctor, but also if they would simply like to be able to do their shopping without taking their children. Or if they are trying to overcome some current difficulties which would be made easier if they had some child care assistance, they can arrange to use the crèche on a regular basis. This is permitted up to three half-days a week and is offered for any local parents whether or not they are registered patients of the health centre. A few adult education classes are also held in the centre: English as a second language, sewing for the elderly. And a women's group also meets at the centre once each week in which discussions focus mainly on problems in close relationships.

The practice has established an impressive range of services, either through direct employment of workers (e.g. a secretary doubles as a part-time welfare benefits rights adviser) or through bringing external organisations or professionals into the practice: a social worker (funded by Social Services) offers counselling on a part-time basis; a Relate counsellor works on a voluntary basis one session a week; and the health authority supports a psychosexual counsellor one day a week. A number of medical specialists also visit the health centre for a few hours weekly or monthly, including a rheumatologist, a paediatrician and a psychiatrist. In addition, the practice has provided waiting room health videos (so far on an experimental basis), and a small health library.

Communication between psychiatry and general practice

The specialist mental health resources available to GPs through referrals to the psychiatric hospital can be used more effectively the more the GP knows about what is available. The traditional referral mechanism, however, is by letter or telephone call from the GP to the psychiatric out-patient clinic. This somewhat distant form of contact has often allowed longstanding poor levels of understanding about what one is looking for and what the other has to offer, to continue (Mitchell, 1985). Personal contact can greatly improve matters. In fact, a major benefit cited for attachment schemes of all other primary care workers in a general practice (including social workers, psychologists, voluntary counsellors) has been improvements to the appropriateness and value of cross-referrals. This has also been shown to be the case when referrals to a psychiatric service have been made to a team seeing patients on the practice premises rather than through conventional channels. McKechnie and his colleagues (1981) showed that patients referred through conventional channels were more likely to have had previous contacts with the psychiatric service, were more likely to be admitted to hospital and spent more time as in-patients than those referred from a practice of a similar size in a nearby town with a practice-based psychiatric team. Both practices were served by the same psychiatric hospital from which they were equidistant, but the psychiatrist held fortnightly clinics at the second practice, the psychologist attending weekly. They and their team's social worker spent one hour a week discussing patients' progress and problems with the GPs. Urgent referrals could still be made directly to the hospital but would be discussed subsequently at their meetings. The close working relationship considerably improved the level of understanding between professionals, *increased* the referral rate to the out-patient facilities, but reduced use of hospital in-patient time. Similar findings have been reported by Fenton and colleagues (1979).

Mitchell (1985) describes several possible ways in which psychiatrists and GPs could strengthen their links to their mutual advantage. They include occasional joint home visits, holding psychiatric clinics in health centres, psychiatrists visiting the surgery to see selected patients, meeting for group discussions in surgeries (discussing patients but not seeing them), and holding joint consultations in the surgery. Of course these models can be combined in any number of ways, but the increased communication and sharing of difficulties from regular face-to-face contacts should increase the confidence of the family doctor in his or her diagnostic and therapeutic role. It should also improve the prospects for early intervention and crisis work, make referrals easier, improve feedback and result in a more efficient use of psychiatric services (Mitchell, 1985). However, whether the benefit will justify the expensive skills of senior psychiatrists being spent in this way can only be determined from further evaluative studies.

In conclusion, there appear to be benefits to health care providers and to their clients in the establishment of formal working links between a wide range of caring organisations and professionals. There is considerable potential for the general practice to become more of a community resource through which their client population could expect to locate useful information, advice, counselling, contact addresses and practical help for health-related problems. Community groups and voluntary counsellors would benefit greatly from the back-up of a medical team and the opportunity to base sessions in the health centre. Doctors would have a range of support to offer patients coping with psychosocial problems that otherwise they may feel they can do little to help. And people coping with a range of stressful circumstances may find the assistance they need either to prevent a crisis developing, to cope with the crisis constructively, or to reduce the likelihood of further crises. Benefits of such may eventually be demonstrated in terms of reduced hospital admissions, better treatment compliance, reduced referrals for misdiagnosed conditions and reduced psychiatric symptomatology. Fortunately many practitioners have not felt they needed to wait for this evidence.

Chapter 4

Preventing relapse in schizophrenia

INTRODUCTION

Nobody knows yet what causes schizophrenia, or even precisely what it is that we have given this name. We can describe how people whom we label as having schizophrenia might behave, and how they might feel, we know that the illness (if this is how it can be described) typically begins in people aged 20 to 30, and that its onset tends to be earlier in men than women. And we know that some people will be seriously affected by the disorder for the rest of their lives, some will recover from a first episode completely, and the larger proportion (about half) will have an up-and-down course where occasional serious episodes are interspersed with periods of relative stability (although usually with some remaining social impairment).

Drugs which are effective in controlling the psychotic symptoms such as delusions, and in helping control excitement and any hostile or aggressive behaviour shown by sufferers, were first discovered and used in the 1950s. This led to a period of great optimism that the disorder could rapidly be brought under control in hospital, and by continuing indefinitely to take a lower 'maintenance' dose of the same drugs, the person could return home and avoid further serious problems. Although the drugs have indeed proved to be invaluable in treatment (Davis and Garver, 1978), have a major role in reducing vulnerability to relapse (Leff and Wing, 1971), and have facilitated the reduction in in-patient numbers, many of their limitations have now become apparent. The neuroleptic drugs do not always abolish the 'florid' or 'positive' symptoms; individuals remain at high risk of relapse even while continuing them (about 50 per cent over two years); the problems of motivation and concentration and other 'negative' symptoms are not helped; and the drugs frequently lead to distressing side effects. In fact, people who have suffered schizophrenia often remain considerably more impaired by their disorder than was anticipated when the drug treatments were first implemented and the reduction in in-patient numbers began. This has contributed to the continuing gap between provision and need for support by people with long-term difficulties who are living at home.

Roughly two-thirds of people treated for schizophrenia return to live with their families after their first admission to hospital. Families therefore have a central role in the rehabilitation phase and in long-term support. And research over the last two decades has shown how important their support can be. This is largely due to the continued sensitivity of the individual to their social environment after a recent acute episode of schizophrenia, even when there are no apparent remaining symptoms (Brown and Birley, 1968; Wing and Brown, 1970; Cutting, 1985).

In particular, the level of emotional arousal created by the person's day-to-day living circumstances has been highlighted as an important factor. Both over-stimulating and under-stimulating conditions can increase the individual's own level of arousal and lead to a raised risk of relapse. For instance, spending lengthy periods with a socially intrusive or very critical relative at home, from whose contact it is not easy to withdraw, can cause a latent thought disorder to redevelop into delusions or odd behaviour (Brown et al., 1972). It is believed that those who live with relatives who can be rated as 'high' in terms of expressed emotion are likely to have heightened arousal levels over long periods of time. It is for these circumstances that the maintenance doses of neuroleptics are considered to be most valuable (Vaughn and Leff, 1976). On the other hand, the seemingly protective but extremely under-stimulating environments in some back wards of the old long-stay mental hospitals (and in upstairs bedrooms at the family home) where sufferers have been allowed to withdraw are now known to have let withdrawal go too far. Patients in such environments also showed a high level of arousal (Wing and Brown, 1970). The optimum environment seems to be one that is structured, where roles are clear cut, and with only as much complexity as the person is able to cope with at his or her stage of recovery. Active encouragement to keep up standards of appearance, work and behaviour can be important. The more the family and the individual understand about the disorder and its management, the better equipped they all can be to control and overcome the existing and new problems. This is true of course for most medical conditions.

After the acute symptoms have subsided, the person is usually well enough to live independently, but will almost certainly be left with many of the so-called 'negative' symptoms which can take a considerable period to overcome. These include a low level of self-confidence, and a poor level of concentration and motivation. Individuals may therefore tend to neglect their appearance and self-care and have some difficulty in going straight back into open employment or running their home life.

Life changes, crises or intrusive events are also known to be linked to risk of relapse, and these findings also have implications for lifestyle (Brown and Birley, 1968; Vaughn and Leff, 1976). It is important that the individual aims to avoid such stresses as far as possible; and where they cannot be avoided it is helpful if they can be prepared for (Wing et al., 1964).

The accumulating evidence on the role of the social environment in relapse and chronicity has led to the development and evaluation of experimental programmes of family therapy, and to community treatment services. Of course, social care and social treatments have always been the mainstay of psychiatric practice, even if they have been, for a time, overshadowed by a heavy reliance on neuroleptics. But Stein and Test (Eds) (1978) describe a number of exemplary and comprehensive community support programmes which provide a much greater level of home support than is ever offered within standard services. And the experimental work in recent years on prevention has been a direct response to the research evidence on the role of expressed emotion, amount of face-to-face contact, and use of maintenance medication in the course of schizophrenia. It has mostly taken the form of family therapy for people treated for schizophrenia who return to live with family members. Essential elements include enhancing the whole family's understanding of the illness, reducing family stress, improving communication and learning coping skills. The results of all these studies have been positive in confirming that psychosocial interventions do add something, particularly during the very vulnerable first months after discharge, to the maintenance treatment of schizophrenia by drug therapy alone. These approaches are the main focus of this chapter.

However, although an individual's mental state may be up and down to some extent from one day to the next, full relapses in schizophrenia are not usually overnight occurrences. There are invariably small changes in the mood and behaviour of the individual's beginning days and often three to four weeks before the marked florid symptoms which characterise an acute relapse surface. These may not be apparent to most people, including the professionals helping the individual, but will often be noticed by the sufferer himself and those people who are in close daily contact with him. Monitoring such 'early warning signs' and responding with rapid drug treatment can sometimes 'abort' relapse (Herz, 1984), and should at least limit the scale and duration of the exacerbation, as well as having other benefits to sufferer and relatives in helping them to feel they have some control over the disorder. Some reference to new work in this area is also made toward the end of this chapter.

PREVENTIVE INTERVENTIONS WITH SUFFERERS OF SCHIZOPHRENIA AND THEIR FAMILIES: THE RESEARCH

In terms of family support, the factor which has perhaps received the most attention recently is the quality of relationships, particularly the level of 'expressed emotion'. A large number of critical comments and an intrusive over-concern for the individual by those people in prolonged daily contact with him increase his susceptibility to relapse (Brown et al., 1972; Vaughn and Leff, 1976). What a review of a number of studies indicates, however, is that, rather than being the primary factor, expressed emotion (EE) is more likely to cause relapse through a circular process (Kanter et al., 1987). That is, it is not that relatives of sufferers of schizophrenia have particularly explosive personalities or are especially critical or intrusive by nature, and that they are the cause of all the individual's problems. Rather, it is the person's disturbed or unusual behaviour which leads to a higher level of tension in the home and to the relative's expressed emotion. The high EE of relatives and disturbed behaviour of the individual fuel each other and the high EE finally leads to relapse (Brown et al., 1972). Intervention studies following this research have therefore been based on the aim of helping relatives to learn to deal with the upsetting, disturbing or even frightening behaviour of the individual in calm, but firm and supportive ways as a means of bringing down the sufferer's own level of arousal. An additional feature of the approach has been to encourage family members to lead more independent, separate lives and to reduce the proportion of each day spent in face-to-face contact with one another below a level of about 35 hours a week, as indicated by the early research (Brown et al., 1972; Vaughn and Leff, 1976). The protective effect of continuing the maintenance medication was assumed.

A programme by Leff and his associates in 1982 (Leff et al., 1982) aimed to achieve these triple goals (lowering EE, reducing face-to-face contact, ensuring adherence to maintenance medication) through an educational programme, a relatives' group, and individual family sessions. The educational programme consisted of four lectures on the causes, symptoms, course and management of schizophrenia, read from a typescript during two visits to the relatives' own homes. The relatives' discussion groups brought together both high and low EE families every two weeks for nine months. Not only was it hoped that discussions about common day to day problems would enable those with the less helpful coping approaches to pick up useful strategies from other relatives, but also that meeting others in a similar position would help to counter the sense of isolation and distress felt by many of them. In the family sessions, a psychiatrist and psychologist met the sufferer and his or her closest relatives in their own home for one-hour sessions (anything from one to 25 times) to discuss their own particular difficulties further and suggest coping responses.

For eight of the 11 high EE families involved in this experimental project, the intervention resulted in either a reduced EE rating or reduced face-to-face contact below 35 hours a week, or both, and none of the disturbed members of these families relapsed during the nine-month follow-up period. One of the remaining three individuals in high EE environments receiving the programme relapsed, while six out of 12 of the control group (high EE, no special family support) relapsed. The programme was therefore judged to have been successful in ameliorating critical attitudes among relatives, in reducing face-to-face contact, and hence in preventing relapse.

Two years after the experimental family intervention, the participants were re-contacted (Leff *et al.*, 1985). Five patients had discontinued their medication at some point during the two years – two of the intervention group, three of the controls. All but one of these five (a control group member) relapsed between one and four months after stopping the drugs. Between the nine-month and two-year follow-ups, few patients of either group received much professional attention although the research team were available for advice and meetings. Nineteen remained on medication throughout the two years, yet nine of these relapsed. Seven of the relapses were control group patients, two were in the experimental group, confirming a marked difference between them (78 per cent vs 20 per cent). However, two other patients in the experimental group committed suicide. Three control group patients also attempted suicide, but survived. For these patients, the management of their difficulties can only be judged as abject failures. This considerably diminishes the success rate of the intervention to 78 per cent vs 40 per cent, but still leaves a larger number of patients in the experimental group who avoid a relapse of florid symptoms.

The two who died were both involved in separating from their closest relative – one girl attempting unsuccessfully to loosen the tie between herself and her mother, the second having recently been left by his wife and children. It must at least imply that extreme care must be exercised in encouraging relatives to break or reduce contact so that the sufferer does not move toward a more, rather than a less vulnerable position.

Other research workers in the field have put less emphasis on reducing face-to-face contact between a sufferer and their relatives. Falloon and his colleagues (1985), for instance, emphasise the positive effects of the household with low EE, warmth and helpful supportive relationships. They argue in fact that *high* contact with relatives who show a good deal of warmth can be health-promoting. Their approach is to help the family improve their problem-solving skills in order to reduce stress of all kinds within the household, and not merely the stresses associated with the behaviour of the sufferer. Stresses are considered as they affect *any* member of the household, and the problems and goals of the sufferer have as high a priority as those of everyone else. Family members are helped to improve their communication skills and their range of activities outside the home, but are *not* encouraged to spend less time together. Nor is reducing EE a specific aim of their intervention study (Falloon *et al.*, 1985), although they work primarily with high EE families. Their aim was to enhance family coping through learning a structured problem-solving method. Considerably fewer of the 19 patients in their family therapy group suffered relapses with florid symptoms of schizophrenia over a two-year follow-up period compared to the comparison group of 19 patients. Furthermore, those in the experimental group who did relapse tended to have less severe symptoms than the relapsers in the control group, and fewer of the non-relapsers suffered minor exacerbations of symptoms.

Hogarty and his colleagues (1986) have also emphasised the need to assist the patient as well as the family in learning how to cope. A combination of family treatment and social skills training for the individual brought about a sustained remission in their controlled study. They randomly assigned 103 patients returning to live with family members rated as high in EE to one of four conditions: family treatment; social skills training for the patient; their combination; or routine treatment. All patients received drug treatment. After one year relapse rates were 19 per cent, 20 per cent, 0 per cent and 41 per cent respectively. This clearly demonstrated the importance of providing education and support for the individual as well as for family members. This support was quite intensive, long-term and well structured, including education, role play, feedback and homework exercises, as well as wider social skills training and empathic support.

Similarly, Tarrier and colleagues (1988) also found that an intensive behavioural intervention including education, stress management and goal setting for both patient and relatives over a nine-month period was needed in order to achieve a significant reduction in relapse rate. Among a sample of 39 participating 'high EE' families randomly assigned to different treatment conditions, 53 per cent of individuals receiving routine treatment relapsed within nine months, 43 per cent of those who also had two education sessions, and 12 per cent of those receiving behavioural intervention. Of 19 individuals in low EE households receiving either routine treatment or education only, the relapse rate was 21 per cent.

Despite the impressive results achieved by Hogarty and colleagues, they remain more cautious than many others in this field in their claims for prevention. They emphasise, in fact, that social interventions do not prevent schizophrenia from following a relapsing course, but act more to delay relapse. And like others since (see Kanter et al., 1987), they also believe there to be considerable potential benefit in working with low EE as well as high EE families, citing young women in low EE households as likely to be vulnerable to relapse, often because of possible or actual impending separation or divorce. In fact, although the concept of expressed emotion has played a crucial role in taking forward preventive programmes for schizophrenia sufferers, it is clear that some workers feel that its causal role has been over-emphasised, and are concerned that a focus on this factor encourages professionals to see families as pathological, and if that happens it may inadvertently *increase* family anxieties about their own role in the individual's distress (Hatfield, 1987). But even with this cautionary note about the need for a careful approach to these issues, it is clear that the basic research on expressed emotion has been the stimulus and focus for a remarkable development of family-based intervention and research in the last 15 years.

PREVENTIVE INTERVENTIONS WITH PEOPLE TREATED FOR SCHIZOPHRENIA AND THEIR FAMILIES: THE PRACTICE

The research on family life has set a climate for experiment and aroused interest in preventive work rather than providing absolute guidelines on the best approach. And the importance of keeping symptoms to a minimum for all sufferers is obviously as important as preventing florid relapses, and this entails supporting all individuals in their efforts to control their symptoms. It is recognised that individuals living with low EE families do not necessarily have warm and supportive relationships with them, and the family is not necessarily exemplary in the way they cope. They may, for instance, be opting for complete disengagement, allowing their relative to sleep all day in his or her room, perhaps. Individuals in this type of household may have a lower risk of a florid relapse, but may nevertheless have a disturbingly high level of symptomatology. A service model will therefore need to find an approach which meets the needs of all their client group.

The work on family education and support, however, has still failed to penetrate services to any great extent in England. Despite over 25 years of research which continues to provide support for its effectiveness, only a handful of centres offered a fully fledged service in 1988, and some of these were offered as part of a research study which was time-limited. Nick Tarrier and Christine Barrowclough in Salford, for instance, were running an impressive service as part of a research programme, although not surprisingly their hopes were that it would continue after the research was complete. Max Birchwood and Jo Smith in Birmingham were the first to establish a service which was a service first and a research programme second. And this only began as recently as 1984. A small number of family support programmes exist in other centres. The only part of the research which has been adopted more widely in the last few years is the discussion group element of Leff and his colleagues' intervention. The National Schizophrenia Fellowship has run relatives' groups in local areas across the country for many years. These were set up as a response to the needs of relatives for this kind of support rather than arising out of the research. But now, social workers in several local authorities have recognised the value of such meetings in terms of the research studies and have set up relatives' support groups of their own which attempt to take a form similar to those described in the research. One example of these is described below.

A SUPPORT GROUP FOR THOSE LIVING WITH SOMEONE WITH SCHIZOPHRENIA

The project described here is in Croydon, Surrey, but is similar to a number of others around the country in its basic design and intention. It aims to copy directly the family work reported by Leff and colleagues: to reduce critical comments and over-involvement of household members; to reduce time in face-to-face contact; and to encourage the individuals to continue taking their maintenance medication.

The project was initiated by two social workers, Graham Collingridge and Jill Steyne, who shared an interest in setting up some group work, after they had attended a lecture by Ruth Berkowitz about the research she had been involved in with Leff and colleagues. It was made clear that the work had a reputable scientific basis, had been shown to be effective, and was something which could be run by social workers. The two Croydon social workers arranged to visit the research workers in order to discuss the work and the best way to go about setting up a service, and attended a one-day training course on running family groups. They received no specific training in family therapy, but their social work training had to a certain extent prepared them for this kind of work. They spoke to the consultant psychiatrist at their local psychiatric hospital who was pleased to hear about their plans, but the project remained wholly within social services.

An outline of the proposed project and its objectives was sent to consultant psychiatrists in the area, the head of the Community Psychiatric Nursing service, to doctors in about 15 of the local practices (those thought most caring about and sympathetic to mental health problems). These professionals were asked to refer patients who had a diagnosis of schizophrenia, who were living with a family in their social services area, and who had a reasonable understanding of the English language. The definition of family was to be flexible and include anyone with whom the patient lived in an intimate or blood relationship. This was assumed to exclude most hostel residents, but perhaps to include some longstanding relationships between landlady and tenant if some emotional involvement had developed.

Obviously, by asking for referrals rather than using medical records to identify and invite everyone who would be eligible, only a small proportion of appropriate cases were located. Just ten referrals were received initially, and all were sent a letter explaining about the group and inviting them to join. No inappropriate referrals were received, but one woman whose husband was ill, who was referred by a GP, was not approached again because her CPN did not consider her to be ready for this sort of work. The remaining nine referrals (from GPs (2), CPNs (2), psychiatrists (2), themselves (2) and another group member (1)) were keen to participate, although one dropped out at an early stage because her husband died shortly after her son became ill and she became too depressed to come to meetings.

Coincidentally, all nine referrals were parents of schizophrenic sons. (It is interesting that these were the people thought by referrers as most likely to benefit from this group, given that it has been argued by Hogarty *et al.* (1986) that the relationship between EE and schizophrenic relapse has been illustrated best among male sufferers living in parental houses.) One of the young men had become ill only six months before his parents joined the project, another about 18 months previously, while the remainder had been ill for a number of years. One of the latter group had never sought or received treatment. Seven lived at home, one lived in a hostel, and one was currently in hospital, probably to be found accommodation away from home on discharge. Only one of the young men was currently working – in a job obtained a week or two before my visit to the group. One other was able to do some building work with his self-employed father. He and the unemployed sons at home were all in high contact with their parents.

At least one other referral was received after the group had been going for a few weeks, but group leaders felt it was not possible to run an open group and accept referrals along the way, as so much ground had already been covered and trust built up between group members. This was an issue that would have to be resolved when plans were made to make the project part of a rolling programme of service provision.

Joining the group

The group took a long time to set up – at least a year from the time the first letters were sent to referrers. When a family had indicated their interest in the project, one of the social workers visited them once or twice at home. During these initial discussions, the family was given a good deal of factual information about schizophrenia based on the understanding of workers of what had been supplied to families by Leff's research team. They also used the first rank symptoms of schizophrenia described by Anthony Clare in *Psychiatry in dissent* (1980) as a talking point.

The group had its first meeting in April 1987 in a spacious room in the area offices of social services. Meetings lasted one-and-a-half hours every alternate Monday evening from 6.00–7.30 p.m. In the first session members were introduced to each other, and informed again about the purposes of meeting (namely to explore some of the difficulties they were having in living with their sons). Rules of the group and issues of confidentiality were discussed, and group members 'brainstormed' a list of problems they wanted to look at which would form the agenda for coming weeks. Jill says that it was evident from this first meeting how much anger and distress the relatives felt. They were almost all traumatised by the experience of losing their hopes for the future life of their son, and the expectation of, very often, a successful career, a marriage and grandchildren; by the stress of living with a person behaving in such a strange, disturbed and sometimes violent manner; by their frustrated dealings with doctors and psychiatrists; and by the difficulties of finding out about the illness, their son's treatment or how they should react. Their indignation at the inadequate help they felt they had received led to some explosive sessions.

Dealing with crisis was chosen as the first subject for discussion. For this meeting, members began by talking in pairs about particular crises and then focusing as a group on all the potential sources of assistance, and on which responses individuals had found helpful, and which they had not. The emergencies which they discussed were mainly those resulting from extremely disturbed behaviour of their sons at the height of the illness. Again the magnitude of the difficulties with which so many relatives had to cope daily became painfully clear. A son who slept most of the day but played music loudly every night to the extent that their neighbours began to become angry and threatening was by no means one of the most serious crises. A more distressing example was when a couple caught their son preparing to set fire to the family home. They reported that too often, crises of the first kind were not taken seriously by professionals consulted and only when a crisis of the second kind occurred was a good deal of help mobilised.

At the third meeting these discussions were continued, and included the legal and practical issues involved in obtaining treatment through a 'Section' (a clause in the Mental Health Act, 1983, outlining legal justification for compulsory treatment). The following meeting focused on finance, but this proved to be one of the least successful meetings and for this particular group of relatives, money did not seem to be one of the major worries. They were, however, anxious to know how best to bequeath money or property to the son for his security after their death. In the fifth meeting they talked about the effect of their son's illness on his siblings, while sessions six and seven focused on the symptoms and nature of schizophrenia. This led on to session eight when management of symptoms was discussed. In the ninth and tenth meetings group members each chose a specific household problem and discussed how they were dealing with it. This was one of the best opportunities for group facilitators to draw attention to the importance of discussing difficulties calmly, and to encourage group members to conclude that the more anxious and angry they became the worse their problems became. Good examples for solutions given by group members could be drawn out. I attended the eleventh meeting.

A description of a meeting

The seating in the room where we met had been arranged into a circle, and the two social workers and I were first joined by a middle-aged man, then by two couples and three women on their own. Everyone was offered a cup of tea or coffee as they sat down, and people greeted each other in a friendly but slightly reserved manner. Another woman came in briefly to apologise for being unable to attend this week, and to distribute leaflets about a forthcoming fundraising event for the National Schizophrenia Fellowship.

The group had at an earlier date decided that they wanted a psychiatrist to come to one of the meetings to tell them about genetics, medication and other possible treatments. Jill brought with her to the group a letter from a psychiatrist (name and hospital removed), giving his reasons why he declined the invitation. His worry was that if any of his statements about treatment conflicted with the treatment or advice received by the patients related to group members, then their confidence in their own psychiatrists would be undermined. This letter was used as the basis for group discussion, and for the group to specify exactly what they would want to know from a psychiatrist which could be explained in the next letter to a potential speaker.

The group's responses were suspicious. 'Feeble', 'defensive', 'he's dodging the issues,' and irritated that they were not trusted by the psychiatrist: 'We could have said we don't want individual cases discussed – we just want to know about the effects of different drugs in a general way.' There was a feeling that as they had deliberately approached a doctor working outside the area so that he would not feel compromised through treating any relatives of group members, his response was disappointing.

The discussion which followed returned several times to the frustrations group members experienced in their contacts with doctors, particularly their exclusion from treatment decisions to which they felt they had much to contribute. 'We know him best . . . we are the only people who see him every day . . .' One man said his son's medication had been reduced twice, leading to a marked increase in symptoms each time. He could have told the psychiatrist his son wasn't well enough then. A woman said she wished the psychiatrist would explain all about the drugs and why they are essential. 'My son had it all explained to him once and he found it very helpful. He seemed to understand and appreciate the need for them.' Two families said they felt the doctors to some extent held them to blame for their son's problems, and how knowing they had other 'normal' children who had been treated the same way was a great comfort.

The majority of the questions the group wanted to put to a psychiatrist concerned the drugs and their effects on their sons' behaviour. Restlessness, lethargy, poor concentration – which were symptoms of schizophrenia and which were caused by the drugs? They also wanted to know about research progress on treatment, the long-term prospect of improvement, life expectancy, suicide risk, the possibility of securing work, and what was going to happen when hospitals closed.

In conclusion, two group members commented that the psychiatrist who wrote the letter was probably afraid of meeting the very emotional parents he might see when a couple's son or daughter is first diagnosed. The psychiatrist was thought not to appreciate how much parents have to adapt – 'It's like adapting to death' – and group members felt that most of them had come through that stage. It was suggested that doctors often did not fully take into account the terrible blow it is to the parent initially. The parents will have had great aspirations for their son, and being forced to revise these hopes was in many ways as difficult to come to terms with as a bereavement. And yet while mourning this loss the person is still with them, often very disturbed, his disorder often creating tremendous problems for the whole family. The points raised during the meeting were recorded on a flip chart by one of the social workers as they were discussed, and it was agreed that these should be the basis of a new letter to another psychiatrist.

The experience of the Croydon group

The social workers running the project told me that they had seen the establishment of the group as a means to an end – reducing EE and preventing relapse in the schizophrenia sufferer 'by providing information to relatives, access to support, and a place to off-load anger' (which might otherwise be directed toward the sufferer). They had occasionally had a rather didactic group set-up when they had been asked directly for information, but on the whole they preferred a much more passive approach to get the message across. However, as the meetings continued, they were becoming more and more aware of the needs of the relatives themselves as distinct from the needs of their sons.

They told me that several of the group members found it difficult to discuss with their sons the fact that they wished to come to these meetings, and so had not informed them that they were doing so.

Case examples – Margaret and her son, Tony

Tony is 23 years old and currently receiving treatment for schizophrenia in hospital where he's been an in-patient for 5 months since setting fire to his parents' house. His parents have been temporarily rehoused by the council. Margaret talked to me about her family and their life before and since their son had become ill.

Tony was always the quietest of their children, and seemed to some extent to live in his brother's shadow. He was in the top stream at school, but at 16 he was beginning to break away from his friends. Margaret and her two other children were committed Baptists, and she at first thought Tony's difficulties were a reflection of his conflicts about whether or not also to become committed to religion. He seemed stronger than the other children, but a bit rebellious. She presumed, however, that with time, patience and support he would resolve his difficulties. This is what happened when her husband had a nervous breakdown at the age of 25. Over a five-year period her husband's problems had diminished (although he was still taking tranquillisers and sleeping pills 20 years later). But at 17, Tony returned from a camping holiday with school friends in a disturbed state. 'It was clear his mind had gone.' Margaret could not persuade him to go with her to see the doctor, and so she 'put up with it' for two years. During the year after he left school his condition worsened. Then he became markedly worse and begin to build violent delusions around a cousin who was being fostered by his mother. Following a night-time episode when he'd been discovered putting white spirit around his parent's bed, they now felt he was potentially dangerous. A CPN who visited would not 'section' him, but succeeded in persuading him to attend the hospital for treatment. However, he absconded the same day, crept home and hid behind the settee until he was discovered at the end of the afternoon in an extremely frightened state. After this he was admitted to hospital under 'section' where he stayed for eight weeks.

His mental state has been up and down since, with periods of improvement and then dropping back. At first he used to swim, meet friends, and have an active social life, but gradually he became quite isolated. He didn't want to see people because he got 'vibes' and 'thoughts' from them. The family were advised that Tony might recover better away from the family home, and although both Margaret and Tony agreed to this, Tony was quite fearful of the move. When a place in a Christian hostel outside the area was offered, his parents encouraged him to take it. However, following a conversation about the plans with his father, Tony left the house in an agitated state, as they found out a few moments later, because he had set fire to his bedroom.

Tony was found later that day at the home of a friend from the church and the police took him to hospital on a six-month 'section'. Now, Margaret says, he is getting a structured day, nursing, social contact, and his drugs are monitored. At home he had been staying in bed all day and was up all night. While at home, Margaret felt there was totally inadequate monitoring, he received medication fortnightly, and the only suggestion if he was ill at home was for him to attend the day hospital, 'but of course he wouldn't go'. 'It takes a dangerous or violent act to get him proper treatment.' In fact, she is remarkably happy about recent events as she says Tony now has the help he needs. 'He's under the best psychiatrist in the borough, he'll get into a house of his own, and I'm getting my house completely rebuilt and decorated.' Margaret had started attending the relatives' support group just three weeks before her son burned the house, while he was at home and extremely ill.

Margaret says she's learnt a great deal from the groups. She now knows, for instance, that there is always an emergency contact officer available through social services, she knows more about the side effects of drugs and the difference between those and manifestations of the illness, and she values the support. She added that it was really befriending her – they were the first professionals who seemed to be on her side. It gave her a tremendous sense of support and sharing of stresses and strains. She also commented that at groups 'You see relatives who are so diverse in personality, class, marital status, so that it reassures you that it can't be your fault your son's ill – otherwise they'd all be like me.'

I asked Margaret if the group was supposed to change her relationship with her son. She said the group had one day had to each choose a problem to discuss and it was supposed to help them cope better. I asked if she felt that she was behaving any differently toward Tony now. She said not, because she already 'had a good feel for it' (especially since reading a book by Sylvano Ariety called Understanding and helping the schizophrenic, *and gets 'a lot of help from the spiritual side'. She says she was already warm towards him, but admits that 'at one stage I gave up everything outside the home for one year so I could devote myself to him and it was my greatest mistake. Diversion is essential.' She intends to continue attending group meetings, and she has missed only one so far, as she finds it helpful and derives great comfort from it.*

Barbara and her son, John

I talked to Barbara and John together. It was a difficult conversation because John kept taking it back to his experiences in Paris some 12 or more years before, which have regularly featured in his fears since. The conversation was not calm and he would shout at his mother periodically as he answered questions or commented on what she said. It was extremely difficult to understand what had gone on in Paris as his story was not logical.

John is now 31 years old and lives with his parents. His mother is very keen to persuade him to move out and live completely independently of them, even suggesting he moves to Manchester or Liverpool, near his brother. John is obviously as unwilling to leave home as she is keen for him to go. He seems very frightened at the prospect and it is mostly when this subject is discussed that he starts to shout. His mother has made appointments for him with a housing aid charity, has got suggestions from the social worker about hostels, and has even given him a deadline to leave. But he has not taken up any of her suggestions. His only attempt to live independently was in a shared hotel room and this ended in failure some time ago.

John is around the house most of every day although he regularly visits the betting shop. He makes himself tea and listens to the football. By weekends he has no money left to do anything anyway. He resents his low income. He takes maintenance neuroleptics orally, but as far as I could gather erratically. He doesn't believe he has schizophrenia and is scathing about psychiatry. Two girls that he has known who have had similar problems to himself are both now dead. So is the man with whom he shared the hotel room. 'So that's what psychiatry has done for them!' 'But I'm in a trap – I can't get any money unless I'm a schizophrenic so I have to be one. But I don't think I am one.'

His problems had begun in the sixth form at school. Although he was still the most hard-working of Barbara's three sons, he was also more sensitive and prone to depression. He found it very difficult to cope with being teased about his girlfriend. Gradually his parents revised their aspirations for a university career for him as it seemed he would be unlikely to cope. He found a job instead in a bank, leaving school with two 'A' levels. He worked late in the evenings and took up music lessons too, and life became too hectic. Suddenly he just went off to Paris, without even taking any money. He obviously had a very disturbing experience there which haunts him still, and he believes someone he met there is now in London and looking for him either to torture or kill him. His parents had had to go to Paris to bring him home, and his first in-patient treatment followed. He has had only one long-term job since, as a petrol pump attendant for one year.

He does not like the fact that his mother attends the relatives' groups, and is clearly not feeling any benefit of her doing so. However, Barbara derives considerable comfort from going to the group and airing her difficulties. 'I let off steam! When I'm furious with John I tell them all about it.' Like when he had taken some money she'd left in her room, and when his odd behaviour had caused the cleaner to resign.

To questions about whether she had learnt more about the nature of schizophrenia, gained ideas for coping with stressful situations, or changed her behaviour in any way as a consequence of going to meetings, she replied in the negative. However, she points out that she had already been coping for 12 years or so and has been an active member of National Schizophrenia Fellowship groups. She is hopeful, though, that she will come to understand more through this group.

Barbara's husband declines to attend meetings as he thinks that he spends every day with the problem already and does not wish to devote his leisure time to talking about it as well. Barbara's main concern is that she and her husband are becoming elderly and she does not relish the prospect of living with a disturbed son in old age, especially if she also becomes widowed. She could afford to buy him somewhere to live and, if she could find a suitably supportive environment, this is what she would like to do.

Mr and Mrs Kay and their son, Nigel

I met Mr and Mrs Kay at their home, and Nigel, who was asleep in his bedroom for most of the morning, joined us briefly only for the last few minutes of our conversation. Nigel is the elder of two sons, aged 25 and 22. He developed schizophrenia soon after leaving school, the first odd behaviour occurring shortly after his 'A' level examinations. Nigel is normally very shy, sensitive and quiet and he was exceptionally worried about his exams. When the results were due he was away from home and had to telephone his parents. He called a day too early and was abusive to his father during the conversation when he couldn't give him the results, which was quite out of character. When the results came they were much lower than his parents were expecting, and he had failed two of three subjects. He retook his examinations twice in the following year, and managed to get work with a solicitor's firm. Throughout this period he was becoming increasingly disturbed.

During that year Mr and Mrs Kay had tried to get help for Nigel but had found it impossible to get anyone to take them seriously. If they persuaded Nigel to come with them to see a doctor, he behaved in a relatively normal way, and even when they finally managed to see a psychiatrist with him, they were told that their son was just play-acting and it was teenage mischief. They became increasingly frightened. Finally one day when Nigel was behaving in a very disturbed way they managed, after an aggressive telephone call, to get the same psychiatrist to see him again, knowing that Nigel would refuse to see another new face. This visit resulted in Nigel agreeing to go into hospital. He was diagnosed catatonic schizophrenic. He had 'sunk so low' that in hospital he would take no medication and just sat or stood without moving. Doctors sectioned him in order to give ECT without consent. Even after the diagnosis, the parents say that they were still made to feel to blame. They also told me that they were made to feel it was unnatural to want to visit their son more than twice weekly, and that they had been spoiling him. He spent five months in hospital.

For three years afterwards Nigel was quite stable, and then he had another major relapse, when, as before, his normal quiet gentle personality was transformed into a noisy, uncaring, unreasonable and aggressive one. Mr and Mrs Kay had similar problems in persuading anyone how seriously ill he was, and experienced the same messages of blame. The CPN they persuaded to visit the house (by saying that father and son would come to blows soon otherwise) persuaded Nigel to go to the out-patient clinic at the psychiatric hospital and made another appointment for him two days hence. He did not inform the parents of these arrangements and when they asked, he told them their son's consultations were confidential. Mr and Mrs Kay knew well that their son would neither take oral medication prescribed nor return for the appointment made. When their fears were confirmed their only remaining step as they saw it was to call the police.

This resulted in a policeman, then a social worker and the GP being called to the house. The GP, known to the family for years, would not speak to the parents. They obviously felt they were being blamed again. He spoke to the social worker and left again, without telling them what he planned. Only when Nigel's behaviour started to deteriorate in front of them as 'he became higher and higher' and the social worker began to get frightened did anything happen. She then called back the GP and eventually Nigel was taken to hospital. Mr and Mrs Kay told me that they and their other son sat and wept after everyone had left. Shortly afterwards the social worker returned to tell them Nigel was safely in hospital, and how distressing the proceedings had been. Nigel had lain down in the street and it had taken four male nurses to get him into the ambulance.

Not surprisingly Mr and Mrs Kay are bitter. They feel that they have not been helped by professionals at any stage in caring for their son. Even when discharged from hospital after the second episode, when it had been agreed that they would look for hostel accommodation and at the very least the hospital would notify the parents in advance of Nigel's discharge, the first they knew of his discharge was when he arrived on their doorstep. They feel that Nigel need never have become so ill on either occasion if they could have obtained some help and treatment at an early stage – perhaps even before losing his job each time. If he'd not slipped so far back again it would have been so much easier to bring him forward again. Instead he was hospitalised for four months. This time he was diagnosed as manic depressive.

He has been unemployed since his last hospitalisation. He spends his mornings in bed, then after lunch he goes into town to look around the shops or the job centre. He returns at the next mealtime, and sometimes goes out for a drink in the evening. As Mr Kay works from home, the family are in high contact.

Mr Kay finds the relatives' groups very valuable as an outlet for his frustration and anxiety. 'I can't sit on it – I like to get it out – to talk about it to someone who is prepared to listen. You can't imagine what it's like. No one can.'

They feel they've learned a little about causes and symptoms – but not in depth. They try to get Nigel to take some responsibility for himself and are always suggesting voluntary work, work experience, and part-time local jobs such as deliveries. The real problems with living with him now are firstly that he can't sit still, and will react childishly to requests to turn down music and so on. Secondly, he is too familiar with his mother, touching her, leaning on her as she works, following her into the bathroom. Neither parent likes this and Mr Kay is making great efforts not to lose his temper when it occurs. It worries them that he has not had a girlfriend ever, and they know he would like to be married.

To questions as to whether the group has increased their knowledge about the nature of schizophrenia, its causes or course, and the effects of treatment, they reply in the negative. In dealing with family stress, they have understood the importance of staying calm – 'counting to ten and so on'. Mr Kay says he now tries much more to avoid losing his temper.

Relatives' groups: how helpful are they in practice?

The case histories above raise many questions and have been described with much of the detail given to me because of the many interesting observations which came out. It was clear that many families had had very difficult encounters with professionals when their sons were first becoming ill and had lived with an extremely worrying situation for weeks, months or even years before receiving the help for him that he needed. Such high levels of stress, lack of support, and often a sense of being felt to be to blame for such a devastating situation must be difficult enough for the family. Subsequently, however, they must adjust to the situation, come to terms with their terrible sense of loss and try to help their son to regain his stability. The sorrow, anger and distress those parents feel when it begins to be clear that the problems are long-term, and that their aspirations are indeed now unattainable, are a trauma to which I heard people refer many times. It is perhaps not surprising, then, to find that the relatives' group meetings had rapidly focused in on the needs of the relatives themselves. But in sharing many negative views about their sons it appears at first sight as though the discussions might actually serve to reinforce and condone such views. The support given is clearly for themselves as carers, and the equally real and distressing problems and anxieties of their disturbed sons became secondary. And when, as here, the group leaders are social workers, with little power to influence the psychiatric service available to these troubled men, one might question how effective in helping the individuals themselves this intervention can be.

Yet an evaluation of a very similar relatives' support group by MacCarthy and her colleagues (1989) suggests that there can be benefits to the individual with chronic mental health problems as well as to his or her family in this approach. As with the group described above, their group members also appreciated first and foremost the opportunity to acknowledge and share some pent-up feelings with others in similar circumstances. MacCarthy and colleagues compared nine families who participated in their relatives' group with 17 other families who all also attended a specialised day care service. All the individuals were currently severely disturbed and had been continuously disabled by their symptoms for a year or more, mostly with diagnoses of schizophrenia or manic depression. Relatives were encouraged to discuss the practical problems and feelings which arose in the course of living with family members with a long-term psychiatric illness. The underlying intention was to focus on issues relating to expressed emotion in order to reduce critical or over-involved attitudes and level of face-to-face contact. They aimed to achieve this by helping relatives to feel more in control of the problems presented; by helping them to see the value of their own coping efforts; by gaining a good understanding of the difficulties of the task they were confronted with; and by learning about the problems experienced by others coping with similar difficulties. Following three educational home visits, the group met monthly for a year for meetings lasting one-and-a-half hours led by a clinical psychologist or a social worker.

Assessments with patients and relatives were conducted at the beginning and end of the intervention. They showed that the relatives attending groups did become less critical than relatives in the comparison group, but levels of warmth and over-involvement did not change significantly. Their knowledge about the disorder was already good and did not change greatly, and level of contact actually slightly increased, although not significantly so. And neither before, nor after the intervention, did relatives feel they had much control over the problems they were experiencing. The factor they most commonly mentioned as helpful was the opportunity to meet and talk to other people with similar problems which they were also finding stressful and bewildering. The project sounds to have been similar to the Croydon group which I visited, although rather more focused toward everyday coping skills and on reducing expressed emotion.

For the patients, who were of course also all receiving the support of a specialised day-care service, the intervention also appeared to have brought some additional benefit. Although (relative to the patients in the comparison group) negative symptoms did not improve, and positive symptoms improved only slightly, their 'independent role-performance' did improve. That is, they became more able (according to relatives' assessments) to perform a range of domestic and self-help skills.

Although at one level these benefits may seem modest, they should be viewed against their low cost (three hours of professional time per month in MacCarthy's study), and against the context of a well supported and carefully monitored patient group. The level of expressed emotion was significantly reduced by a method which was not sophisticated, did not explicitly focus on EE, and could be taken up relatively easily by other workers. MacCarthy and colleagues concluded that

> this sort of specific, time-limited group needs to become a routine part of the clinical service offered by community care facilities, even if relatives and patients have achieved an equilibrium in the context of persistent chronic and severe difficulties. Ideally, this should be initiated early in a patient's career to avoid the development of persistent failures of communication between the clinical team and carers.
>
> (MacCarthy et al., 1989)

In the Croydon service the costs were marginally higher, as they met on a fortnightly basis. Each family referred was also visited at home before meetings began by one social worker on two occasions.

The Croydon service was still only half-way through its first programme when I visited. They planned to do detailed work with individual families in their own homes after the group had been meeting for at least nine months. From my interviews and from the regular attendance of the members, the relatives clearly derived considerable support from the group meetings, but it did not seem as though discussions had so far given much detailed consideration to the ways of coping with specific common day-to-day problems. The group seemed to focus more on wider issues, general points and coping with crisis. I was left with the impression that without thoughtful individual work on day-to-day living, looking also at the problems from the point of view of the individual diagnosed as having schizophrenia, changes to coping styles and family relationships may not be as great as they could be. To have the maximum preventive effect, such groups almost certainly need to be just one part of a more comprehensive programme. A rather different service model of a more comprehensive nature is described below.

A COMPREHENSIVE PREVENTION PROGRAMME AS A COMPONENT OF A MENTAL ILLNESS TREATMENT SERVICE: WEST BIRMINGHAM

The first service to implement fully the growing research findings on the influence of family coping and knowledge on the course of schizophrenia was set in motion by Max Birchwood in 1982 in Birmingham All Saints Hospital. Birchwood had recently completed his PhD on this subject and began to prepare an educational course for relatives for use by the psychology department. By 1985, he and his colleague Jo Smith had produced five booklets which were published by the Health Promotion Unit of West Birmingham Health Authority. Birchwood and Smith set up a family intervention service in October 1984 based in the Family Centre for Advice, Resources and Education, a house at the edge of the hospital grounds. Most of the first year was spent on developmental work, the full educational programme beginning in Autumn 1985. 'Psychoeducation' was to be the primary method through which they aimed to improve family coping, family relationships, medication compliance and knowledge about schizophrenia, and hence the course of the disorder suffered by the individual. They offered their support to all sufferers who lived with relatives or in a household with family-like relationships, or had regular every day contact with their family, whether or not those relatives were high in EE. Several years after the education programme was established, the programme was extended to include a systematic approach to symptom monitoring with the aim of identifying early warning signs of imminent relapse.

The clients

All Saints Hospital has a catchment area in West Birmingham covering 250,000 people and in 1988 was also covering the neighbouring district of Sandwell (population 200,000). All patients admitted from these districts to All Saints with a diagnosis of schizophrenia were eligible to receive the programme. In order to reach a larger number of families, part of the education programme was also offered through two local day-centres for people with chronic schizophrenia, and to meetings of relatives organised through the National Schizophrenia Fellowship. Through the four centres, some 200 families were involved in the basic information programme during the first two years. However, the full programme involving the whole family was much more intensive and was received by just 40 families and patients from All Saints Hospital.

Individuals and their families were recruited in the following way. Two technicians attached to the Family Centre went around the hospital wards regularly in order to identify people who had recently been admitted with either a definite or possible diagnosis of schizophrenia. Their name, presenting problem, ward and home accommodation circumstances were noted and relayed back to the two psychologists. One of the psychologists then arranged an interview with the patient to confirm the diagnosis and to offer their services to them when they were ready to leave the hospital. If the patient was interested in this, their permission was then sought for the team to approach their relatives. The family could then be contacted during a hospital visit and arrangements made for them to meet one of the psychologists to hear about the programme offered. The risk of relapse for people with a diagnosis of schizophrenia was explained, and the aim of the programme in helping families to help their relative to regain his or her stability and improve social recovery. Some families do not wish to take up the service offered, of course, but they were very much encouraged to give it serious consideration, and would be asked why they were not interested. Those who did wish to participate were then interviewed further to look in more detail at the kind of help they most needed. The questionnaire completed during this interview included information about the social functioning of the patient, the way in which the family was coping with the symptoms, and the level of family burden.

About one in three patients or their families declined this offer of help. In some cases (usually those experiencing a first episode), this was because the individual did not accept either the diagnosis, or the view that difficulties might continue or recur. Other refusals were because the family took this view, that is, that the difficulties would in all probability resolve themselves over a period of time. In other cases the reason was related more to a general hostility toward professionals, sometimes because they had had great problems in obtaining treatment and unhappy dealings with professionals in the meantime, sometimes because they had received a good deal of conflicting advice and information from professionals which had reduced their confidence in their expertise.

The programme

The family work had three stages: educational, 'enabling' and problem management. Each consisted of four one-hour meetings although the schedule was flexible to take account of individual needs. The relatives and the sufferer received their four educational sessions separately, and this stage was primarily an information-giving exercise – about symptoms, cause, course, diagnosis, management, medication and so on. It also set the scene and explained the rationale for subsequent work.

The enabling phase was intended for relatives alone, and focused on the impact of schizophrenia on family life. By discussing how the condition of the individual was affecting the health of the key relative most closely involved in the caring role, and of other family members, these sessions could help to reduce the over-anxious responses and over-involvement in the sufferer's life which may have developed. They would discuss how, for instance, close relatives sometimes become so involved in the difficulties of the individual and the problems these have caused in the home that they have neglected their own well-being. And how some families feel they cannot leave the individual alone in the home even for a few hours. Families in this position would be advised that the health and welfare of each family member was equally important, including their own, and for some, this straightforward professional sanctioning of their right to a life of their own would be enough to encourage them to become more active. Others might need to be encouraged to experiment with a short evening out in order to test the validity of their fears that the individual would burn a pan dry/leave the house without closing the front door/come to harm. An uneventful evening should encourage them to plan other activities.

During the enabling phase, there were also discussions about the damaging effect of strongly expressed emotions, and about unhelpful emotional responses such as guilt and embarrassment. Discussions would consider the irrational basis of the emotion (e.g. a feeling of being to blame for a son's illness) and work through the consequences of this feeling (e.g. doing everything for him at home), and consider the potential effect of this on his recovery. The psychologists tried to involve as many of the family as possible in at least one of these sessions in order to help them offer support in the most positive way. They would also encourage discussion about whether the key relative was neglecting other members of the family because of their concern for the sufferer. Of course, although these discussions focused on the relatives' coping strategies, the changes which were encouraged were intended to benefit the disturbed individual as much as his or her relatives.

The third stage focused on managing specific problems. Sufferer and close family members were usually (but not invariably) seen together to look at particular issues: coping with aggression, alcoholism, relationship difficulties, delusions and hallucinations, for instance. They looked both at the skills needed by those living with the person with schizophrenia, and the problems that the sufferer saw in living with his family.

Some of the advice was quite prescriptive – there were certain 'do's' and 'don'ts' which were emphasised, but for the most part, the advice was modified by the families' own ideas on how best the approach could be implemented. The sessions were highly structured and there was a booklet for the family to take away with them which summarised the key issues of the discussion. Often it included a 'homework' exercise in which the relative had to consider possible answers to problems similar to those they had discussed. During the educational phase, for instance, one session was devoted to symptoms of schizophrenia, to help relatives to have some insight into the reasons which might underlie some of the individual's disturbing or annoying behaviour. An example given was of a woman who noticed that her husband refused to eat anything she had cooked, but would eat the same food cooked by someone else. In this case it was found that the husband believed she was trying to poison him. A 'homework' exercise following this session was: 'Mrs Green noticed that her husband suddenly kept on shutting the curtains even when it was still daylight. He also began refusing to answer the phone or the door. What symptoms could he be having?'

The potential benefits of all three phases are clear. If relatives become less absorbed by the individual's problems and allow him and themselves more independence, if they learn to deal with their own guilt, embarrassment and anger and discuss problems at home calmly, and if they understand that some of the infuriating behaviour of the sufferer is caused by a particular delusion rather than being done with the intention of annoying them, the climate in the home is almost certain to be improved. This in turn should have a positive effect on the individual and lower his or her level of arousal, and risk of relapse. Particular problems of each family can be drawn out during the final stage. They might draw up a target sheet of things they would like to change – their own lack of social life, their guilt, the sufferer's lack of motivation, perhaps. And they could plan detailed steps to achieve each goal. After the 12 sessions, families could (and usually did) return to see one of the two psychologists monthly for up to a year, depending on how much further support they felt they needed, and during this time the lessons could be consolidated and applied. With this kind of support, the individual and his family should find that the disorder becomes less of a problem for all of them than it would otherwise be.

Case example: Mrs Z and her son, Mike

Although Mike and Mrs Z don't live together, and haven't done for several years prior to his becoming ill, she is in regular contact with him and is the only person he spends much time with. Mike's father died seven years ago. Mrs Z has an excellent relationship with Mike and wants to do the best she can to help him overcome his illness. She has considered asking him to come and live at home with her again, but has decided against this because she realises that the main incentive he has to get himself out of bed, organised and out of his flat is to come to her house. Without this he would probably be much less active.

Mrs Z is part way through the programme. She has attended four sessions of information, four on family well-being or 'enabling' and has come today for a session on management skills. Each session has involved a one-to-one weekly one-hour meeting with the clinical psychologist. The focus today is showing approval and disapproval. Mike has also had four sessions of patient information and the clinical psychologist is now working in a less structured way with him on quality of life issues – trying to encourage him to become more active, and to help him to overcome his remaining negative symptoms. Both had agreed to let me sit in on their discussions and to talk to me afterwards about the programme.

Mike and Mrs Z will shortly begin joint sessions on 'target setting', and will continue to have these less structured follow-up meetings monthly for nine months.

Management session: Mrs Z

A trainee clinical psychologist was participating in the meeting, and she introduced the session, using the overhead projector to highlight the key ideas. She began to talk about how, when just discharged from hospital, a person treated for schizophrenia would usually be unable to do all the things he was capable of doing before the illness, and how in addition, he would almost certainly be feeling very unsure of himself. She talked about how easy it can be to draw attention to and seem to focus on what the individual is still unable to do, and this of course would do nothing to help boost his low level of self-confidence. Often the improvements in his abilities since the more acute stages of illness will go unnoticed, and progress unremarked upon because it is taken for granted that he can do those things that came easily before the illness began. The points which were emphasised were to avoid focusing on deficits, to notice and remark upon progress, and to help the individual regain his confidence.

Mrs Z turned the conversation to Mike's current capabilities. She remarked that things had changed since the last session in that where she was seeing Mike three or four times a week, she was now getting him to come to her house every day for a meal because he seemed to be withdrawing and not looking after himself. The psychologist expressed understanding of Mrs Z's intentions. She could see it was helping him to be more active but said she was a little worried it might encourage dependency on her and that they were obviously working toward Mike having both a more active and independent life.

They then went through the homework from the last week, before returning to the approval/disapproval theme. The psychologist talked about praise and rewards, and Mrs Z immediately related one or two examples of her already appropriate use of praise. She praised her son if he washed up the dishes after she had cooked a meal and described how she got him to do the washing up in the first place without showing that she expected it of him. 'I don't say "I've cooked the dinner so you've got to wash up" although that's what I think to myself. I'd say "I've got to rush off now – would you mind washing up for me? You'd be doing me a real favour." And next day I'll praise him for it.' Mrs Z also said she had been noticing a few things he was beginning to do for himself again. She has been encouraging his concentration in watching television quiz programmes by saying, for example, 'You were slow there', when one question came up she knew he would have been able to answer if he had been listening properly. Now he would sometimes follow bits of them and pick up on them. He was reading one or two articles in the papers and mentioning them. She always made it clear that she had noticed and was pleased. (Concentration is something the psychologist had been working with Mike on too.) Mrs Z also described how she was getting Mike to do more by finding things she would ask him to do which she would normally expect (and want) to do for herself. Recently, when she was going out to her night classes, she had asked him to walk her to the bus stop and pick up a paper for her and take it home, and added 'Would you mind feeding the cat for me when you get back?' And, using the excuse that it was the first time she had gone to the new later class, and it would be dark, she asked him if he would come and meet her out of her class and walk her in to town to the other college.

Having shown her already excellent use of praise (her night classes were on psychology!), they then discussed disapproval. The psychologist emphasised the need to avoid nagging, criticism, shouting, using force, and keeping quiet and ignoring the problem. A helpful general approach was to (list shown on the overhead):

1 *keep your voice calm, but firm – never shout*
2 *say* exactly *what he has or has not done*
3 *let him know how it makes you feel – upset, irritated, or embarrassed, etc.*
4 *say exactly how you would like him to change his behaviour*
5 *say something as soon as possible after the problem occurs (don't bottle up anger)*
6 *and show how pleased you are if he follows your suggestion.*

Both the psychologist and Mrs Z each gave examples of good and bad instances of each part of the approach, and Mrs Z said that she had already discovered for herself how shouting 'is the worst thing you can do to him'.

Mrs Z was then given her homework sheet – to record examples of two things Mike was doing that she was pleased with and that she had commented upon. And to also record one or two instances (if any occur) of behaviour she has disapproved of and how she dealt with it.

Management session: Mike

Shortly after she left, Mike arrived for a half-hour meeting with the psychologist. The focus was on helping Mike to overcome his lack of motivation and his tendency to withdraw from life. They began by talking about the possibility of Mike getting work. Would he be prepared to do voluntary work for a while? Yes. What kind would he prefer? Physical/ mental, with people/alone . . .

From the examples listed, Mike said he would like landscaping out in the country – gardening. The psychologist said she knew of some conservation work that was being done on the canals by groups of people, and she could give him names and addresses. He agreed that he would like her to do so. Alternatively, she suggested he could consider joining teams doing gardening for elderly people. The only payment would be travel expenses and a free lunch. Mike said he liked the sound of that too. They turned to discuss what he was going to do with his time meanwhile, and the psychologist suggested they have a good look at his week to see if they could extend his activities more, and give a structure to his time. He was asked about every detail of his day – what he eats and when, if and when he cleans the bath, hoovers the carpets, does his washing, goes shopping, goes to the job centre, as well as his social activities. Mike claimed to do everything he was asked about around the flat. But he said his friends were all working, and his best friend was also married now, although he does still occasionally see him in the pub on a Friday or Saturday night.

The psychologist asked if he would spend some of his day in sport if he could. Yes. She gave him a leaflet about a local sports centre, told him how to get there, and that it was free for unemployment benefit card-holders . . . The psychologist ended up with a list of five tasks which he was to try to make sure he did before their next meeting in two weeks' time:

– to enquire (not necessarily enrol) at the sports centre about sailing, swimming and other sports;
– to get his passport to leisure ticket sorted out;
– to set a particular weekday for going to the job centre and go;
– to contact his friend Steve one evening;
– to invite his mother to come to his flat for a meal.

She even planned it out, day by day, on the left-hand side of a form, on which he was to complete the right-hand side with comments about when the activity took place and how it went, with the request that he should bring it back with him in two weeks' time.

Then they turned to another of his remaining negative symptoms – poor concentration. The psychologist explained to him that it was one of the first things to go in an illness like this, and one of the last to come back, and that it was something you have to 'train up'. She suggested that he practice forcing himself to read one extra paragraph in the newspaper when he had reached the point where he found he was no longer concentrating. Also, to force himself to sit still for five minutes if watching something on television.

Mrs Z

Both Mrs Z and Mike agreed to tell me about their experiences. I talked first with Mrs Z. She described the years leading up to Mike's first onset of schizophrenia, at the age of 26 years. It was clear that he had become acutely disturbed quite suddenly, with very few signs that he was experiencing any difficulties more than a few weeks before. Mike and Mrs Z both had very constructive encounters with their respective GPs, who both immediately recognised the seriousness of Mike's symptoms, and he was given an appointment at the psychiatric hospital by Mrs Z's doctor for the following day.

At this point, Mrs Z interrupted her story to say that when first faced with bizarre behaviour in someone you know well, and when you have never seen anything like it before, 'You assume he's play-acting – you think they're putting it on – and then you feel so guilty afterwards. You believe there couldn't possibly be that much wrong to behave in such a way.' But when she took him home to stay overnight with her before taking him to the hospital, she saw he was terrified, deluded and persecuted. During the night he cut his wrists, but fortunately the cuts were superficial. Mike was admitted to All Saints the next day.

The first diagnosis was manic depression. After eight weeks he was discharged to his own flat, his mother being discouraged from taking him into her own home. Within six weeks he had relapsed and was readmitted. He had begun to complain about people talking about him 'and I recognised these symptoms as not being right this time, so I got in touch with the hospital, and they asked me to bring him in to see them the next day. The doctor decided he needed to come back in. 'Mike was in hospital for another two months, and diagnosed as suffering from schizophrenia.'

Mike had come out of hospital five months before I met him. 'He's had his ups and downs since, and recently he's been getting a bit withdrawn, quiet. That's when I started enticing him out – getting him to come up for meals. And there is an improvement in him – whether or not it's a coincidence I don't know . . . You don't know what to do for the best. Some people like their own company best . . . but I felt he needed some stimulation . . .'

Q What part of the programme here have you found most helpful?
A I'd say it was all helpful really. Some of it I've already sussed out for meself. I picked up quite a lot on me own, but it's always nice to know it's verified . . . to know what you are *doing is the right thing, or to know*

what you aren't *doing is the right thing, and to hear about all the pitfalls you could fall into. Because there can be pitfalls, I don't care who you are, you could quite easily fall into things. I'm glad I've been coming here. Even if I've been doing something right already, it's just as important to know that you definitely* are *doing it right.*

Q You don't meet any other families coping with schizophrenia here, do you? Would you like to?

A I don't know. I think I'd rather have the information individually – cos they say that no schizophrenic has all the symptoms all the time, and that, and to be quite honest with you, the only person I'm interested in is my Mickey. The only thing that might be helpful is in coping with the guilt, especially if you'd thought that what was going on at first wasn't for real. And then you think – my God, how can I have thought that? What kind of person am I? Then you start thinking, how can this come about? What kind of mother was I? And you start remembering when you smacked them, were you too hard on them . . . and you start questioning yourself. (But she says she's got her own friends to talk to for support, so does not really need a group.)

Q Do you think this course has made you solve any problems differently?

A That's a difficult one, because this course is really for people who live together, and when you live separately you go about things differently . . . I've got fewer problems . . .

Q Has it increased your knowledge about the nature of schizophrenia?

A It certainly has.

Q Has it enabled you to understand better which parts of his behaviour are due to the illness rather than laziness or whatever?

A Oh most definitely.

Q . . . the cause?

A No.

Q . . . about the drug treatment?

A Yeah. But I got some of this from the psychiatrist too. My family also want to know a lot of this information. My other son is divorced and he's got a girlfriend and he's got two children and there's a possibility that they might get married and my son's girlfriend is in on all this too because she wants to know, because the man that she's going to marry has two children whose uncle has schizophrenia, and she might also have children. So we want to discuss all this, about what's going on. And she gives me a lot of support, but we keep it to ourselves and she won't go telling people about him.

Mike

I talked briefly to Mike. His account of the onset of his illness was exactly as his mother described, sudden and acute. One morning he heard voices telling him to get out of bed . . . he also thought people everywhere were talking about him, and that some people 'were out to get me'. He is confused about who has treated him and calls the psychiatrists 'the doctors', and refers to the psychologists who have been helping him since his discharge as psychiatrists.

Q *Did the doctor explain a lot about the illness?*
A *Yeah.*
Q *And about the drugs?*
A *Can't remember.*
Q *Did he tell you you had schizophrenia?*
A *Funnily enough, no he didn't. Me mam told me.*
Q *Has it all cleared up now?*
A *Oh yeah. I feel a lot better in meself.*
A *Did you feel better right away, or are you gradually getting better?*
A *Gradual. When I first came back home I felt very weak, and very unsure of myself.*
Q *Has that come back now, as good as before you were ill?*
A *Not quite, but it's slowly coming back.*

He also understands that he needs to keep having injections to stop the illness returning.

Q *What is it that's not back to normal?*
A *Concentration.*
Q *What do you think coming here is supposed to be for, for both of you? What do you get from it?*
A *They make me do more things.*
Q *Have they explained much to you about the illness?*
A *Oh yeah, I had five lessons about that. I found it very interesting.*
Q *Did they tell you a lot of things you didn't know?*
A *Oh yeah.*
Q *Has it made you behave differently . . . for instance, I heard Jo trying to get you to do more, is it making you make more efforts that you wouldn't be doing if you weren't coming to see them?*
A *Yeah, that's it, yeah.*
Q *What do you think you'd be doing each day if you hadn't been in touch with them?*
A *Nothing.*
Q *Do you think you'd start to become ill again?*
A *That's what the doctors say, and Jo. If I stop in the flat on my own, doing nothing, just thinking all day, there's a strong possibility of the illness coming back again.*
Q *And if you weren't seeing them – that's probably what you would be doing?*
A *Mmm.*
Q *Have you ever talked to anyone else who's had the same illness?*

A No – (in hospital no one asked each other what was wrong).

I commented that it must feel strange, as if you're very unusual if you've never known anyone else with the same illness, then 'But there's quite a lot of people get it aren't there? . . . I think it's one in a 100 isn't it?'

A Yeah, and if two couples who've had schizophrenia are married, and have children, there's a strong chance of four in ten.

Q Have any of your relatives had it?

A No.

Q So the risk in your family is less then isn't it?

A One in ten, yeah.

Mike said he'd never tell anyone he's had schizophrenia, 'because they take it as if you're mad, like you've a split personality, but it's nothing like that. Because I wouldn't have thought it was like an illness – I thought it was a split personality.'

I also asked him if there is anything that happens that makes his illness worse and he said yes – if he has something to drink. 'I start getting paranoid . . . And before I was taking the tablets, a lot of things got on me nerves – people talking, people in general. I'd criticise them, and I'd think they were talking about me . . . Now – I just take things with a pinch of salt.'

He also said a stressful job would probably make it worse.

'And since I've been on the tablets and getting injections, I've got on a lot better with all the family.'

Q What's the most useful thing you've got out of this course?

A Teaching me about the illness that I've had and getting me to do things.

Q Are you going to carry on coming?

A Oh yeah – it's all help isn't it? In a way coming here to see Jo – she's pushing me – not too hard – in a gentle way – and it does work. You've just got to say to yourself – get up off your butt and do it. Cos I like to keep meself occupied. It makes the day go a lot faster.

Evaluation

A first consideration which gives a crude but quite valuable indication of the effectiveness of a service is its success in enlisting the target audience. What proportion of the people living with schizophrenia and their relatives in the catchment area are offered the service, and what proportion of those who are wish to attend? An examination of refusers and drop-outs then reveals further information about its perceived usefulness.

In terms of reaching the target audience, the service is extremely effective. By running groups in day centres and through National Schizophrenia Fellowship meetings, as well as personally contacting every in-patient and out-patient in All Saints Hospital with a diagnosis of schizophrenia, a large proportion of the potential target group will, after a few years of its existence, have been offered this help. However, almost one in three individuals or families did not take up the offer of help, or dropped out after one or two sessions (Smith and Birchwood, 1990). Although this was sometimes due to a lesser need and a relatively low sense of burden (high stress and high EE were not a criterion for entry to the programme) this was not the most common reason, except among Asian families. Asian families were less likely than other families to take up the offer of education, and this was thought to be partly explained by the finding that Asian patients had a considerably lower relapse rate than individuals from Caribbean or white English families and also sometimes because of their conflicting constructions of mental disorder (Birchwood, personal communication). As already discussed, most of those who chose not to participate in the programme were people who either did not accept their diagnosis (or the likelihood of continued problems), or who had had dealings with professionals that made them hostile toward further involvement. Those running the programme have endeavoured to counter these objections firstly by attempting to improve the amount and consistency of information given to patients and families by hospital staff (through staff training days, see p. 161), and secondly by working with community mental health teams to encourage take-up. Some of the families or patients declining involvement after a first episode may, of course, decide to take up the service at a future date if they come into contact with services again and their views about their problems change.

In terms of affecting the expressed emotion of close relatives, the intervention demonstrated modest benefits (Smith *et al.*, 1991; Birchwood, *et al.*, 1991). Their evaluation of 49 patients and their families randomly allocated to intervention or control groups examined outcome over a two-year period. It was intended to be an assessment also of the service validity of the method and therefore did not pre-select patients according to EE status, and included information about a further 15 drop-outs, and 36 people who refused offers of support. The intervention was provided by psychologists blind to whether families would formally have been assessed as high or low EE. Instead information on EE status was obtained in separate interviews with families (by other workers) before and after the intervention. The intervention also assessed family 'needs', i.e. stress, fear, burden, coping.

They found, first, that 'need' correlated well with EE status (that is, families assessed as having greater needs tended also to be those assessed as high EE). And secondly they found that the intervention was effective in meeting those needs, i.e. in reducing family stress, fear and burden, and in improving coping. High EE families in the intervention group more often than high EE families in the control group did, therefore, reduce their expressed emotion, and this (perhaps because of their concern to reduce burden) was particularly reflected in reduced emotional over-involvement rather than reduced criticism. The twist in the tail of this apparent success story, however, was that there was not a corresponding reduction in rate of relapse.

Given the number of replications of the link between expressed emotion and relapse in schizophrenia, this finding is puzzling. It may be partly explained by the sample: the individuals studied by Birchwood and colleagues tended to be recovering from a first or second episode, whereas most earlier studies tended to recruit people with a longer history of the disorder. Perhaps a change in the family's approach to coping with the situation has more significance after they have been coping with it for some time, and after it has become clear that the problems are long term. Or perhaps a greater change to critical comments is necessary to produce effects on relapse – other styles of intervention which have had effects on relapse have reduced critical comments far more than over-involvement. Further evaluation of the Birmingham and other intervention programmes will shed more light on this. This fascinating study raises many questions which should not, of course, detract from the finding that there were marked benefits to family life for those participating in the programme.

Monitoring early warning signs of relapse

There are almost always signs during the days or weeks before a sufferer of schizophrenia relapses that a relapse is imminent. Chapman (1966), Docherty and colleagues (1978), Heinrichs and colleagues (1985) and others since have described the 'prodromal symptoms' in schizophrenic relapse. Often they begin with an increase in anxiety, poor concentration, depression and withdrawal, before more obvious signs of psychosis occur such as delusions or hallucinations. They will differ from one sufferer to another, but will usually be the same from relapse to relapse for each person. Sometimes they are recognisable only a day or two before a full episode recurs, but usually they are present at least two weeks before.

Many individuals who have experienced more than one relapse will be aware of their own early warning signs and will be the first to recognise the implications of a change in their health. Similarly, relatives or close friends will also very often become aware of the warning signs, and may spot them soon after the individual becomes aware of them. One of the many advantages of an intervention which establishes a working partnership between professionals and clients in the management of the disorder is that such information can be rapidly relayed to clinicians and acted upon. And it has been shown that if maintenance medication is increased to a therapeutic dose at this early stage, then a full relapse of florid symptoms can sometimes be averted (e.g. Herz, 1984).

A family programme is a particularly helpful context for a systematic approach to monitoring early warning signs. This is not only because the family provide a second source of information, and because it needs a well-informed family to carry out effective monitoring, but also because for some individuals, their insight into their own health status begins to diminish as a relapse becomes imminent (Birchwood *et al.*, 1989). Birchwood and Smith therefore set up a monitoring system on an experimental basis in which both the individual and close relatives were trained.

The first step was to develop a brief questionnaire suitable for the individual and for relatives to complete on their own at home. The assessment of early signs developed by Herz (1984) had involved regular interviews by professionals, and was therefore not appropriate. Birchwood and colleagues (1989) gathered information from the family informants of 42 schizophrenia patients about changes noticed prior to the most recent relapse. Four separate groups of changes were discerned: anxiety/agitation (irritability, sleep problems, tenseness); depression/withdrawal (quiet, depressed, poor appetite, withdrawn); disinhibition (restlessness, aggressiveness, violent behaviour, stubbornness); and incipient psychosis (says he is being laughed at, or talked about, behaves oddly, behaves as if hearing voices). Most relatives observed some of these signs of relapse two to four weeks before the individual was admitted to hospital.

These signs were used to form a 34-item measure on which relatives scored items (such as losing his temper) from 0 to 3 (not a problem – marked problem). The test–retest reliability of the questionnaire for relatives was found to be good, and the version for use by sufferers themselves was even more reliable. There was also a strong correlation between how observer and individual rated his mental state, particularly when he was relatively well.

Birchwood and colleagues (1989) then set up a prospective pilot study with 19 schizophrenia out-patients and their 'informants' (relative, key worker or hostel worker). They were not a random sample of patients, but were people who were willing to enter the trial. On the whole, they were young and in work and therefore an unrepresentative group. The individual completed the form with the psychology technician on their fortnightly visit for maintenance medication, and informants received their form by post, completing it and posting it back on the same day as the sufferer visited out-patients. Non-returns were followed up by a home visit. At monthly intervals, a Psychiatric Assessment Scale was also completed.

Both the individual and those people whom he had agreed could act as informants were found to be more than willing to fill in the questionnaires on a regular basis as they were glad to have the illness monitored so closely. As the forms took just five to ten minutes to complete, it was not an onerous task. In fact, when the nine-month trial period was over, half the families requested that the monitoring process continue. After a short time, these forms provided a 'baseline' of symptoms, mood and behaviour against which changes could be assessed.

In none of the 11 sufferers who did not relapse were early signs detected.

That is, there were no 'false positives'. Eight sufferers relapsed within nine months. Early signs were spotted in four cases, in three more the patient stopped coming to the clinic, and in one early signs were absent. So it seemed that both non-attendance at the clinic and early signs were predictive of relapse. Two of the relapses were rapidly controlled by an immediate increase in medication following detection of early signs.

These exciting results from the pilot study led the team to plan a larger scale replication and further research into the clinical implications of monitoring 'early signs' using a standardised monitoring system. The procedure was also integrated into their family education programme to become a routine part of the service.

Other additions to the service following evaluation: improving the consistency of information given to relatives

Given the changing climate of opinion in recent decades on the causes of schizophrenia, and the controversies which continue, it is not surprising that professionals hold different views from one another on this subject. This means that relatives may get quite different answers to the same question, depending on whom they ask. Clearly this does not help relatives in their efforts to support the sufferer, nor will it enhance their confidence in the service providers. Nurses are often the professional seen most frequently by relatives, and some nurses may in fact have started out with relatively little initial training specific to the aetiology, prevalence and course of schizophrenia. And although they may have a long experience of helping people in hospital with major mental health problems, they may not have kept themselves fully abreast of advances in research and thinking, or be aware of the role families can have in helping the individual to control the disorder.

In order to improve the consistency of information offered to relatives, and to encourage staff to recognise the importance of giving information to individuals and their families, Smith and Birchwood arranged regular staff training days. Two half-day sessions were provided on giving information to relatives, and a separate course of two half-day sessions on giving information to the patient. The first session often began with a knowledge test – a multiple choice questionnaire. After individuals had completed it, answer sheets were given out to enable staff to examine for themselves where the gaps in their knowledge lay. They would not be asked about their scores. A second exercise would be for each participant to imagine themselves as a close relative of a sufferer of schizophrenia, and consider what information they would wish to know. Discussions in small groups enabled them to work through key questions, to think about how important that information would be, and to consider the most helpful answers that could be given. During the second session, they might view a video prepared by the psychologist on giving information to families, and look at the available information booklets. They would also be told about the research which shows the frequency with which readmission follows discontinuation of the medication, how in many instances their families do not know what the drugs are or why the individual would benefit from choosing to keep taking them when he has seemingly recovered. This kind of example was found to be particularly helpful in convincing staff of the value of education.

Costs

The principal psychologist at All Saints devotes approximately one-third of his time to the family programme. A senior clinical psychologist works on the programme full-time, and a secretary part-time. The secretary has a background in social work and is therefore invaluable to the team as she can also visit families, act as receptionist to patients and families, and respond to a range of incoming queries on her own initiative as well as perform a secretarial role. There are no other staff costs to the programme. Two technicians are part of the team, but one is on a 'sandwich' course, while the other gives her services voluntarily in preparation for a clinical psychology training course.

The premises (four rooms on the upper floor of a house close to the hospital), its heating, lighting and telephone bills were the only other costs.

CONCLUSION

Both the research and practice point to the need for a service that educates and supports both the sufferer and his or her family. Schizophrenia can be a frightening and distressing disorder, both to the individual and those close to them. Viewing it as an illness that can be at least partly controlled by medication, and the course of which can be influenced by other factors, including action by the individual and their family, may help to reduce fears. It may also provide individuals and their families with a sense of control over the situation. The more insight relatives gain into unpredictable behaviour, coping with everyday difficulties, the role of medication, available resources for schizophrenia sufferers, and the importance of looking after their own needs too, the more they will feel in control, the less stressed or burdened by their circumstances, and the more optimistic about the future. This in turn will lower the emotional temperature in the home, and help to reduce the arousal of the individual and hence his or her susceptibility to both minor and major exacerbations of symptoms. The individual too can learn much to give them the sense that they are not powerless against this distressing condition. Whether or not a recurrence of the disorder is preventable, and it would seem that relapses can be delayed and reduced in frequency rather than completely prevented, the way in which the individual copes, the way the family help them to cope, and the extent to which services support them both in coping can markedly affect the entire family's quality of life.

It would appear that there are advantages to linking a preventive family intervention service with existing treatment services, and this is particularly necessary if early warning signs of relapse are to be monitored. Set within the treatment services, probably in a psychology department, it may also help to ensure the recovery and functioning of the individual remaining as central a focus as the needs of family members. Liaison with community teams, day centres, and other services in the community would also seem necessary to ensure it reaches as many of those who would benefit as possible. However, there is also a valuable role for support groups established by services or organisations outside psychiatry if none exist within the psychiatric service.

There also appears to be an issue, not fully addressed here, but discussed in the concluding chapter, of how services might be more efficient in providing support, information, advice and treatment before a person's symptoms reach the acute florid stage when their problems are obvious to everyone. Given that each relapse is believed to further damage long-term social functioning and increases susceptibility to further relapses, and given the considerable stress suffered by individuals and their families sometimes during this prodromal phase, it would seem particularly important to link individuals and their families with support services as early as possible. Monitoring early warning signs will address this problem for people with an established illness, but in the early stages of the illness when contact is probably with general practitioners, there is more which could be done. A service in Buckinghamshire which has set up an early identification method with general practitioners is described in the final chapter.

The work on early warning signs, linked with targeted use of neuroleptic medication, is promising to have exciting implications for long-term sufferers of schizophrenia. Such close monitoring of symptoms will make it easier for treatment services to set maintenance doses at the lowest possible level, but may also, in a small proportion of cases, mean that maintenance medication can be discontinued and replaced by intermittent targeted usage of the drugs. Research is continuing on this approach, but it will probably be most appropriate in the context of a family education and support programme.

Education and support for sufferers of schizophrenia and for the families and friends on whom they will depend in their efforts to re-establish a normal life are gradually becoming more commonplace. However, at the end of 1988 the availability of high quality preventive care remained the exception rather than the rule.

Chapter 5

Preventing mental illnesses among elderly persons

The two most common psychiatric disorders among elderly people are dementia and depression, and they each affect a similar proportion of people. Murphy (1984) gives a figure of 12 per cent of the population aged over 65 years as suffering from depression severe enough to warrant the attention of medical services, and Cooper and Sosna (1980) give a point prevalence rate to dementia among the same age group as approximately 12 per cent. But while dementia, of course, becomes increasingly common with increasing age (the majority of cases are aged over 75 years), depression is a condition which affects people at all stages of adult life.

What marks out the depression experienced by elderly people from depression occurring at other stages of adult life is its tendency to chronicity, and its link with physical disability and premature death. Murphy (1984) found that 60 per cent of a community sample of depressed elderly people also had a serious physical illness which was likely to reduce their life expectancy and which was currently interfering with their daily lives. In another study, she found that only one in three of a sample of 124 depressed patients (aged 65 to 89 years) made a good recovery within the one-year study period, despite the fact that they were all receiving treatment. This compares with a recovery rate over a four-month period of more than half an adult (non-elderly) sample studied by Tennant and colleagues (1981), and two-thirds (over a nine-month period) of a sample of women studied by Brown and colleagues (1985). Those elderly persons in Murphy's study most likely to remain depressed, or to relapse after a brief recovery, were those who had the most serious symptoms, who also had a physical illness, or who were from a low socio-economic group. There is also some evidence that depression itself can have an effect on life expectancy among elderly people (see Millard, 1983).

It may be helpful to begin with a brief summary of the indications for prevention from what is known about the onset of depression and dementia.

THE DEVELOPMENT OF MENTAL ILLNESS IN OLD AGE

Dementia can be subdivided into two main groupings: multi-infarct dementia, and progressive degenerative (or senile) dementia (of which Alzheimer's disease is a common type). The cause of senile dementia is unknown. Multi-infarct dementia, however, which accounts for 15–20 per cent of the dementias of old age is caused by a series of minor strokes. It tends to begin earlier than other dementias, typically between age 60 and 70 years, but to have a slower and more variable course. Either kind, however, is characterised in the early stages by a memory loss for recent events, and an increasing inflexibility of thought.

In the early stages of dementia, as the individual perceives themself as 'beginning to fail', they may also suffer episodes of severe depression. It is a progressive disorder, of course, and gradually the person becomes confused, and finds difficulty in giving attention to more than one thing at once (so may concentrate on getting to the other side of the road but forget to look to each side first). Their vocabulary will also diminish and their judgement will become impaired. As the disorder becomes more distressing and worrying to those close to the individual, they may themselves begin to be less distressed by it, losing insight into their condition and awareness of their deficiencies. After several years of deterioration (although the time scale can vary considerably), speech eventually becomes incoherent, thought content becomes aimless, personal habits deteriorate and incontinence develops. A person who lives long enough to progress to these stages will of course have become totally unable to care for themselves.

There are some obvious opportunities for the prevention of multi-infarct dementia through attention to physical health. As it results from a series of strokes, the prevention, early detection and control of hypertension in middle age and later years should be preventive. The routine blood pressure testing of every person over the age of 40 consulting their family doctor for any reason should be helpful in this respect (Murphy, 1984). And as general-population health education strategies begin to affect the country's dietary and smoking habits, the prevalence of coronary artery disease and cerebrovascular disease may begin to decline in Britain as they have already begun to do in many other countries (Rose, 1981).

Depression probably comes about for much the same kinds of reason in old age as at other ages, and here social factors also appear to play an important role (Murphy, 1982). Events which represent a marked long-term threat of loss, or long-term social difficulties, can cause depression to develop in vulnerable individuals. For elderly people, four kinds of loss experience are particularly common: retirement, bereavement, deterioration of certain physical capacities, and the lessening of authority and feelings of control (Bohm and Rodin, 1985). And society's expectations and the restrictions on the roles open to elderly people mean that they often lose the status and identity which they may have enjoyed while members of the working community. These kinds of losses appear also to be associated with life expectancy, and increased death rates are reported among men during the six-month period following bereavement, retirement, admission to hospital, and transfer to a residential home (see Millard, 1983). Social support is widely considered to be protective against depression in the face of major social difficulties or loss events, but among elderly people, relatives and friends who move away or die are often not replaced by new relationships.

Although at first sight these factors should mean that rates of depression are particularly high among elderly populations, in fact there are a number of studies which indicate that grief (particularly following bereavement) among elderly people is not the same as grief at younger ages (see Kasl and Berkman, 1981). The fact that deaths are more likely, and can be to some extent anticipated, may help elderly people to be more accepting and less likely than might otherwise be expected to become seriously depressed. Nevertheless, as discussed in Chapter 3, loss events offer an obvious opportunity for preventive counselling by primary care workers, and the same considerations as suggested for younger adults regarding vulnerability (and likelihood of benefiting) would apply. That is, for those individuals without a partner, close relatives or friends nearby, and whose circumstances, expectations or commitments mean that the event has particularly distressing long-term significance, counselling, or at least additional supportive attention by primary care staff would seem justified in preventive terms. One in three elderly people coming to terms with bereavement, for instance, have no remaining living family members, and family doctors and community nurses are among the most acceptable outside visitors at such times. Routine visiting by family doctors to bereaved elderly people may, since the new contract for general practitioners was introduced in 1990, have become more common. Certainly in 1982 it was not commonplace – Bowling and Cartwright's study showed two-thirds of elderly widows had not received a visit from their doctor in the six months after bereavement.

Other opportunities for preventive counselling (which may be more specific to the prevention of anxiety rather than depression) occur in general practice at the time of diagnosis of frightening physical disorders or when a frightening event is planned, such as admission to hospital or to residential care. Many devastating assumptions may be made by the patient about diagnoses of 'stroke', 'coronary', 'diabetes' and 'cancer', some of which may be quite inaccurate. Whether their fears are justified or not, it would be helpful to explore and discuss these at the time of, or soon after, such a diagnosis (or after the need for hospital or residential care is determined), as this sort of 'psychological' help is very often more acceptable when provided at the same time as practical assistance. Also, as depression often accompanies physical illness or disability, the early treatment of physical disorders and the alleviation of accompanying handicaps could be expected to have an impact on the occurrence of depression (Murphy, 1984).

People with dementia do not usually visit the surgery, and half live without relatives who might report their failing capacity, and GPs will often be unaware of a large proportion of their elderly clients with depression or dementia (Murphy, 1984). Often dementia is not diagnosed until a crisis occurs, when repeated wandering or minor accidents at home generate anxiety in relatives or neighbours that they can no longer tolerate. Or the extent of the disorder may only be revealed following a sudden change of environment or death of a supporting partner. Murphy suggests that GPs should arrange regular visits (by themselves, a trained practice nurse or the health visitor) to clients over 75 years so that early signs of dementia could be recognised and monitored, and an effective management plan worked out with relatives. In fact, such regular visiting of elderly patients is now required by the 1990 GP contract and should bring an improvement in the preventive mental health care of this age group.

FOCUS OF THIS CHAPTER

On the whole, the social and mental health needs of old people, and the services which are appropriate for them, are the same as for younger adults (see Chapter 3). The main differences between their lives and those of younger adults relate to a sometimes diminishing social network and, for many, an increasing physical frailty. A proportion (particularly of those over 75 years) will also develop a psychological frailty. Mobility problems will affect their capacity to take up health and other services which do not have a domiciliary element, and frailty may mean that they have an increasing need for help with self-care and home-care tasks for which other adults obviously have no need. The level of support at home by close relatives and friends will determine how far the individual needs the support of outside services.

It might reasonably be expected that losses to the social network or losses which relate to an individual's health that have a profound impact on the individual's capacity to continue to lead an independent life will be associated with a raised risk of depression. And these sorts of loss events will be those most feared by elderly people, and those likely to affect this age group more than younger adults. The transition from a position where the person has been accustomed to making choices and exerting control and having an active social life to one of feeling comparatively helpless, isolated and powerless will almost certainly have consequences for mental health. For instance, for an elderly and frail couple who had managed to support each other's needs in a balanced way, the death of one of them will bring the other's own infirmities into the light. The survivor may need to become reliant on younger relatives, and may perceive themself as a burden to them. In the absence of support from relatives, the survivor may need to give up their own house to go into some form of residential care, and, particularly if this has not been planned for, this will bring an even greater sense of loss.

The extent to which deleterious mental health consequences follow a change in living arrangements for a frail elderly person will depend on a number of factors. Essentially these relate to a balance between what is lost and what gained by the change. Better housing, a safer neighbourhood, and the availability of health and social facilities may to some extent offset the effect of a bereavement and loss of contact with neighbourhood friends, particularly if contact with relatives is maintained, and the arrangement offers a good deal of choice and independence in day-to-day activities. If the frailty is associated with the early stages of dementia it is likely to add to their confusion and worsen their condition to move to a new neighbourhood.

The focus of this chapter is on this time of transition: when events such as bereavement or gradually increasing frailty lead to a reappraisal of the suitability of the individual's living circumstances; and relatives are either unable or unwilling to provide the level of support needed to enable the individual to retain an independent life in their own or a family home. It is not an uncommon experience among this age group, and carries a profound threat of loss. Service provision can offer support to enable the individual to remain in their own home, or provide accommodation in supported housing schemes, or in a residential home for elderly people. It is hoped that the descriptions of services in this chapter throw some light on to the ways in which the individual's sense of control, autonomy, and social support can be maximised from the way in which that support is provided.

While the services described are included in this review as good practice in preventing mental illness, there is in this area perhaps the weakest evidence that mental illness is prevented by such intervention. Although, given our understanding of the causes of depression, the loss of one's independence coupled with a lack of social support would seem highly likely to be associated with depression, longitudinal research has not adequately confirmed that this is so. There are numerous studies documenting the apathy, withdrawal and depression among residents of residential homes, and a raised rate of illness and death in the 12-month period following admission. And many workers in the field and government recommendations about quality of care in such homes have elaborated the commonly held view that the lack of individual choice, independence and autonomy is at least partly to blame for this, and good practice should aim to minimise these limitations of the environment. But without a carefully controlled longitudinal study of people before entering residential care and after one or two years in a home, the possibility that the poor health of residents is simply a matter of selection bias cannot be ruled out.

But it is not the role of a review such as this one to decide such matters. Work is described as good practice because it concurs with our current understanding of aetiology of disorder, and with prevailing views about good practice; because maximising individual control over one's own life is part of the underlying rationale of this review; and because of humanitarian concerns about the dignity and well-being of our elderly population. No doubt research will eventually resolve some of the complex issues about effectiveness (in mental health terms) of these approaches. In this respect, it is important that these services continue to be evaluated as they grow and develop. But, as discussed in introductory chapters, service providers cannot wait for conclusive evidence, and must move ahead on the basis of current knowledge.

FRAILTY, SUPPORT AND INDEPENDENCE

Whether or not an individual is able to live independently until death depends primarily on their health and their network of support. Unfortunately, much of what is publicised in the media about old age encourages the view that old people all eventually become dependent and burdensome. Many inaccurate conclusions are drawn from statistics: for instance, that the numbers of old people living alone represent the number who are socially isolated; that all people aged over 80 with dementia, or who are living with relatives, require a high level of care and close supervision and so on (Wenger, 1986). Such conceptions add to the view that the growing numbers of people living longer than 80 years will necessarily have a devastating effect upon our health and welfare system. In fact, living alone but a short distance from close relatives is increasingly the arrangement preferred by old people, and most people with symptoms of dementia living at home, and elderly people living with relatives, are only mildly disabled.

How great are the dependency needs of elderly people in reality? Some indication of this is given by the 1980 General Household Survey of 4,553 people over the age of 65 years living at home (Office of Population Censuses and Surveys, 1982). One-third of this sample lived alone, nearly half with their spouse, the remainder (18 per cent) with younger household members. The most common difficulties experienced (by one-fifth and one-third) were in getting shopping and cutting their toenails. The latter problem was nearly always dealt with by social or medical services, but shopping was done mostly by younger relatives (56 per cent of those needing help) or by friends or neighbours (20 per cent). Social services helped 21 per cent and 3 per cent took paid assistance. Less common difficulties were unscrewing jars, washing laundry, bathing, cooking meals, walking outdoors, and in a very small number (about 0.5 per cent) getting in and out of bed. Statutory services were quite often involved in help with bathing (52 per cent of those getting help), washing laundry (33 per cent) and cooking meals (25 per cent).

Elderly couples coped between them with almost all difficulties which either or both of them experienced, other than toenail cutting, rarely getting much assistance even from family or friends. Similarly, those elderly people who lived with other younger relatives received almost no help from outside the household with any of their difficulties, except for a small proportion of those needing help with toenail cutting or bathing. When a carer is clearly identified inside the household, help from other sources is limited or non-existent.

Elderly people living alone are more likely to receive help from outside sources when they become infirm, and for those who could not manage to bath, cook meals or wash laundry, the help was provided by social/medical services in 52 per cent, 25 per cent and 33 per cent of instances respectively. Friends and neighbours helped with shopping (for 20 per cent who couldn't manage their own); unscrewing jars and so on (36 per cent); and walking out of doors (37 per cent). Relatives were the main source of help for domestic difficulties: cooking; washing laundry; shopping; getting in and out of bed; and walking outside.

Most people living in their own homes want to retain a home of their own (although not necessarily the same one) rather than be cared for in community homes or hospital wards if they become infirm. A home of one's own to most people is synonymous with independence, having the freedom to do as one wants, look after oneself, and avoid being beholden to others (Sixsmith, 1986).

The research evidence and general climate of opinion support the contention that it is better for the physical and mental health of individuals to remain, if possible, in their own homes (though perhaps within a sheltered housing scheme) throughout old age, if this is what they wish to do. There are studies showing that residential homes are potentially harmful places in which to live (Hughes and Wilkin, 1980), and apathy, helplessness, withdrawal and disorientation is widespread amongst residents (Booth, 1986). Several health and social service review bodies have now concluded from this and other research that a loss of expectation, need for independent action, and the removal of the need for self-help can cause rapid deterioration, both physically and mentally, in relatively active old people (see Booth, 1986).

Following from this, most reviews also conclude that homes should therefore strive to maximise the degree of independent living which is possible, by routines which are flexible and by enabling residents to do as much as they would like to do for themselves. By this reasoning, homes with such resident-oriented regimes should have more active, self-reliant residents with better physical and mental health. Those whose policies tend toward the other extreme would be expected to have residents who are more passive and helpless, in poorer health and who die sooner. Homes which allow people to have as much choice over their everyday lives as possible, which encourage residents to look after themselves as far as possible, and which help them to keep up their existing relationships and activities in the community should prevent the deterioration so commonly associated with institutional life. For this reason, a home is described below which has been assessed as exemplary in this respect. In a survey of 18 local authority homes for elderly people in Wiltshire which were rated in relation to being resident-oriented, Hawthorne House ranked second highest (Dixon, 1986b).

HAWTHORNE HOUSE

For some years, Wiltshire has built all new residential homes to a bedsitter design, for which they have attracted a high reputation. This is the design most favoured by the consumers according to Peace (1983). By 1988 they had five bedsitter homes while the remainder were mostly older, purpose-built styles with both single and double rooms and more emphasis on communal areas. Hawthorne House is one of the latter group, but with a manager-in-charge strongly committed to promoting independence, choice and personal control among residents, and striving to train her staff to have similar attitudes to care. Hence it scored highly in Dixon's survey of the 18 local authority homes in Wiltshire in terms of maximising resident choice, control and independence, comparing well with the bedsitter homes.

Hawthorne House is in the centre of a village in a wealthy area of Wiltshire. It is unremarkable in its physical design. Two units each for 15 people are separated by a sitting room, dining area and kitchen, hobbies room and quiet work room. Two other small sitting rooms enable those who want to relax with relatives or friends away from other residents to find a comfortable quiet place, as individual bedrooms do not have sufficient space to sit more than one or two visitors.

The guidelines for the home's policies when it was set up took account of all the latest ideas on excellence in residential care. The document stated: 'The philosophy is comparatively simple. The keywords are normalisation, activisation and integration.' Staff were expected to see themselves not as 'running a home', but as providing an enabling service according to individual needs in the place where the resident group lives. Starting from scratch, with no built-in inhibitions of past tradition, it was to be an attempt to establish a different approach to resident–staff roles and relationships. The aim was to maximise resident independence and areas of decision-making. Residents were to be expected, within their own capacity, to look after their own rooms. The domestic cleaning service was to be provided according to need, and the amount and timing of the cleaning to be negotiated at regular intervals. Unless too frail to be able to make the short journey to the post office, or too confused to handle their own finances, residents should make their own arrangements to collect their pension and see themselves as paying their way for their accommodation. A resident's committee was to discuss mealtimes, meal choices and facilities for self-catering, and other important day-to-day issues. They were to be encouraged to bring as much of their own furniture as they could fit in, and allowed to bring pets with them provided arrangements could be made for their care. Staff were not to be permitted to wear uniforms or colour-coded clothing to indicate their status, and were to be given titles that were less dominant (manager rather than matron) and to be known by their first names. The possibility of establishing a library, a resident-run shop, and providing a telephone were to be considered. To enable the new practices to become established, it was proposed that most residents be taken direct from the community and until the first complement of 30 was established, to keep transfers from other homes and hospitals to no more than a quarter. After this, restrictions on entry were to be dropped.

I visited the home early in 1988 and was shown around by the manager. A group of residents were watching television in each of the two sitting rooms. A few individuals sat in the dining room and hobbies room, and I was introduced as we went through. A small kitchenette where anyone, staff or resident, could make tea or coffee adjoined the main sitting room in each wing, but although regularly used by staff, almost no residents used them at all, choosing instead to drink only at the times when drinks were made by staff. None of the care officers wore uniforms but domestic staff were recognisable by their overalls.

I was shown two or three bedrooms which were small, about 10 feet square, with fitted wardrobe, washbasin, mirror, bed and chair. In the first room I saw, the resident had brought almost no personal additions, and the walls were painted in the colour chosen by staff. The next two rooms, however, were papered and had several pieces of furniture brought from home. Residents could have their own television or radio and many did so. They also had a telephone point and electric sockets, but in fact none of the residents had a telephone, toaster, or kettle, and no one prepared any food or drinks in their rooms. Two of the 30 rooms were double bedrooms, although one had been converted back to a single room and the other was currently being used as a single. One of the single rooms was used for short-term and respite-care placements for which it was almost continuously booked. On six days of the week, the home could also take up to three day-care clients brought in from surrounding villages by volunteer drivers. The number of days they attended was variable and currently a total of 11 such day-care clients could be accommodated. The respite-care and day-care facility was used by some local families to enable them to support a frail elderly relative in their own homes.

Staff

The manager had two deputies, and seven care officers, six of whom worked part-time. Between them they worked the two day shifts on a six-week rota system (7.00 a.m.–3.30 p.m. or 2 p.m.–10 p.m.). Senior staff worked one weekend in three, care officers alternate weekends. Six other care staff were employed to cover the night shift. In addition, there were six part-time domestic staff, one full-time and one part-time cook, and a part-time 'handyman'.

The manager had established a key worker system in which staff each took a special responsibility for and interest in particular residents. This was clearly very popular with the residents, but it had taken a while before staff could adapt comfortably to the extra responsibility towards individuals. The number of key clients for each key worker varied according to the number of hours worked and the physical dependency of the client. The key worker helped the resident (if necessary) to bath, and might also, for instance, help the resident to arrange appointments with a doctor or chiropodist, and remember events like the date of a son's birthday (and perhaps remind a forgetful resident to buy a card). Of course, the development of close relationships of this kind meant that it was especially difficult for the key worker when the resident died, so they would be given some time to themselves on the day. With about 12 deaths a year this was an event, of course, with which most soon became familiar.

The residents

Clients were taken from a waiting list (shared by five other residential homes) of people in the area wanting residential care. The list was ordered for priority by social services. Those coming from their own homes had usually been known about for some while before a place became available, and were offered day-care or respite-care in the interim. This arrangement helped to familiarise them with the home and to help them prepare for the move. There were currently 31 residents with an average age of 86, 21 women and ten men. All were white, and of Church of England or United Reform Church religion. Five came directly from a local long-stay psychiatric hospital, two of the youngest residents from centres for mentally handicapped adults. Four residents had Alzheimer's disease and one other was in the early stages of the disease. Many residents easily became confused and in the manager's view 22 of the residents had some degree of mental impairment or disorder. Twenty-three residents needed a walking frame or stick and 13 needed a great deal of physical help with washing, dressing and going to the toilet. Other common problems were deafness and partial sightedness. No one was currently completely wheelchair bound.

Maximising autonomy

When the present manager first came to the home, it had, as so many other homes do, a bathing rota for residents in which people were helped to bath at fixed times, usually weekly, not necessarily by the same person each week and in which, if time was short, the least popular residents were missed out. (The policy guidelines for the home do not appear to have guided the practice to a great extent in the early days.) With the successful introduction of the key worker system in 1984, residents needing assistance could negotiate with their key worker to bath at a mutually convenient time, and not necessarily the same time each week. Another change instigated by the present manager was to the routine for changing bed linen. Previously done corridor by corridor, she wanted bed linen to be changed at the same time as residents were bathed, that is, at times to suit the residents' routine rather than the domestics' work routine. This was greeted with reluctance by domestic staff but soon easily accommodated.

Residents were offered a cup of tea in bed each morning, between 7.00 and 7.30 a.m. and if they wished they then dressed and went to the dining room for breakfast. However, this was not obligatory; they could ask to be left to sleep on, or to have breakfast brought to their room on a tray (although this was rarely requested). This was again a change to existing practices, which had been for residents to be woken as early as 5.45 a.m. to ensure everyone was dressed ready for breakfast at 8.00 a.m. It meant a change of hours for night staff, which was opposed by staff, but which their union supported when the reasons were understood.

The staff also helped residents with continence difficulties to control the problem without needing to rely on incontinence pads or to risk embarrassing accidents. Staff were trained in an approach in which the individual was helped to monitor their own routines and schedule assistance in visiting the toilet at regular times determined by this assessment.

Residents could invite relatives or friends to the home, and could buy them lunch there which would be served to the family unit privately in the hobbies room. One lady was also able to arrange for her sister to stay at the home in the short-stay room when it was free, for a short holiday. The staff were trying to minimise the help given, although recognising that it was more time-consuming than the traditional style of care. They would walk slowly behind someone with a wheelchair ready to help them if and when they needed it, rather than push them quickly back to their room. Instead of feeding residents with particular difficulties, they provided special plates. They would assist individuals needing help with washing and dressing rather than do it for them. The manager told me that it took some time for staff to appreciate that doing things less well *with* the resident was at least as caring an approach as doing it 'properly' *for* them. Staff training was continued every month, and those who have found the approach difficult to adjust to have left. In 1986 the manager introduced meal choices at lunchtimes.

Activities

The inevitable bingo, board games and television were available daily. There was also a video club, and weekly sessions for 'liquid embroidery', painting, cooking, and 'movement to music'. Outside the home, a number of the people had kept up their membership of social clubs but as none of these activities were free, most residents chose not to go. Residents received visits from and sometimes went on outings or holidays with relatives. A small group of residents went on a holiday organised by staff. Some residents were already too frail to take up many activities when they moved in (the last admission was a person of 97 years).

Christine

Christine is 77. She moved to Hawthorne House a year before I met her. She had had her name on a waiting list for nearby warden-controlled bungalows, but before gaining accommodation her health had deteriorated and her GP felt she would be well advised to seek a place where more personal assistance was available. She suffered from angina, Parkinson's disease and arthritis. Her health had improved since moving into the home, largely because the constant warmth had greatly improved her movement. Before admission she had needed to walk with a stick, but currently had no need of it. She had been dieting carefully and had lost three stone in weight since admission.

Christine had become unable to cook for herself some while previously and had been coming to Hawthorne House for day-care, and was therefore familiar with the home. It was situated in the village where she had lived for many years and where she still had many friends. She also received occasional visits from her son.

She described her typical day to me. She is woken up and brought tea in bed at about 7.15 a.m., washes, dresses, tidies her room, and joins the other residents in the dining room for breakfast. Afterwards she likes to help the kitchen staff by clearing the tables and washing up the beakers. She goes back to her room but returns with another lady to the dining room to dry the cutlery after it has been sterilised. It is then time for morning coffee, a read or a walk to the shops, then to lay one of the tables for lunch. After lunch she takes her tablets, then returns to the dining room to dry and put away the cutlery. She then usually watches television and knits. One afternoon a week she is taken by a volunteer driver to a local club. Otherwise she relaxes in the communal sitting room until it is time to lay the tables for tea. After eating, she waits for the cutlery to be ready for drying and putting away. After a hot drink at 7.00 p.m. she washes the beakers, and retires to her room at 8.00 p.m., and either watches her own television or reads in bed, sleeping by about 11 o'clock.

I asked her if she would not sometimes like to have breakfast in her room, but she said not. I felt her answer at least partly reflected her desire not to put anyone to any trouble on her behalf. She told me that she did not regret coming to live at Hawthorne House 'one bit'. 'They are all wonderful here – they're all nice.'

Robert

Robert is 95 years old, and has lived in Hawthorne House for the past eight years. He seems to have made more of a personal home life around his private space than most of the other residents who live conspicuously public and communal lives. He listens to the 7 a.m. news on Radio 4, then gets up. He gets washed and dressed, makes his bed, and goes out to sit in the dining room until breakfast is served at 8.30 a.m. (As he prefers a cooked breakfast to the choices offered, he supplies his own eggs.) Then he comes back to his own room to read the daily newspaper that he has arranged with the handyman to bring him each day. He takes tea at 10.30 a.m. and retires back to his room again to read and snooze until lunchtime. Immediately after lunch, he comes back to his room again. He watches snooker or other sport on his own TV until teatime. He feels his own TV is better than those in the communal sitting rooms, and he prefers it. He returns to his own room after tea. Most evenings he plays cards on his own and then goes to bed at 9.30 p.m., reading for another hour before sleeping. He likes to stick to a regular set day for his bath. His niece visits him occasionally, his two or three other nearby relatives visiting infrequently. But he has a lively social life and was previously one of the 'ringleaders' of the local Derby and Joan club. He now gets a lift to a club every Thursday and alternate Wednesdays he goes by bus to a nearby village to see old friends. Other friends who live further afield he has now stopped seeing.

Robert has given up a certain amount of his self-care activities in moving to Hawthorne House. In his own house, he got up at 9.00 a.m. and made his own breakfast. He did his own shopping twice a week, and his own cleaning and washing. Most of his spare time was spent gardening, and 'leaving the garden was the hardest part of moving here'. The friends he now sees once a fortnight he saw twice weekly.

He now has just two real friends at Hawthorne House, feeling that he could not hold much of a conversation with most of the residents. He had become very friendly with one of the new day-care clients, but the man had died a week ago. But Robert told me he is happy at Hawthorne House and says the staff are all very kind. He is organising a birthday party for himself on the coming Saturday, to celebrate being nearly 100 (just in case he doesn't live long enough to celebrate his hundredth on the right day and while still fit enough to enjoy a party!). He has bought the drink (and presents for the staff), and will hold it in the main sitting/dining area.

Ruth

Ruth has lived in Hawthorne House for two years. She is a lively and articulate 79-year-old woman who unfortunately now gets very confused about recent events. She had come to live in Hawthorne House after a seven-month hospital stay following a fall at her home when she had broken her hip. She was no longer able to reliably monitor her own medication or diet (essential because she was also diabetic) and so could not be discharged to her own home. In her confused state, she gave elaborate stories when asked about meals, so that no one (least of all herself) could be sure if and what she had last eaten.

Ruth had worked as a telephonist in London for most of her working life. Her daughter had lived with her until her marriage, after which Ruth had moved to Dorset to live with the couple. This arrangement had not worked very happily and Ruth moved out to live alone in a flat nearby, where she lived for 11 years before coming to live in Hawthorne House.

At Hawthorne House she spends most of the day in the communal sitting or eating areas. She spends a lot of time watching television as her eyesight is too poor for reading. If it is good weather, she sometimes strolls out into the garden with her walking frame, and sometimes she comes back to her room to listen to her 'talking book'. She usually retires to her room at about 8 p.m., watches the 9 o'clock news and is in bed by 10 o'clock.

Her daughter visits her once a month, and occasionally her granddaughter brings her new great grandson to see her. She is particularly friendly with Christine (above), but likes many of the residents.

Evaluation

These case histories reveal a good deal about institutional living. Most people enjoy having meals made for them, not having to think about what to buy, and being looked after – having life made easy. It should perhaps not be surprising to find that the residents interviewed had adapted to this passive role. And it appeared that they did not wish to seem ungrateful or troublesome by asking for different treatment from the others. They made choices about matters on which they were actively encouraged to make a choice – how their room was furnished and decorated, when they would take a bath. Other choices which were available, but perhaps not so actively encouraged, were the possibility of staying in bed after others got up, taking breakfast in their own room, making snacks or drinks for themselves.

Only Robert exercised his right to choose to do things a little differently from other residents, and was possibly less worried about staff going to extra trouble on his behalf (to make him a boiled egg for breakfast).

Hawthorne House scored second highest in Dixon's survey of local authority homes in Wiltshire in relation to being resident-oriented on the Evans Analysis of Daily Practices Schedule (Dixon, 1986b). The aim of this assessment is to

judge particular organisation practices or features according to their tendency to facilitate or limit resident freedom, to facilitate administrative efficiency at the expense of resident needs, to regiment residents and subject them to block treatment, to depersonalise residents by eroding individual differences or limiting decision-making powers, to maintain social distance between residents and staff.

(Evans *et al.*, 1981)

It also scored well on staff attitude to resident autonomy. It had quite obviously successfully established a resident-oriented approach to care. However, this did not appear to have been reflected as far as might have been expected in the daily lives of individual residents. The three case histories were deliberately selected from the more articulate residents. Many less physically or mentally capable residents will have been more limited in their capacity to make choices, and it is unlikely that a different set of case histories would have illustrated greater independence.

Other research has indicated that in fact changes in routines to offer choice and encourage individual autonomy are more easily achieved than actual changes to resident autonomy (Dixon, 1986a). Furthermore, a large-scale research study attempting to demonstrate the effects on residents' functioning of the regime of the home failed to find any evidence of an effect. Booth (1986) followed up 3,412 residents of 175 local authority homes over a two-year period to test the 'induced dependency hypothesis'. Information (from structured staff interviews) on the functioning of individual residents was used to create four dependency scales: self-care (mobility, ability to wash, dress, feed, etc.); continence; social integration; and mental state (confusion, disorientation, wandering, etc.). The routines and management practices of the homes were also assessed on four dimensions, in this case: opportunities for choice; respect for privacy and personal identity; scope for participation in running the home; and encouragement to keep up links with the wider community. Real differences were found between homes in rates of improvement and deterioration among residents, as well as in rates of mortality and survival. After controlling for initial differences, more residents deteriorated or deteriorated faster, and died sooner in some homes than in others. However, he did *not* find that these differences correlated with his measures of quality of residential life. His interpretation of this result was that the common features of institutional living are so dominant in their effects that changes to their style can have only minor impact. That is, that the scope for encouraging self-determination in communal settings like these is too limited to have much impact on residents, or to counteract the pressures acting in the opposite direction (Booth, 1985).

It would appear that regimes offering opportunities for choice, privacy, and social contact are probably not sufficient alone to influence resident functioning greatly. However, Booth's research did establish differences between homes on morbidity and mortality that were not explained. It leaves open the possibility that other qualitative assessments of staff–

resident relationships may have been related to the differences in resident functioning between homes. For instance, claims to respect privacy may not be born out by practice, and choices may exist but not be encouraged. Dixon (1986b) describes how one manager who emphasised the importance of the resident's right to privacy and dignity showed her into a resident's bedroom without knocking on the door first, or introducing her to the occupant.

This possibility that choices must be encouraged as well as available in order to affect resident functioning would explain why the research by Rodin and her colleagues seems to conflict with that of Booth. Langer and Rodin (1976) assessed the effects of an intervention designed to encourage elderly North American convalescent home residents to make a greater number of choices and to feel more in control of day-to-day events and found marked benefits. Compared to another group of residents living on a different floor of the same block, the residents given greater responsibility became more active, showed greater improvements in alertness, in health and even showed differences in death rate over the following 18-month period. Twice as many of the comparison group died. A later controlled study by one of the same researchers with a slightly younger and much fitter group failed to replicate the benefits of such straightforward encouragement to take more responsibility (Rodin, 1983). However, in this later study, the group who were taught stress management techniques did experience substantial health benefits. They were taught over a period of three weeks to become aware of their own negative self-statements ('Nothing ever goes right for me here'), to emit new positive self-statements when they caught themselves thinking this way ('It's my choice to work this out if I want to . . . I'm not going to let today get the better of me . . . I will not sit here and do nothing') and to apply them to everyday problems. So in this research, it appears that staff attitudes and personal relationships with residents in actively encouraging and sometimes training residents to feel in control are beneficial.

The comparison group in the first study who engaged in fewer activities, had poorer health and a higher death rate were residents of the *same* establishment as the experimental group (see Langer and Rodin, 1976). The same choices and activities were theoretically open to both groups, but staff looking after the experimental group were trained to actively encourage residents to exercise choice and responsibility. The comparison staff group cared for residents in the more traditional way, with the unspoken messages that 'We'll take care of you' and 'You don't have to worry about anything – it will all be taken care of.' It is widely believed that residents adapt to the expectations of staff. So if it is easier for staff to serve breakfast for everyone at 8.00 a.m. in the dining room, anyone taking up the option of eating in their room at 9.00 a.m. might feel that they run the risk of being branded as 'difficult' or 'privileged' unless actively encouraged to exercise that choice.

It seems likely that most people living in an environment where staff will provide meals, cleaning, regular drinks and wash laundry will quite rapidly (and quite happily) become less active and independent. Who would choose to do for oneself what others will do for them? No doubt there are many elderly people for whom this amount of care is an attractive option. Many others, however, who would welcome having help with self-care tasks, which because of increasing physical infirmity are becoming difficult to manage, would prefer to retain as much of their independence as possible and live in their own home. But in the United Kingdom, our current approach to caring for elderly people as they become physically frail is to look for the right match along a kind of conveyor belt of different services to meet increasing levels of dependency (Harris and Kelly, 1986).

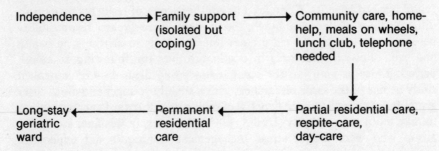

However, by making the kinds of support in the community flexible enough to meet all kinds of needs at all times of the day, night or weekend, then the numbers of people who would require residential care or hospital care could be substantially reduced, as case management schemes have demonstrated. In fact, even very severely dependent people who would be too handicapped for a residential home like Hawthorne House have been enabled to live out their lives in their own homes when they have wanted to do so. Knowing that comprehensive support services were available and that the above model of care need not apply, would help many more elderly people reluctant to enter residential care to choose instead to stay at home.

THE KENT/GATESHEAD COMMUNITY CARE SCHEME

An elderly person with disabilities which make some self-care, self-catering or household management tasks difficult clearly needs assistance. If the individual is keen to stay in their own home, then just what assistance they need in order to do so needs to be worked out in detail form the viewpoint of the elderly person. The approach to the Kent/Gateshead community care scheme does not start by considering which of the existing support services (meals-on-wheels, home-help, district nursing, etc.) would be helpful and then attempt to fit the person into this pattern of provision. Rather, it begins with a consideration of the person's own family and neighbourhood supports and whether with co-ordination and support these sources of assistance could be strengthened. And if support is needed that relatives, friends or neighbours cannot or do not wish to provide, or of a kind which falls outside the existing services, this can be provided by a specially recruited helper. If the assistance most needed is more for physical aids or minor adaptations to the home these can be purchased from the community care budget. The scheme aims to solve a range of care problems which might otherwise precipitate an admission to residential care. These were summarised by Luckett and Chessum (1985) as follows:

1 Gaps in basic physical care: difficulties in preparing meals, getting in and out of bed, washing, dressing, toileting, taking medication, and so forth.
2 Gaps in health care: inappropriate use of drugs, untreated illness, lack of rehabilitation.
3 Loss of motivation or low morale arising from loss of family, deteriorating health, lack of social contacts.
4 Unacceptable level of burden on carers or on formal services leading to threatened withdrawal and breakdown.
5 The elderly person's refusal to accept the traditional services.
6 Certain 'risk' factors: for example, fear of falling, vulnerability to attack, loss of self-care abilities.

In other words, the community care service aims to bridge the gap which currently exists between the level of care provided by traditional community services, and the total care available in residential homes. Its key element is flexibility – about the kinds of tasks it undertakes, the hours it covers and the resources it is able to provide.

How the scheme works

The 'case management' approach to community care as pioneered by social workers in Thanet and Dover in Kent involves the decentralisation of control of resources to individual field workers so that they can develop individual packages of care. These case workers can then co-ordinate an effective and appropriate service to the individual. This has obvious advantages to the traditional approach in which each of the relevant organisations (working under their own co-ordinator) works independently from each other with the same client group: home-helps, meals-on-wheels, Age Concern, social work and district nursing. The combination of such services received by each individual is often to a large extent fortuitous. But the greatest resource of the community care scheme is the possibility of recruiting helpers from the local community to assist particular individuals in ways and at times not covered by existing services.

Thanet in Kent was the first area to implement this case management approach, initially as a three-year pilot project, in 1977. Its development was monitored by the Personal Social Services Research Unit at the University of Kent. Thanet is a seaside resort with the highest proportion of retired elderly people anywhere in the country. Many couples who choose to retire here do so because they have spent many holidays here in the past. This means that they are often moving many miles away from their former homes, friends and relatives. A common type of client of the Community Care Scheme (or CCS) in Thanet was a woman whose husband had died since moving there, whose main social contacts had been through her husband, who was not able to drive, who had become socially isolated, and who had herself become increasingly disabled. Thanet's meals-on-wheels service was only available three days a week, and the home-help service only operated in the mornings. Anyone who needed help to cope alone at home could not be supported by the traditional services either at weekends or on weekdays in the afternoon or evenings.

When an elderly person was brought to the attention of social services because their needs could not adequately be met by these existing services, the CCS workers would visit the individual to determine the kind of help needed and, if appropriate, offer their own support. They could draw on a special budget in which the expenditure on each client was not to exceed two-thirds of the cost of a residential ('Part III') placement. Project workers were free to use their budget to buy in the services of other helpers (existing services, neighbours or volunteers) in order to put together a package of care that was appropriate, acceptable to client and carers, and cost-effective (Saunders, 1982). In this approach, clients have a much greater role in determining their own future than is often possible, discussing with the social worker both the nature of the problem and the alternative solutions.

In 1981, the success of the Thanet project led to the appointment of a Community Care Organiser in Dover, who operated in a similar way to his colleagues in Thanet, but expanded his range of helpers to include existing voluntary agencies. His clients were as infirm as those helped in Thanet, and in describing the service which he offered in 1982 he gave an indication of its scope: a night sitting service, incontinence washing, giving prescribed medication on a rota with the district nurse, weekend meals, day-care in helpers' homes through to befriending and bereavement support (Saunders, 1982). Costs per client were on average under half the cost of 'Part III' placement. One of the advantages of the Dover service was that the co-ordinator and his one assistant were based in a large health centre in a central shopping area and helpers were regularly able to call in to discuss problems and progress.

The Gateshead scheme also began in 1981. Their team consisted of a team leader, senior social worker, two social workers, a research monitoring officer and a clerical officer (Challis et al., 1983). The team operated as a specialist unit, separate from other social work teams, and concerned only with vulnerable elderly people who were encountering difficulties in remaining in their own homes in one social services district. Like the Kent scheme, the budget restriction per client was two-thirds the cost of a residential placement. This costing had also to take into account all other social services help being supplied so that the total cost of a client to the department in any one week stayed within the limit.

The budgetary control of project workers not only allowed the response to the old person to be flexible from the beginning, but also allowed the worker to make continual detailed adjustments to the help given as the elderly person's circumstances changed. This could be done quickly with no time-consuming administrative procedures or reference to centralised control, because accountability was not attached to specific items of expenditure, but to overall expenditure (Challis *et al.*, 1983).

Examples of support provided

A good description of the many ways in which specially recruited helpers can support elderly people unable to carry out basic self-care tasks and maximise their control over their difficulties is provided by the research workers from Kent University who have monitored and evaluated the scheme (Challis *et al.*, 1988). They illustrate how by building up a trusting relationship, a helper can enable an individual to, say, overcome fears about attendance at a hospital clinic, possibly taking them in their own car. And how helpers with training in physiotherapy exercises can help the client regain or improve certain physical functioning. They describe some of the advice a trusted helper can offer, from the best ways of getting out of bed, how to fall more safely, or how best to minimise problems of incontinence. Their reports also offer advice to community care scheme co-ordinators in how to introduce a helper to a moderately or severely confused client; and in how to introduce their services to clients with psychiatric problems such as depression or schizophrenia (see also Challis and Davies, 1986). And they give practical tips like replacing an ordinary kettle with an automatic one if a client is forgetful in order to avoid the risk of its boiling dry. The evidence that this case management approach to care can prevent the need for institutional care of even the most severely disabled individuals is best illustrated by some case examples.

Mrs Glass

In Gateshead, in 1988, I met Mrs Glass, one of the first referrals to the service when it started, and described in Challis and his colleagues' article in 1983. She is now 75 years old, having retired from full-time work as an office manager at the age of 59 years because of worsening rheumatoid arthritis in the knee. She moved into more convenient housing and lived alone, able to look after herself for several years with the assistance of a weekly home-help. By the time she was 67, her mobility had deteriorated so that she really needed help every day. She frequently fell over, and required help from the district nurse in the mornings to get herself up and dressed. Following one short hospital admission to a geriatric ward while her daily home-help was on holiday, her GP advised her that she should seriously consider looking for nursing home or geriatric hospital ward care. Mrs Glass was appalled at such a prospect, telling her GP she would sooner die. However, although alert and intelligent, she was now bedfast, hardly able to use her hands, needing help to use the commode, dress herself, and even comb her hair. In this crisis situation, she was referred to the community care scheme. Her morale was extremely low, and she was sceptical that they could help her.

The CCS worker introduced Mrs Glass to a helper, Jan, with nursing experience, whose assistance would resolve the most urgent need for weekend commoding. The traditional services were able to cover Mrs Glass's needs at bedtime and during the day until mid-afternoon. The district nurse could help her to get up, toileted, washed, dressed and into her wheelchair in the morning. A home-help could come on weekdays to help her with her breakfast. Three days a week her lunches were provided by meals-on-wheels, two by the home-help. At weekends Mrs Glass used her attendance allowance to employ a helper at breakfast time, and neighbours often helped at lunchtime. But teatimes and early evenings could not be covered either by the home-help service, which was available mornings only, or by the nursing service where the day service ended at 4.00 p.m. and night staff did not come on duty until later in the evening. Jan also stepped in to help out at this time. Quite soon she persuaded Mrs Glass to move out of her cold bedroom into the warm, pleasant sitting room with access to both telephone and television.

In fact, this helper and client became very close. The heavy commitment required raised anxieties with CCS organizers at this stage who could see Jan taking on rather too much responsibility. They needed to introduce a second helper who could share the workload, but to do so with great care in order to avoid causing Jan to feel displaced. This was achieved and provided a stable pattern of care for three years. After 1985, the CCS helpers took over some of the lunchtime support previously given by the home-help service, and the late-evening getting ready for bed service of the district nurse. Seven CCS helpers were involved by 1988 and Mrs Glass had a good relationship with each of them.

When I met her she was cheerful and full of praise for the service, particularly valuing Jan's friendship, and becoming acquainted with Jan's relatives. She was able to keep abreast of the arrangements and any weekly variations, and passed messages from one helper to the next. Her greatest anxiety was that someone might fail to turn up, but the six years of unbroken support had done much to boost her confidence. She received visits from her brothers, from two former work colleagues and from neighbours. She enjoyed crosswords, memorising answers until her CCS helper arrived who could write them in. When a visitor was present she would have a cigarette.

Mrs Glass is an example of how it is possible to support even those people with excessive physical dependency needs, if they wish to live at home. However, she is a very unusual client in an extreme situation, and is also one of Gateshead's most expensive clients. It is not usual for so many different helpers to become involved with one client. However, even for Mrs Glass, institutional care would cost more.

Edith

I also met a community care client who was considerably physically disabled in Thanet. Edith answered the door of her specially adapted bungalow in her electric wheelchair. She showed me into her sitting room. She told me she had been fully independent until six years previously when she had suffered a stroke. Since then she had experienced increasing difficulty with movement, and became in need of a wheelchair. In the last two years she had found it impossible to get in and out of the chair, and her visiting medical specialist had told her she should seek more help. She was put in touch with the CCS team. The CCS organiser visited her and asked her what she needed help with. She was and remains adamant that she wants to stay in her own home and would not like to go into residential care. Her main problems in self-care were getting out of bed, to the toilet, and into her chair in the morning, and conducting the reverse process at night.

Two CCS helpers were currently helping her with this, one coming seven mornings and four evenings, the other covering the remaining three evenings. Edith would dress herself as far as she could while still in bed and eat her cereals which would have been left nearby the night before. And at night she again prepared as much as possible herself so that her helpers were able to do their work quickly. She did not like to be putting anyone to any trouble. She had difficulty in sleeping, so her helper usually made her a flask so she could drink tea and listen to the radio during her sleepless hours. She told me how delighted she was that her helpers were so happy to help and did not even seem to begrudge coming on Christmas Day. She could not speak highly enough of the scheme. Once in her chair, she was able to manage (if slowly) most other things herself despite her arthritic hands. She also had friends who visited occasionally, a niece who came to see her most weekends, and she went by ambulance once a month to a club for arthritis sufferers. She would talk to her neighbours by telephone, as they were all also disabled which made meeting them difficult. She told me that she was not really interested in going out more.

It is also possible to enable people coping with psychiatric difficulties as well as physical frailties to remain in their own home. I met one such client in Gateshead, another in Dover.

Betty

In Gateshead at their Wednesday lunch club I met Betty, an 88-year-old lady who was very confused because she suffered from senile dementia and was rather deaf. In recent years her physical health had also been poor. She had had home-help support for about ten years but in the last two years had needed more help since being treated in hospital for a burst ulcer. Hospital staff had been anxious about discharging her to her own home as it was clear that she was in the early stages of dementia and unlikely to be able to effectively monitor and control her own diet and medication as necessary for recovery. As another CCS client was receiving treatment on the same ward at the same time, the ward staff were aware of the service and able to contact CCS helpers directly.

When Betty returned home, the CCS assessments showed that she was depressed and lonely and not coping on her own at all. She was not bathing, doing housework or washing, nor was she able to handle money. A CCS helper was asked to visit Betty, initially to provide some company. But as the helper had nursing experience, she was also able to help out when Betty was discharged from hospital after another operation a short time later. The consequence of the physical difficulties were that Betty's walking was not steady enough to allow her to risk leaving the house. This was in one sense helpful to her prospects for remaining at home because she had been liable to wander and get lost.

Betty had very few visits from relatives. Only one of her two sons ever visited her and he only once or twice a year. However, her memory was now so poor that she may have had other visits of which she had no recollection. Her confusion was such that she was unable to understand the explanations given about CCS, and she believed that her helper was simply a new rather helpful neighbour. However, her mind was clear enough to respond to all enquiries about her needs to the effect that she did not wish to leave her own home or to go into residential care.

Mr and Mrs White

In Dover, the CCS organiser took me to visit Mr and Mrs White. Mr White was a friendly, articulate man who welcomed any opportunity to have an intelligent conversation. His wife was completely disabled by senile dementia, unable to do the most simple task for herself such as picking up fingers of bread to put into her mouth. She was doubly incontinent and a district nurse came daily to get her up, wash and dress her, and to put her to bed at night. Her husband prepared most of their meals and fed her. She was propped up in a chair in the sitting room when I visited. Mr White told me he wanted his wife to be able to stay with him at home, and had no wish for her to be taken into a nursing home or hospital. And although her continual 'speech' was unintelligible, he told me 'she's company just how she is'. A community care sitter came for one to two hours one afternoon a week so that he could go to the bank or do other errands, but in fact he was rather unsteady on his feet himself now and so preferred not to walk outside the house. The CCS 'sitter' visits were still felt to be important, however, so that at least they could 'see another face'.

Mr White had spent his working life in the insurance business, and so had provided quite well for his retirement. He could afford to pay someone to come in to do his gardening, and to send most of their washing to the laundry. Their regular CCS helper (June, see below, p.190) took their shirts home and ironed them. She also did most of their shopping, although some meat and groceries were ordered by Mr White and delivered by a local shop.

The couple had no local relatives who could call in to see them. A sister-in-law who had visited sometimes in the past had now become too old and frail herself. No neighbours called in to see them either, probably because they saw the great needs of the couple and feared they would become burdened if they were to become involved.

Recruiting clients

Both the Kent and Gateshead services rapidly reached their maximum caseload and their budget ceilings, and developed waiting lists. Admission to the schemes therefore began to operate much like that for residential homes. The team office in Gateshead kept a list of people needing community care which was monitored monthly. If a vacancy arose, a team meeting would decide which case would be accepted.

Most of the clients had had some experience of residential care – either a hospital or a residential home, perhaps after an illness or to give informal helpers a respite, and had decided it was not for them. They were at least 60 years of age with some kind of chronic disability. Sometimes their disabilities included dementia. In fact at one stage nearly one in three of the Gateshead clients were sufferers of dementia, although at the time of my visit the proportion was smaller. Such clients of course presented the team with particular difficulties, and some judgement often needed to be made about acceptable risk. Where there were anxieties about personal safety, precautions taken might include, for instance, switching off the mains electricity supply to the cooker to prevent the client from using it. Some aspects of independence may have had to be sacrificed in the interests of safety. Helping these clients could sometimes be less rewarding for helpers, who may have found that the client mistook them for someone else, or accused them of stealing their money, as well as causing them anxiety about their safety when on their own.

A first visit to a new referral by the CCS organiser included completing a questionnaire covering health, financial needs, management of daily living, housing circumstances, help and support received. Neighbours, friends and relatives were also spoken to about what they were happy to do and what they would prefer not to do any longer for their elderly friend. The community care organiser in Thanet maintains that experience has shown that relatives visit more often once they know that CCS has taken over the practical things. A relative may dread calling around if they suspect there may be a pile of laundry waiting, that the house will be in a mess, and her relative in need of a bath. A social call then becomes a whole day's work, and something to be avoided.

The average age of clients of the Thanet service was just over 80. Most were not mobile enough to go out of the house and had lost contact with their friends. Many had become quite socially isolated. At the first visit the CCS organiser would investigate potential and actual informal support. If, for instance, there was a church magazine on the table, he may ask the client if it would be all right with her if he asked the vicar if someone from the church might be able to do her shopping. Sometimes a small increase in social contact through such strategies could greatly improve a person's capabilities. Where some informal helpers were still available, the CCS organiser aimed, through patient, tactful negotiations with any friends, family or existing services which were currently helping the individual, to co-ordinate their efforts to the maximum benefit. This might have meant persuading them to alter what they were doing and when they were doing it, to increase their input or to decrease their frequent random visits in order to provide a more regular visiting pattern and high quality contact. All this needed to be achieved without interfering unreasonably in other people's lives and relationships and without making them feel displaced in their caring role. The gaps that were left would be those for which CCS would need to bring in their own helpers.

Recruiting helpers

Most of the additional help CCS clients needed involved personal assistance from caring people. The helpers recruited were predominantly local people with a caring motivation who had been judged by the scheme's staff to have the personal qualities to enable them to care in a neighbourly way for an elderly client (Luckett and Chessum, 1985). They did not need any formal qualifications related to caring, and very few had any. Nor did they necessarily need any previous experience. Their attitude to and support toward the concept of supporting frail elderly people to enable them to remain in their own homes was, however, important. Obviously, those who felt that the more disabled clients ought to be cared for in institutional settings would have been unsuitable.

Many helpers hear of the service through the existing network of helpers. In Dover they also increased their list of helpers by encouraging a local newspaper to write an article about them once every six months, and by advertising in local doctors' surgeries, libraries, the Volunteer Bureau, and through organisations such as Age Concern. Helpers in Kent, and initially in Gateshead, were paid a set fee for providing an agreed amount of care for a particular person, with no rigid prescription of hours or duties. Helpers therefore had considerable autonomy and were expected to exercise their discretion and initiative. It meant they could vary what they did from day to day, and fit in with what other carers might offer to do. The project social worker needed to keep a check on the arrangements to ensure that neither the client nor the helper were exploiting the relationship, and to ensure that the helper was not taking on too much work or worry, both of which might threaten the success of the arrangement.

The CCS organiser aimed to find helpers who were geographically as close as possible to their clients, partly because it made it a more neighbourly relationship, but also because it kept expenses to a minimum. But perhaps more important, during bad winter weather when visits were essential, it reduced the chance that the helper would be unable to get to the client's home. Helper and client were also matched as far as possible in personality, for instance, avoiding putting a particularly unassertive helper with a bossy client or vice versa, and by looking for factors which indicated that the two were likely to get on well. The helper also needed to be able to cope with the particular physical or emotional demands of the tasks, and sometimes proximity had to be sacrificed for a good match. Care also had to be taken, however, to avoid allocating to the most capable helpers too high a proportion of the most demanding and unrewarding clients.

Before taking on their own 'client', a new helper might accompany an established helper on one of her visits. He or she would also be offered some rudimentary training by the back-up service, especially for tasks involving lifting the elderly person. Some feedback from the client would be sought, about the quality and reliability of the help provided, and the organiser might also occasionally carry out unnotified visits to check on the arrangement.

The CCS organisers in Kent and Gateshead differed from each other in their approach to the employment of helpers. The co-ordinator in Dover preferred to have helpers who would support just one or two elderly people close to their own homes. Although a few of his helpers had a large number of clients and aimed to work full-time as carers, earning an economic wage from their role, this was not how he wanted the scheme to work. He would willingly employ pensioners to do just one or two visits a week, and his helpers ranged in age from 30 to nearly 70.

In Gateshead, the CCS organiser believed that helpers were entitled to a predictable and regular income and some sick and holiday pay if they worked at least 15 hours a week. However, she was also wary of taking on a helper who wanted to make the work so much like a regular job that they expected clear hours of work, as this would have made their aim to respond flexibly to client needs difficult to achieve. She therefore offered a contract to helpers working more than 15 hours a week, guaranteeing that she would employ them every week for that number of hours, but not necessarily at the same times or on the same days. In practice, few helpers wanted this contract, as they preferred to have the flexibililty to refuse a new client needing support at times of day that were not so convenient as a previous helping role had been. However, their helpers tended to be much younger than Kent helpers, predominantly aged 25 to 45, and more reliant on the income. One helper who wanted, and received, this guarantee of regular employment was Jan.

A CCS helper in Gateshead

Jan was one of the first helpers recruited to the community care scheme in 1981. She had begun by supporting one elderly man, spending a total of seven hours a week with him. Her involvement had steadily increased and she was currently working 34 hours in supporting four clients and helping each day at the lunch club. Two of her clients were those described above, Mrs Glass and Betty. Each client lived a short car journey distant. Jan described to me how her time was spent.

Each day was different, but on a Tuesday, for instance, she began with a visit to Betty. They would chat while Jan helped her to bath, and while Jan then tidied and washed up. She would also go to collect Betty's pension and shopping. At the beginning of their friendship, Betty was able to walk with Jan to the shops and the hairdressers, but her mobility was now too poor. Instead Jan sometimes took her out by car, and would do her hair for her at home. After leaving Betty, Jan was free until four o'clock in the afternoon, when she was expected at Mrs Glass's home. She would spend one-and-a-half hours there, and they would do crosswords together while Jan prepared the tea. Jan then drove the short distance back to her own home to prepare tea for her teenage sons. At 10 p.m. she went again to Mrs Glass's house for half an hour to settle her for the night.

A CCS helper in Dover

I met one of the helpers in the Kent scheme who described how her time was spent. She had three CCS clients – a married couple both aged 88 who lived in her street (Mr and Mrs White, see above, p.186), and a single lady of 89 who lived a five-minute walk away. Neither had any regular visitors other than paid services. She was also supporting another neighbour of 81 years 'off my own back', receiving no payment for this as the elderly man was not a CCS client. She was paid to do an average of one visit a day to give 'social support' to each of her two CCS households, seven days a week. At £3.50 per visit, she earned £49.00 each week (1988). In practice, she put in much more time than she was paid for. This was partly because she felt she could be most helpful if she visited each house twice a day rather than once in order to help plan and prepare the two main meals. She would stay about 40 minutes (once between 10 a.m. and 12 noon, once between 4 p.m. and 6 p.m.). In addition, she would sometimes prepare extra portions of her own family meals (which of course she would have paid for herself), and reheat them in her microwave to take them over hot. She also brought ironing home with her.

During visits to Mr and Mrs White, she would discuss with Mr White what they would eat for their next meal, and sometimes stay to help feed Mrs White. She had been visiting them for five-and-a-half years and admitted to being very involved with them. She had also begun visiting Mrs Spencer five months previously since her partner had died after which she had become extremely depressed and withdrawn. June's main role here was to try to help Mrs Spencer regain her interest in life and learn to cope with her new circumstances and drop in income. (As her partner was not married to her, his pensions had died with him.)

The Wednesday Lunch Club

One of the commonest worries about clients referred to the CCS was that the individual was neglecting their diet. This was not always because of their physical frailty making cooking difficult or hazardous, or because of their confused state of mind. Frequently depression played a major role. Many depressed elderly people live alone, and have no desire to prepare solitary meals. Often they have neither appetite for nor interest in food anyway. For these old people, providing meals-on-wheels or even home-cooked meals does not overcome the problem. An early solution for the Gateshead team was to bring a few clients together in a helper's home one lunchtime a week to stimulate their interest in food and improve their diet. It meant that several clients at once could be encouraged to eat a meal, but meetings had other far-reaching benefits for the clients. Many elderly people become artificially housebound because they have nowhere to go, are afraid of falling, or have no transport. Then with few social contacts, some gradually lose interest in self-care and their appearance. Informal lunchtime meetings helped all these problems. The clients often looked out their best clothes for the event, and made sure they looked well groomed. In fact, this had further spin-off benefits for the CCS scheme. It helped to increase trust in the helper–client relationship, and made clients more likely to take up offers of help in bathing or hairdressing, particularly on the day before a lunch meeting. The gentle reintroduction to socialising greatly improved morale and in some instances encouraged clients to take up other day activities (such as going to day-centres) which had previously been seen as too demanding, risky, overpowering or frightening.

At first, three or four people met in the helper's home. However, most helpers had homes with upstairs toilets and many elderly people had difficulty climbing stairs. One small group continued, but clients in another district met instead in a larger group in a neighbourhood centre. The larger group usually consisted of ten elderly people who met each Wednesday from 11 a.m. to 3 p.m. They were driven there by a volunteer who had been obliged, by local authority policy, to retire from paid work for CCS at the age of 65 years. He now used his own car to transport the group members, and he received only his expenses in return. Three helpers made lunch and organised social activities. A physiotherapist came for half an hour and tried to encourage the group to participate in a few exercises. Most of the group members lived alone and had severe mobility problems, limiting their capacity for going out of their home either to socialise or shop.

Evaluation

As a real alternative to residential care for frail elderly people, CCS has clearly been highly successful. When the Gateshead scheme began, it accepted 60 referrals in the first 18 months, and this was reflected in a dramatic reduction in the division's waiting lists for residential vacancies. In fact, the division drew up plans for alternative uses of some of the beds. Only two of the 60 old people needed to be admitted into residential care, the other 58 being maintained at home until they died or needed hospital care (Challis et al., 1983). However, as the budget for the scheme did not grow substantially, a waiting list soon built up. This in turn caused the waiting list for residential beds to begin to grow again. It would appear that without an increasing level of financial support, the scheme may have only temporarily taken the pressure off the residential service.

In fact, by 1988 the demand for CCS in Thanet was considerably greater than the service availability. One hundred clients in Thanet were being supported by CCS, but 20 further referrals remained on the waiting list because of lack of money. Some of these were being supported by friends or neighbours until CCS could take over. Others were paying for temporary private help until their money ran out or CCS took over. Others were unworried, but their neighbours were extremely anxious about their safety. Still others were waiting in residential care but were desperate to return home. Of course, 20 names on a waiting list was not an accurate indication of unmet need. Many other cases were not being formally referred once it became known that there was already a considerable waiting list.

Table 1 Outcome of follow-up of CCS clients in Kent

		After 1 year	After 3 years
Remaining in their own home	CCS clients	69%	35%
	comparison group	34%	12%
Entered local authority homes	CCS clients	4%	22%
	comparison group	22%	31%
Died	CCS clients	14%	32%
	comparison group	33%	53%
		(N=74)	(N=74)

Challis and Davies (1985) report the first results of the 'quasi-experimental' evaluation of the Kent service. Cases receiving CCS support were matched one-to-one with similar cases from adjacent areas receiving standard services. Independent assessment interviews were undertaken with elderly people and their carers immediately prior to receipt of the service, and these interviews were repeated after one year. Seventy-four pairs, client and comparison cases were identified, matched by factors likely to be predictors of survival in the community: age, sex, living group (household composition), presence of confusional state, physical disability, and receptivity to help.

The results, as shown in Table 1, were impressive, clearly showing the effectiveness of the scheme in enabling people to remain in their own homes.

No differences between the two groups were found which were likely to be associated with survival chances, such as functional status, incontinence, poor memory, or other correlates of organic brain disease. If anything, the CCS group showed a higher degree of frailty. However, a higher proportion of CCS clients than the comparison group were in hospital care after three years: 8 per cent against 1 per cent. This was to be expected as they lived at home often until too frail for residential care to be a realistic option. The low number of the comparison group in hospital after three years does not accurately reflect the numbers of this group receiving long-term hospital care, however, as 5 per cent had been admitted to hospital within the first year and three of these four elderly people died before the end of the third year.

Challis and Davies attribute the superior survival rate of CCS clients primarily to the fact that fewer needed to move out of their own homes.

Fifteen CCS clients moved into care in the first year and three died soon afterwards. Thirteen of the 32 comparison group who went into care died within the year. However, these authors also attribute improved survival to the protective effect of the social support given to CCS clients, whose help had provided emotional and social support as well as practical assistance.

> At follow-up, survivors living in their own homes were asked whether they had anyone in whom they could confide. Whereas 58 per cent of the comparison group could not identify a confidante, only 15 per cent of the community care group felt this to be the case. Much of this difference was accounted for by the greater number of community care cases who would confide in their social worker or scheme helper.
>
> (Challis and Davies, 1985)

Other comparisons showed equally marked benefits for CCS clients compared to those receiving standard care. The quality of life of the individuals improved significantly more for CCS clients in terms of morale, depressed mood, loneliness and 'felt capacity to cope'. For those with an identifiable carer (about one in four), the support of the CCS helper had brought the carer a considerably reduced sense of strain and burden. It had also to some extent reduced the disruption to their social lives and household routines. There was no evidence that CCS caused informal helpers to provide less, however. In fact in some cases the presence of additional support seemed to be a factor which made carers less likely to give up.

The Gateshead service has also been evaluated through a comparison of matched pairs (Challis et al., 1988). The CCS scheme operated in two of the six social services districts and comparison cases were drawn from three of the other areas. Both samples came from both inner- and outer-city districts. As in the evaluation of the Kent service, independent interviews were conducted either immediately before receipt of community care or as soon as they were identified as suitable high-need comparison cases, and matched on factors likely to be associated with the outcome of care. The interviews were repeated after one year, and costs over the period were monitored. Ninety pairs were studied, each of whom faced extreme difficulties in coping at home, despite the input of services, and for each, residential or long-term hospital care was a realistic consideration. The comprehensive assessments which had been developed by the CCS team were used, and these took into account the circumstances of the elderly person, their carers, any formal services received, an evaluation of risk and of the individual's retained abilities or strengths.

The circumstances of elderly people in Gateshead differ in many ways from those of elderly people in Kent, not least because they are much less likely to have chosen to move there after retirement age. This meant that many more had an identifiable principal carer (about two-thirds). The Gateshead CCS therefore worked more with carers. Carer stress was a serious problem in nearly half the CCS cases, and traditional services tended not to offer help to carers. Yet with the right kind of help, some carers were willing and able to maintain their very dependent relatives at home until the end of their lives.

In fact only 1 per cent of the CCS clients in Gateshead were in a residential home after one year, compared with 39 per cent of those who received the usual range of services, an even better result than in Kent in this respect. However, the finding in the Kent study of a higher survival rate of CCS clients was not replicated. Perhaps this reflects the more extensive natural support available to the comparison group in Gateshead than in Kent, reducing group differences in the latter region, or the fact that clients of the Gateshead service tended to have a greater level of dependency than clients of the Kent service. The CCS sample showed considerable improvements in depressed mood, loneliness, social visits and satisfaction with life compared to the comparison group.

A breakdown of outcomes was analysed according to whether the old people stayed at home or went into care. It was found that clients staying at home and receiving CCS *or* going into a residential home experienced considerable benefits. Those staying in their own homes but receiving standard services were those who fared badly, and it was concluded that 'for this highly dependent population the standard range of domiciliary services, despite the best efforts of those involved in providing them, is insufficient to meet their needs' (Challis *et al.*, 1988). The pattern was the same in terms of benefit to informal carers, their practical stresses being reduced whether the elderly person received CCS or went into a home. However, considerable guilt was often felt by carers when an old person went into a home, which was not experienced in relation to CCS.

Cost

The service is costed against a 'Part III' bed, that is, a place in a local authority home for elderly people, which in January 1988 was roughly £112 a week in Kent, £120–£130 per week in Gateshead. The CCS is seen as an alternative to the 'Part III' bed and this therefore sets the background against which expenditure is viewed. The target is to keep the cost per person down to a maximum of two-thirds of this, i.e. £70 in Kent, £82 in Gateshead, although occasionally they will spend more. In fact, Thanet's average cost per client was well below this, at £48 per week. The more physically disabled clients, the more confused clients, and those without existing caring networks tend also to be the most expensive clients for CCS to help. Where, for instance, help is limited only to relief sitting to enable a relative to have an evening 'off', the service will be very cheap. This means, however, that there will be difficult choices when there is little spare money in the CCS budget. The lady who already has a good deal of informal support who is a low-cost potential client will probably be accepted, at least in Kent, rather than a referral who needs more support from CCS helpers. The latter client would then have to apply instead for a residential placement which is of course much more expensive, but which was in 1988 funded from a different budget.

CCS is not entirely free to the client. In Thanet, clients were asked to pay £4.90 per week (January 1988 prices), unless they were already paying toward a home-help service.

The CCS budget in Dover was £59,000 in 1987, but cut to £52,000 for 1988. With this, the CCS organiser and his assistant maintained 58 clients. They had 115 helpers on their books, and several voluntary agencies. Not all of these were currently active as helpers. The Gateshead service had 80 to 90 helpers for their 55 to 60 clients. Five or six worked a 39-hour week, a further 20 worked between 15 and 30 hours, while the largest number worked for fewer than 15 hours a week.

The evaluation by Challis and Davies (1985) costed the care provided for the CCS sample over their first year against the comparison group. There was very little difference overall, the CCS sample costing slightly less per month of survival, but costing slightly more over the year because more of them survived. Their support cost the social services department less, both monthly and annually, and the NHS less monthly, but because of their longevity, the NHS costs averaged more over the year. This was not from greater use of long-stay beds, but from a more frequent use of domiciliary and acute services. In fact in the care of very dependent people, the CCS appeared to be a substitute for long-term hospital care, producing cost-savings to the health service for these patients. But Challis and Davies argue that the more appropriate and important question to answer is not 'Is this care cheaper?', but 'For whom is this mode of care the most cost-effective response and the best use of resources?' This requires a consideration of outcomes alongside costs, and their analysis showed two groups of people for whom the service was particularly cost-effective, for social services departments and for society.

> The first [group] was the extremely dependent elderly person with both mental and physical frailty who receive a considerable degree of informal support. The second group was the relatively isolated elderly person, with only a moderate degree of dependency, suffering from a non-psychotic psychiatric disorder, people whose difficulties may be particularly likely to remain undetected in usual circumstances.
>
> (Challis and Davies, 1985)

The evaluation of the Gateshead service also found that the cost to the social services department for providing community care was no more or less than the standard provision to the comparison group. The cost to the NHS was also similar, except for those comparison group cases who lived in an inner-city area who had confusional states and carers under stress. For them the NHS costs were *cheaper* if they didn't receive CCS, presumably because their needs were not met. Further analyses will reveal more precisely which elderly people can derive most benefit from CCS so that future schemes can be targeted most effectively. However, it may be concluded that the considerable benefits in terms of lower rates of admission to institutional care and improved welfare of elderly people and their families can be achieved at no greater cost over one year than the standard provision.

SUMMARY

This chapter focused on elderly people who have reached a crisis point in their home lives: they are unable to care adequately for themselves at home any longer because of physical or mental infirmity, and their needs cannot be met satisfactorily either by traditional home support services or by informal carers. It is a crisis more likely to occur in old age than at younger ages and is a situation often feared by elderly people. Decisions made at this time about how their needs are to be met can potentially affect the individual's vulnerability to mental illness for the rest of their life, and may shorten or prolong life expectancy. Provision of care in a home for elderly people or a hospital ward is sometimes the option preferred by the individual, and current research and the climate of opinion support the view that these institutional settings should be managed in ways which maximise individual autonomy, choice, dignity and privacy. One home which has successfully implemented 'resident-oriented' regimes has been described above. However, it appears that physical design features of the home (such as individual bedsitters rather than individual bedrooms) play an important role in shaping both staff and resident attitudes to resident autonomy. In addition, making choices must be actively encouraged by staff; it is not enough that choices exist.

Most people, given the choice between a home for elderly people and staying in their own home with help and support choose the latter. (Other possibilities, including sheltered housing with warden support, may some-times be preferable to either, but are not described here.) With a case management approach to community care, even the most disabled individuals can remain in their own homes if this is what they choose to do, and this approach has been described above. Whether disabilities are moderate or severe, a home support service based on what the individual feels is needed and in the way he or she chooses to receive it will have beneficial effects over the often piecemeal support of traditional service provision. It should help to preserve a sense of control, autonomy and choice. It has been shown to improve depressed mood, loneliness and satisfaction with life among clients compared to clients of traditional home support services, and to reduce the stress experienced by informal carers.

The community care scheme was considered by an evaluation team to be most appropriate for extremely disabled people who already have a good deal of informal support, and for less disabled clients who are isolated and depressed. Long-term support from one or more specially recruited local people can bring valued friendships as well as practical assistance.

The community care scheme is a good example of a service which fulfils all three criteria for good practice suggested at the beginning of this review. It targets a vulnerable group, focuses on maximising their control over their own lives and their self-esteem, and makes the maximum use of the existing natural and community support networks.

Conclusions: Prospects, pitfalls and possibilities

This book is the result of the second stage of a prevention research project commissioned by MIND. The first stage was a literature review which drew conclusions about where the best hopes for social strategies for prevention should lie on the basis of research on the prevalence, distribution, cause and course of disorders such as depression and schizophrenia. A brief overview of experimental social interventions aiming to prevent either a first onset or a recurrence of disorder was also given, along with a description of the evidence of their success.

Many of the pointers for prevention arising from that review were for actions already covered, to some extent, by existing services. This is not surprising given the social factors linked to depression: long-term social difficulty, traumatic events, poor parenting, pre-marital pregnancy, institutional care, and so on. A large range of services, projects, and voluntary groups have been established to offer support for people in such situations. The aim of this second review was therefore to look afresh at existing services from the point of view of their potential contribution to the prevention of psychiatric disorder, and to describe those which seem particularly promising in these terms.

Of course some services and projects of these kinds will grow willy-nilly – those which catch the imagination or public sympathy, where it is clear that something is needed, or those which are set up by a charismatic leader with enthusiasm for the approach, and which, perhaps, seem to fit well with the priorities of funding agencies. And sometimes these services in a sense develop a life of their own – once set up they are difficult to change. Increasingly, however, there is a demand for evidence of effectiveness, and given the limited funds available for support programmes for vulnerable groups, an ethical argument can be made for evaluation of effectiveness. The focus in this review has been on effectiveness in terms of preventing psychiatric disorder, and on this basis the projects are judged as being 'good' practice. However, it is not the purpose of a review such as this to conclude by arguing for more widespread implementation (even if humanitarian concerns leave this hope in mind). Preventing psychiatric disorder is only one aspect (and for some, a narrow aspect) of what they are trying to achieve.

But given that planners and practitioners need to make decisions about priorities for action, it is essential to maintain a continuing dialogue between research and practice. And a regular appraisal of its potential for prevention should at least help to strengthen the coherence of a growing service. These beliefs underpin this review, and the aim has been to bring together some of the conclusions arising from the research with what is going on in the field in relation to preventing mental illness. Much aetiological research and theory are not tested in experimental programmes or translated into practical recommendations and, equally, service development often seems to pay scant regard to research insights (even from evaluative data from similar enterprises). Bringing the two sides together reveals a number of valuable lessons about both.

In this chapter, I draw some brief conclusions about aspects of service delivery that appear to be particularly important in contributing to effectiveness, and raise some questions about certain aspects of current mental health care planning. What emerges, I feel, from a study of the approaches described in this review is the relative ease with which vulnerable people can be identified, and how it often seems quite straightforward to specify what needs to change in order to help them become less vulnerable. Providing something that will be acceptable to them, and that they will find helpful, is less straightforward, but quite feasible. Particularly important, in this respect, is the client's own role in specifying the kind of help needed, and in bringing about the desired changes. The greatest challenge, however, is in demonstrating that even the most carefully planned service, using strategies that research has clearly indicated as likely to reduce risk (whether of depression, acute psychosis, child neglect or other potential outcome), can actually produce those benefits. The crucial importance of bringing research and practice together in this field is clear. We will learn more about prevention from experimental epidemiology and long-term in-depth service evaluation, than from either aetiological research or evaluation of practice in limited terms alone.

What also emerges, is the way in which services will need to make some fundamental changes in their relationships with other agencies if they are to become more effective in their preventive role. Greater collaboration and liaison will be needed between voluntary groups and professionals, between primary and secondary care workers, and between professionals and clients. Such changes will also have implications for diffusing skills.

FACTORS INFLUENCING EFFECTIVENESS

Politics and new developments in services

Many people in caring professions are motivated in their work by helping distressed or ill people to resolve their difficulties and/or get well, through changes that are visible to client and provider alike. Preventive work does not have this kind of immediate reward, and can be experienced as less satisfying and less important. With heavy demands on a practitioner's time from people with marked difficulties, it is understandable that in many services prevention receives a lower priority, particularly where, as is usual, success is invisible and difficult to measure.

A financial inducement has been used in primary care services to help shift this balance, and the 1990 contract for general practitioners sets fees for immunisation targets, targets for preventive screening (for cervical cancer), and for health promotion checks. This has greatly increased activity focusing on the potential for preventive work in general practice, but it needs to be noted that both the strategy and the work resulting from it are very largely aimed at physical rather than mental health. There is potential, however, for interested practices to increase their activity and obtain financial support for their work in the mental health area: the changes accompanying the contract have brought a relaxation of regulations determining the kinds of ancillary staff whose salary is eligible for reimbursement (at 70 per cent) by the family health service authorities; and the post-graduate allowance for general practitioners is linked to a minimum number of sessions of further training. It follows that practices can now more easily employ counsellors, and general practitioners may choose to obtain further training on matters relating to mental health care along the lines suggested in Chapter 3. There is also the possibility that in the longer term, the changes may bring benefits to mental health care even among those currently without much interest in this part of their work. The focus on prevention will require more collaborative work practices, decisions on priorities for the team, close monitoring of the health and health needs of the client group, and measures of their effectiveness, and this may bring mental health issues more to the fore.

Other recent political moves relevant to the mental health prevention strategies described in earlier chapters include the 1989 Children Act, the Griffiths Report (1988), and the NHS Community Care Act of 1990. The Children Act includes advice to local authorities that they should more fully involve children in their care in decisions about them, and that they should provide adequate support until they reach 19 years. The Griffiths Report made a number of recommendations about the way much social care is funded, which has been taken up in legislation, including the NHS Community Care Act. In particular, these changes should remove the conflict for social workers and others in their decisions about the kind of care which is suitable for an individual or family, and the source of funds for this. For instance, the choice between a hostel and bed-and-breakfast accommodation for young families, or between accommodation in a home for elderly people, hospital or at home with social services support was sometimes influenced by budgetary considerations, not because the chosen option was cheaper, but because it could be paid from a different budget in which there was greater flexibility.

Other kinds of 'political' concerns may affect preventive services too. For instance, media interest in child abuse can influence social services departments in their allocation of funds to client groups. Services for children are more likely to be well-funded than those for elderly clients or people with mental health problems, for instance. Deaths among the latter groups would be less publicly noticeable as they are less likely to be assumed to be preventable.

Both time constraints and financial restrictions may limit preventive work. The provision of supportive hostel accommodation for pregnant young women from disadvantaged backgrounds (such as St Michael's, Chapter 2) is reliant on the ability and willingness of the social services to pay the fees. Financial limitations have meant that the client group now served (1990 onwards) by St Michael's have greater difficulties than those of earlier years (only the more severe cases will be supported by social service grants). They are now more likely to be women who have already developed worrying parenting difficulties, whose children are on the 'at risk' register, or who are known to have had other major difficulties like abusive family backgrounds, or a violent partner. This is a clear shift toward dealing with existing difficulties rather than the previously preventive emphasis. It would be surprising if women with more problems were not at greater risk (of mental health difficulties, or neglecting or abusing their children); and given this, the change might be presumed to be a more cost-effective use of resources. Equally, it can be argued that women with problems linked only to a background of poor parenting, depression, and an absence of current social or practical support will be helped sufficiently by such intervention to make a real difference to their vulnerability for some time to come.

Does the service ensure it supports the intended client group?

It is widely understood that services set up to meet the needs of one client group often find themselves, after a time, serving a rather different group. This shift may be for positive reasons – that other groups have been identified as having similar needs, and providers step in to fill a perceived gap in services. It may also be explainable in more negative terms – that the intended client group are difficult to recruit, might have entrenched long-term problems, and offer less job satisfaction to carers in their efforts to help them. Part of 'good practice' would be a clear policy statement that included a description of the needs of the client group, what the service was intended to help them with, and how. In order to ensure care continues to go to those for whom it is intended, a service would need to establish a means of self-monitoring.

A well-documented example of what happens without gate-keeping and monitoring mechanisms is the Community Mental Health Centres movement (Levine, 1981; Leighton, 1982; Brown, P., 1985). Boardman and colleagues (1987) have described a typical pattern in which the community team who develop an expertise in supporting discharged patients with chronic difficulties gradually shift toward spending most of their time seeing a less severely or chronically ill client group. They evaluated one of the longest running Community Mental Health Centres in Britain which had a 'walk-in' service to which a large number of people were referred, usually by their family doctor. This produced a substantial rise in new patients, primarily seeking counselling. New referrals continued at a high rate, year by year. The new client group obviously consumed considerable professional resources, counselling being provided by CPNs, social workers, a psychologist or psychiatrist. While initially a new service like this one can cope, and shows benefits in terms of reduced referrals to out-patient departments and admissions, after a time it becomes swamped. When this happens, many referrals are sent on elsewhere and a proportion of clients, particularly those with long-term problems and those most severely ill, are referred back to hospital departments.

A similar observation was made by Brown and colleagues (1966), who documented how people chronically and severely handicapped by symptoms of schizophrenia often in time dropped out of a service set up specifically to cater for them, and the community workers tended to visit those who wanted to be visited. In the United States, these factors have contributed to growing numbers of people with long-term mental health problems seen in nursing homes, boarding houses or on the streets (Brown, P., 1985). Despite the awareness, among managers and staff of the new CMHCs being established in Britain, of this tendency for care to drift away from clients with chronic and severe problems, almost none of them have set up a caseload monitoring system geared to checking this (Patmore and Weaver, 1991).

However, before a gate-keeping system can be established, a service obviously needs to have carefully specified their target group, and to have set up a service which provides resources which match their needs. It is also important to appoint a manager *before* the service begins to recruit clients so that they can ensure the service develops along the lines intended (Patmore and Weaver, 1991). Although this may seem self-evident, many services become operational in a piecemeal fashion which can allow conflicting practices to become established. Also important, if drift toward doing what staff enjoy most is not to work against service aims, is to attend to the issue of staff motivation and morale.

Not only must the service avoid recruiting too many clients who are not part of the target group, but it must ensure it recruits as many as possible who *are* part of the target group, and that they remain involved for long enough to benefit. This suggests that services will often need to establish appropriate means of 'outreach', and to be prepared to meet clients in the setting most acceptable to them.

The projects and services described in this review fulfil these basic requirements of good practice. They work with clearly defined client groups, design the support specifically to their needs, have managers who ensure the focus remains with the client group, and/or financial constraints acting against catering for additional groups, have outreach mechanisms to recruit those people for whom the support is intended but may not otherwise receive it, and deliver support in appropriate settings. The notable exception is the provision in general practice; unlike the other services it is generic, and does not work with a specified client group with specific needs, and the issues faced are therefore quite different.

Are the intended methods correctly implemented?

Political factors and aspects of service planning and management influence the effectiveness of a service in their aim of supporting a particular client group. However, it must also be clear what the service is aiming to change, and how, and that the people involved in offering support fully understand and agree with these goals. (It goes without saying that the goals must also have been carefully considered as feasible, equitable, and matching need, etc.). Mechanisms are needed to ensure that as well as working with the intended clients, the providers also continue to offer support in the way intended.

Some of the provision described in the central chapters did not have goals which were as well defined as they might have been. And some of those with clear goals did not ensure as well as they might that workers were providing support in the way intended. For instance, the Child Development Programme (Chapter 1) has clearly specified goals, for a clearly specified client group, and guidelines on how these should be achieved. Nevertheless, individual workers varied considerably in their practice, even though they might voice support for the avowed approach, to have understood what it entailed, and even believed that they were working in the way intended. Dixon (1986b) made a similar observation about the way residential homes for elderly people were run in Wiltshire. One manager who had emphasised during the interview that both she and her staff aimed to maximise the independence and autonomy of their resident group was described. However, her interpretation of what this meant varied substantially from that of the research workers. Believing it important for individual autonomy to have a private room, she denied the request of two women arriving together to share a room (which they had done for many years previously), causing them considerable distress. Believing that it was important for residents to contribute to domestic tasks, she insisted that everyone contribute to clearing up after meals (even if so severely disabled that carrying items of cutlery across the room was as much as they could do). Encouraging independence had essentially been translated back into a 'we know best' policy.

Monitoring systems should therefore include an examination of work styles as well as client group characteristics. But does this then ensure client benefit?

Attending to detail – quality issues

Unfortunately, even appropriate targeting of care and careful ongoing training for workers does not necessarily ensure that the service will bring the expected benefits. However, those with the means to gain evaluative data on their effectiveness will be better able to modify their approach to improve the service. If they are capable of being, and willing to be flexible in their strategies, the quality of the service can be much enhanced.

For instance, the evaluation of the 'psychoeducation' service in Birmingham (Chapter 4), found that nearly one in three people being treated for schizophrenia turned down the offer of education and support from the psychologists. Exploring the reasons for this led the psychologists to set up staff training days to ensure that patients and their relatives received more consistent advice and information, and to extend their service to facilitate closer working links with other agencies in the community through which they could reach their client group. And they have evaluated different approaches to providing information to clients and their families (in groups, by post, from videotapes) to enable them to make decisions about whether their methods could be improved. Their outcome evaluation has revealed many benefits for the daily lives of clients and their families. It has not, however, proved that the rate of relapse has been reduced by their intervention.

Evaluation of Newpin (Chapter 1) has also provided valuable insights into the way in which it could improve its effectiveness. It was found that the organisation was successful in reaching and engaging their target group (Cox et al., 1990). The ongoing support and training ensure that befrienders maintain the intended style of support. And the evaluation has indicated that the benefits to client women are greatest for those who remain involved the longest (Cox et al., 1990). However, a newly trained befriender, still usually learning much about her own difficulties, may be less supportive in a first friendship than in later ones. (Two women who talked to me indicated that they had initially found it difficult to offer emotional support.) In some instances the friendship may not become established sufficiently to encourage a new client to come to the Newpin centre, and if there is no other follow-up support, then these women will slip through the Newpin net. This has implications for the level of supervision needed for women beginning their role as a befriender.

The evaluation showed that there were considerable benefits for the mental health of the women involved in Newpin. However, it did not find conclusive evidence to demonstrate that the benefits gained by women were reflected in improvements in their parenting, and the possibility remains open that to achieve this goal fully, additional specific work on parent–child relationships may be needed.

In projects where the managers are not the innovators of the approach, but are attempting to replicate an intervention demonstrated elsewhere to be effective, and where they have not had the benefits of direct involvement in a service evaluation, it is likely to be more difficult for them to attend to such issues of detail. The support group for relatives of individuals suffering from schizophrenia (Chapter 4) was implementing an approach of demonstrated effectiveness, and working with the client groups, goals and methods described in the literature. However, the social workers received minimal training and no support from psychiatric services staff. The lack of guidelines suggest that the project will in all probability lose some of the specific concerns about the daily lives of the individual experiencing symptoms of schizophrenia which characterise the research. Inevitably this will affect its effectiveness in preventive terms. It could be argued that clinical psychology services should provide much greater support for these kinds of initiatives, whether they are based in social services departments, or voluntary organisations.

Can the service be proved to have prevented anything?

These discussions help to explain why evaluating services is so problematic, and why so frequently, the results are disappointing. It may be straightforward to look at who is, and who is not receiving the service, and why. It is more complex to examine whether or not workers are providing support in the way intended, and to what extent appropriate support is meeting the immediate needs of the client in the way intended. (For instance, information may be provided, but is it understood?) Studies sometimes conclude that an intervention is ineffective when a closer examination of what was actually happening would have shown that where it was operating as intended, it was successful, and negative effects were explainable in terms of faults in the way in which the method was applied rather than faults in the method itself.

What is most troublesome to measure is the extent to which the service is actually achieving its goals in relation to prevention. Central problems are:

first, that it is usually extremely difficult to establish with any certainty what would have happened to clients without the intervention; and second, that many benefits do not become apparent until long after the intervention took place. No doubt an evaluation of help given by schools to young people with a poor level of parental care would have concluded that they derived little or no benefit (in terms of self-esteem) from their time at school, compared to many of their peers. Yet several years later, Quinton and colleagues (1984) were able to demonstrate a subtle but important role that school experiences had played for some of them, in terms of helping them to plan their lives. Similarly, evaluation of the pre-school compensatory educational programmes set up in the United States also showed that the benefits of the programme appeared to 'wash out' in the months following the end of the intervention. Yet some years later, further follow-ups revealed lasting effects (Lazar et al., 1982).

Rigorous evaluation of services is rare in the field of preventive mental health care, and the research on Newpin and the Birmingham 'psycho-education' project are extremely unusual in the close scrutiny which they have undergone. With carefully planned and managed services such as these, they will undoubtedly continue to refine their strategy. There are subtle issues of quality of service content and delivery which will finally determine whether a good idea based on relevant research can translate into a service which can achieve its aims. It behoves research workers to address those issues fully, and to monitor outcomes over a period sufficiently long for effects to become clear, before coming to conclusions about benefit.

POSSIBILITIES: LESSONS ABOUT METHOD

Helping people to take control over their lives

A consistent theme throughout this review has been for a view of good practice in terms of an individual's sense of control – helping people to find their own solutions to problems, to recognise their key role in shaping their children's futures, and to see themselves as able to control, or at least influence their own health and welfare. As has been made clear, this focus has implications not only for the form of support to be offered, but also, of course, for the way in which it is provided. All the approaches described involve a move away from the traditional provider–client relationship toward a partnership of care.

The partnerships involved in supportive arrangements are not necessarily between a professional and client. Support is also provided by lay people, voluntary groups and families, and it is clear that such arrangements have much to offer. Not least among their benefits is the equal status of client and helper, the chance that the relationship has benefits for both, and the greater control it often provides the client in determining when, how often and for how long support is given.

One of the characteristics of more equal partnerships is the greater role for clients in specifying the kind of help that is needed. This was perhaps most apparent in the community care scheme for elderly people (Chapter 5), in the Birmingham family support programme for people treated for schizophrenia (Chapter 4), and in the support scheme for young people leaving care (Chapter 2). The collaborative style is likely to lead to greater self-respect for the recipients of services in so far as they are genuinely treated as capable of making these decisions.

However, choices are only meaningful if there is no obvious or covert pressure to exercise it in a particular direction, and this also has implications for the way in which support is offered. Residential settings, for instance, can provide choices about mealtimes, self-catering, privacy and so on, but in practice it may be difficult to do much that is different from anyone else. For instance, if an individual is not asked whether or not they would like a lock on their room door, even if a lock would be provided should they ask, they are likely not to ask. There is thus a need to provide opportunities for choice (by offering to have a lock put on the door, say) as well as making choices possible in principle (being willing to put a lock on the door if asked).

Creating mechanisms for inter-agency support

An issue which comes to light from many of the projects described, is the extent to which providers in one setting relate to professionals with responsibility for people with mental health problems. Given that the client groups of these projects are deemed to be particularly vulnerable to psychiatric disorder – what back-up, referral, training or other support should psychiatric services be offering? Voluntary groups may sometimes be supporting people whose problems have not been prevented but who have become quite seriously disturbed, or are showing very worrying inadequacies in their parenting, or be involved in seriously violent relationships, for instance. At the other extreme, carers in one agency may seek to involve carers in other agencies in an excessively large number of cases. Clearly, it is important to get the balance right and to establish good channels of communication. Otherwise social workers, say, with their statutory accountability for children officially deemed to be at risk, will not want to risk devolving any responsibility for family support to voluntary agencies, despite the obvious benefits the family might stand to gain from a befriender. And the more support general practitioners receive in the practice setting, in their dealings with mental health problems, the more skilled they will become themselves, and the greater the proportion of mental health difficulties they will be able to contain at the primary care level.

Similar issues arise, of course, in relationships between natural carers (relatives and friends) and providers (whether voluntary or statutory), and also between the individual and caring agencies. The issues are essentially about diffusing information and skills to enable people to help themselves, relatives to provide effective support for their family member, primary care and voluntary care workers to be better able to support their client group. If professionals can recognise, value and support the role of lay people in their own care, or in supporting others, it should also have benefits to the quality of the service they are able to provide. In fact, there is evidence that inter-agency collaboration is a concept that has already gained a good deal of support. Strathdee and Williams (1984) found, from a postal survey, that as many as one in five consultant psychiatrists spent some of their working week in general practice settings – arrangements that they had usually established between them on an informal and *ad hoc* basis.

Increasingly, Community Mental Health Centres are taking on the role of co-ordinating a wide range of support for a wide range of clients, and at first sight appear to be in an ideal position to improve inter-agency support. What seems to be happening, however, is that they are absorbing many of the client groups themselves. A survey of the aims of 67 British CMHCs in 1988 (Sayce, 1988) showed that preventive work was frequently named as an important part of their role. Sixty per cent said 'improved professional liaison' was one of their aims, 51 per cent said 'accessibility', 45 per cent 'primary prevention/health promotion', 39 per cent 'building community links', 33 per cent 'secondary prevention' and preventing admissions, and 32 per cent 'multi-disciplinary work'. Other aims stated by between 26 per cent and 16 per cent included reducing stigma, long-term support, training, and consumer involvement. Services most commonly offered by British CMHCs in 1988 included counselling (73 per cent), assessment (54 per cent), medical treatment (46 per cent), psychotherapy (43 per cent), family therapy (40 per cent) and group therapy (40 per cent). About one-third also offered support groups, training, health education and rehabilitation. Twenty-one per cent also claimed to be 'facilitating' self-help groups, 19 per cent offered crisis intervention, 18 per cent offered support for carers, 9 per cent education for users. However, although at one level their co-ordinating role may be a valuable one, evidence from this survey and from other work discussed earlier, shows that this is usually to the detriment of the client group for whom their services were intended: namely, the recipients of psychiatric services before they became community based.

One other problem arises from the broad focus of Community Mental Health Centres, in that where they exist (and they are being established at a rapid rate across the country, over 150 so far), and where they have such a wide remit, it is easier for general practices to refer patients to them, and leave decisions about appropriate support to CMHC staff. This strategy conflicts with the suggestions put forward here for encouraging general practice to become better equipped to deal with psychosocial problems. With more specialist work taking place outside of the practice setting, it is more likely to reduce, rather than enhance, the skills of the general practitioners. All the accounts of arrangements with counsellors, psychologists and psychiatrists working in the general practice setting cite improvements to the GP's understanding, skills, and sense of support in the mental health aspect of their work as a major benefit. It also effectively creates another tier to service provision. The approach taken in this review would support the maintenance of existing divisions between primary and secondary care services (though not usually based in mental hospitals) alongside a greater collaboration between primary and secondary health care workers.

Alternative models could at least be considered. Buckinghamshire, for instance, allocates individual community psychiatric nurses to particular general practices. The family doctors and psychiatric nurses therefore get to know each other well, and can discuss individual patients whom the doctor feels require specialist psychiatric help. The nurse will decide which cases to deal with themselves, and which they feel should be referred to the psychiatrist or to another member of the mental health team (all of whom are based in the community). The CPNs are trained in a highly structured behaviour management approach which has its roots in family work with people with a history of schizophrenia pioneered by Ian Falloon, who is also the initiator of the Buckinghamshire service. The community mental health team includes a social worker, who is the main link between the team and the community. She helps to build links with community groups and voluntary agencies, and has prepared a list of all available local resources, (from toddlers groups, voluntary counselling facilities, support groups, welfare rights advice, to home-care schemes). Where she sees a gap, she can establish a new group, such as a support group for people trying to break their dependence on minor tranquillisers. Of course this model of service may not be equally suitable for other areas and it is not put forward as in any sense an ideal model. Service developments will inevitably vary according to local circumstances.

In the services described in this review there have been many parallels in objectives for which differing solutions have been applied for different client groups. It may be that workers in one area may find this exercise useful in considering new approaches which have been found effective in other areas. Why not, for instance, a voluntary befriending scheme for care leavers? Perhaps as foster Aunts or Uncles for particular individuals as they approach their final year in care: someone who could go with them to look for accommodation, to find cheap furnishing, to look for work, and be at the end of a telephone for advice.

There is much yet to learn about how mental illness might be prevented. Humanitarian concerns for people with the range of psychosocial problems described in preceding chapters will ensure that such services and projects continue to be needed. Current knowledge on how social action might best be focused in order to prevent mental illness is a reasonable yardstick against which to measure the quality of that provision. Regular critical appraisal of its success will help to inform judgements about future service development.

Bibliography

Abramson, L. Y., Seligman, M. E. P. and Teasdale, J. D. (1978) 'Learned helplessness in humans: critique and reformulation'. *Journal of Abnormal Psychology 87* No 1 pp 49–74.

After-Care Team (1987) 'Bradford After-Care'. Briefing paper prepared for delegates of a conference in Bradford, October 1987.

Albee, G. W. (1959) *Mental health manpower trends.* New York, Basic Books.

Alberman, E. and Berry, C. (1979) 'Prenatal diagnosis and the specialist in community medicine'. *Community Medicine 1* pp 89–96.

Balint, E. and Norell, J. S. (Eds) (1976) *Six minutes for the patient.* London, Tavistock.

Barker, W. and Anderson, R. (1988) 'The Child Development Programme: an evaluation of process and outcomes'. Evaluation Document 9. Manuscript, University of Bristol, Early Childhood Development Unit.

Barnard, K. E., Hammond, M., Mitchell, S. K., Booth, C. L., Spietz, A. and Elsas, T. (1985) 'Caring for high-risk infants and their families' in Green, M. (Ed.) *The psychosocial aspects of the family.* Lexington, Massachusetts, D.C. Heath.

Barnard, K. E. *et al.* (1987) 'Clinical nursing models'. Unpublished project summary. NIMH Grant MH 36894. University of Washington.

Bebbington, P., Hurry, J., Tennant, C., Sturt, E. and Wing, J. K. (1981) 'Epidemiology of mental disorders in Camberwell'. *Psychological Medicine 11* pp 561–79.

Birch, D. (1986) 'Schoolgirl pregnancy in Camberwell'. MD thesis. University of London.

Birchwood, M., Smith, J. and Cochrane, R. (1991) 'Family intervention in a dedicated service setting: impact on clinical outcome and EE status at nine months and two years' follow-up'. In submission to *Psychological Medicine.*

Birchwood, M., Smith, J., Macmillan, F., Hogg, B., Harvey, C. and Bering, S. (1989) 'Predicting relapse in schizophrenia: the development and implementation of an early signs monitoring system using patients and families as observers, a preliminary investigation'. *Psychological Medicine 19* pp 649–56.

Birley, J. L. T. and Brown, G. W. (1970) 'Crises and life changes preceding the onset or relapse of acute schizophrenia: clinical aspects'. *British Journal of Psychiatry 116* pp 327–33.

Boardman, A. P., Bouras, N. and Cundy, J. (1987) The Mental Health Advice Centre in Lewisham, service usage: trends from 1978–84. Research Report No 3. London, Research and Development in Psychiatry.

Bohm, L. C. and Rodin, J. (1985) 'Aging and the family' in Turk, D. and Kerns, R. D. (Eds) *Health, illness and families: a life-span perspective.* New York, Wiley Interscience.

Booth, T., (1985) 'Finding out some home truths'. *Community Care* October pp 24–6.

Booth, T. (1986) 'Institutional regimes and resident outcomes in homes for the elderly' in Phillipson, C., Bernard, M. and Strang, P. (Eds) *Dependency and interdependency in old age: theoretical perspectives and policy alternatives.* London, Croom Helm.

Bowlby, J. (1969) *Attachment and loss. Vol 1. Attachment.* London, Hogarth Press.

Bowlby, J. (1973) *Attachment and loss. Vol 2. Separation, anxiety and anger.* London, Hogarth Press.

Bowlby, J. (1980) *Attachment and loss. Vol 3. Loss: sadness and depression.* London, Hogarth Press.

Bowling, A. and Cartwright, A. (1982) *Life after death.* London, Tavistock.

Bronfenbrenner, U. (1975) 'Is early intervention effective? in Gultentag, M. and Struening, E. L. (Eds) *Handbook of evaluation research.* Beverly Hills, Sage.

Brook Advisory Centres (1986) *Annual Report 1985-6.* London, Brook.

Brown, G. W. (1989) 'Depression: a radical social perspective' in Herbst, K. R. and Paykel, E. S. *Depression: an integrative approach.* Oxford, Heinemann Medical Books.

Brown, G. W. (1990) Paper given at a conference entitled Prevention of Depression and Anxiety: the role of the practice team. March 1990.

Brown, G. W. and Birley, J. L. T. (1968) 'Crisis and life changes and the onset of schizophrenia'. *Journal of Health and Social Behaviour 9* pp 203–14.

Brown, G. W. and Harris, T. O. (1978) *Social origins of depression.* London, Tavistock.

Brown, G. W. and Harris, T. O. (Eds) (1989) *Life events and illness.* London, Unwin Hyman.

Brown, G. W., Bifulco, A. and Andrews, B. (1990) 'Self-esteem and depression: III Aetiological issues'. *Social Psychiatry and Psychiatric Epidemiology 25* pp 235–43.

Brown, G. W., Bifulco, A. and Harris, T. O. (1987) 'Life events, vulnerability and onset of depression: some refinements'. *British Journal of Psychiatry 150* pp 30–42.

Brown, G. W., Birley, J. L. T. and Wing, J. K. (1972) 'Influence of family life on the course of schizophrenic disorders: a replication'. *British Journal of Psychiatry 121* pp 241–58.

Brown, G. W., Craig, T. K. J. and Harris, T. O. (1985) 'Depression: distress or disease? Some epidemiological considerations'. *British Journal of Psychiatry 147* pp 612–22.

Brown, G. W., Harris, T. O. and Bifulco, A. (1986a) 'Long-term effect of early loss of parent' in Rutter, M., Izard, C. and Read, P. (Eds) *Depression in childhood: developmental perspectives.* New York, Guildford Press.

Brown, G. W., Bone, M., Dalison, B. and Wing, J. K. (1966) *Schizophrenia and social care: a comparative follow-up of 339 schizophrenic patients. Maudsley Monograph No 17,* London, Oxford University Press.

Brown, G. W., Andrews, B., Harris, T., Adler, Z. and Bridge, L. (1986b) 'Social support, self-esteem and depression'. *Psychological Medicine 16* pp 813–31.

Brown, P. (1985) *The transfer of care: psychiatric deinstitutionalisation and its aftermath.* London, Routledge.

Caplan, G. (1964) *Principles of preventive psychiatry.* New York, Basic Books.

Challis, D. and Davies, B. (1985) 'Long-term care for the elderly: the community care scheme'. *British Journal of Social Work 15* pp 563–79.

Challis, D. and Davies, B. (1986) *Case management in community care.* Aldershot, Gower.

Challis, D., Chessum, R. and Luckett, R. (1983) 'A new life at home'. *Community Care* 24 March pp 21–3.

Challis, D., Chessum, R., Chesterman, J., Luckett, R. and Woods, B. (1988) 'Community care for the frail elderly: an urban experiment'. *British Journal of Social Work 18* Supplement pp 13–42.

Chapman, J. (1966) 'The early symptoms of schizophrenia'. *American Journal of Psychiatry 112* pp 225–41.

Child Development Programme (1987) 'Consistent and significant improvements found in home environment and nutrition of intervention children'. Evaluation Document 8. University of Bristol, Early Childhood Development Unit.

Child Development Project (1984) *Child Development Programme*. Booklet produced by the University of Bristol.

Children Act (1989) Chapter 41. London, HMSO.

Clare, A. (1980) *Psychiatry in Dissent*. London, Tavistock.

Clark, E. (1991) 'Growing up fast: adult outcomes of teenage motherhood', (commissioned by St Michael's Fellowship) Brighton, Trust for the Study of Adolescents.

Cohen, S. and Syme, S. L. (Eds) (1985) *Social support and health*. New York, Academic Press.

Cooper, B. and Sosna, V. (1980) 'Family settings of the psychiatrically disturbed aged' in Robins, L. N., Clayton, P. J. and Wing, J. K. (Eds) *The Social consequence of psychiatric illness*. New York, Brunner/Mazel.

Corney, R. H. and Briscoe, M. E. (1977) 'Social workers and their clients: a comparison between the primary health care and local authority settings'. *Journal of the Royal College of General Practitioners 27* pp 295–301.

Costello, C. G. (1982) 'Social factors associated with depression: a retrospective study'. *Psychological Medicine 12* pp 329–39.

Cox, A. D., Pound, A., Miller, M. and Puckering, C. (1990) 'The assessment of intervention: the evaluation of a home-visiting and befriending scheme for young mothers: Newpin', unpublished manuscript, final report to the Department of Health.

Craig, T. K. J. and Brown, G. W. (1984) 'Goal frustration and life events in the aetiology of painful gastrointestinal disorder'. *Journal of Psychosomatic Research 28* pp 411–21.

Creed, F. (1981) 'Life events and appendicectomy'. *Lancet* pp 381–5.

Cutting, J. (1985) *The psychology of schizophrenia*. Edinburgh, Churchill Livingstone.

Davis, J. M. and Garver, D. L. (1978) 'Neuroleptics: clinical use in psychiatry' in Iversen, L. L., Iversen, S. D. and Snyder, S. H. (Eds) *Handbook of psychopharmacology Vol 10*. New York, Plenum Press.

Davis, J. M., Schaffer, C. B., Killian, G. A., Kinard, C. and Chan, C. (1980) 'Important issues in the drug treatment of schizophrenia'. *Schizophrenia Bulletin 6* pp 70–87.

Davis, K. (1987) 'Research and policy formulation' in Aiken, L. and Mechanic, D. (Eds) *Applications of social science to clinical medicine and health policy*. Princeton, New Jersey, Rutgers University Press.

Department of Health (1990) *Health and personal social services statistics for England*. London, HMSO.

Dixon, S. (1986a) 'Away from institutional dependence: towards a more resident-oriented institutional environment' in Phillipson, C., Bernard, M. and Strang, P. (Eds) *Dependency and interdependency in old age: theoretical perspectives and policy alternatives*, London, Croom Helm.

Dixon, S. (1986b) 'Towards resident-oriented environments in elderly persons' homes'. Unpublished Ph.D. thesis, University of Bath.

Docherty, J., van Kammen, D. P., Siris, S. G., and Marder, S. R. (1978) 'Stages of onset of schizophrenic psychosis'. *American Journal of Psychiatry 135:4* p 420–6.

Dohrenwend, B. S. and Dohrenwend, B. P. (Eds) (1974) *Stressful life events: their nature and effects*. New York, Wiley.

Drake, M., O'Brien, M., Biebuyck, T. (1981) *Single and homeless*, Department of the Environment and Social Survey. London, HMSO.

Earll, L. and Kincey, J. (1982) 'Clinical psychology in general practice: a controlled trial evaluation'. *Journal of the Royal College of General Practitioners 32* pp 32–7.

Elliot, S. A., Sanjack, M. and Leverton, T. J. (1988) 'Parents' groups in pregnancy; a preventive intervention for post-natal depression?' in Gottlieb, B. H. (Ed) *Marshalling social support*. London, Sage.

Epstein, S. (1983) 'Natural healing processes of the mind' in Meichenbaum, D. and Jaremko, M. E. (Eds) *Stress reduction and prevention*. New York, Plenum Press.

Evans, G., Hughes, B., Williams, D. and Jolley, D. (1981) 'The management of mental and physical impairment in non-specialist homes for the elderly'. Research Report No 4. University of Manchester, Psychogeriatric Unit.

Eyken, W. van der (1982) *Homestart: a four-year evaluation*. Leicester, Homestart Consultancy.

Falloon, I. R. H., Boyd, J. L., McGill, C. W., Razani, J., Moss, H. and Gilderman, A. M. (1982) 'Family management in the prevention of exacerbations of schizophrenia'. *New England Journal of Medicine 306* pp 1437–40.

Falloon, I. R. H., Boyd, J. L., McGill, C., Williamson, M., Razani, J., Moss, H. B., Gilderman, A. M. and Simpson, G. M. (1985) 'Family management in the prevention of morbidity of schizophrenia: clinical outcome of a two-year longitudinal study'. *Archives of General Psychiatry 42* pp 887–96.

Feinmann, J. (1985) 'Community psychiatry: an experiment paying dividends'. *Health and Social Services Journal, Vol XCV* No 4963, 3 October pp 1228–9.

Fenton, F. R., Tessier, L. and Struening, E. L. (1979) 'A comparative trial of home and hospital psychiatric care. One year follow-up'. *Archives of General Psychiatry 36* pp 1073–9.

Finlay-Jones, R. (1981) 'Showing that life events are a cause of depression: a review'. *Australian and New Zealand Journal of Psychiatry 15* pp 229–38.

Finlay-Jones, R. and Brown, G. W. (1983) 'Types of stressful event and the onset of anxiety and depressive disorders'. *Psychological Medicine 11* pp 803–15.

First Key (1986) 'Floating support – we have the technology'. *First Key Notes* Issue No 8 pp 6–7.

Freeman, G. K. and Button, E. J. (1984) 'The clinical psychologist in general practice: a six-year study of consulting patterns for psychosocial problems'. *Journal of the Royal College of General Practitioners 34* pp 377–80.

Garber, J., Miller, W. R. and Seamen, S. F. (1979) 'Learned helplessness, stress, and the depressive disorders' in Depue, R. A. (Ed.) *The psychobiology of depressive disorders*. New York, Academic Press.

Gask, L., Goldberg, D., Lesser, A. L. and Millar, T. (1988) 'Improving the psychiatric skills of the general practice trainee: an evaluation of a group training course'. *Medical Education 22* pp 132–8.

Gask, L., McGrath, G., Goldberg, D. and Millar, T. (1987) 'Improving the psychiatric skills of established general practitioners: evaluation of group teaching'. *Medical Education 21* pp 362–8.

Gillie, O., Price, A. and Robinson, S. (1982) *The Sunday Times self-help directory* 2nd Edition. London, Granada.

Glass, D. C. *et al.* (1980) 'Effect of task overload upon cardiovascular and plasma catecholamine responses in Type A and Type B individuals'. *Basic and Applied Social Psychology 1* (3) pp 199–218.

Goldberg, D. and Blackwell, B. (1970) 'Psychiatric illness in general practice: a detailed study using a new method of case identification'. *British Medical Journal 2* pp 439–43.

Goldberg, D. and Huxley, P. (1980) *Mental illness in the community: the pathway to psychiatric care.* London, Tavistock.

Goldberg, D. P., Steele, J. J. and Smith, C. (1980a) 'Teaching psychiatric interview techniques to family doctors'. *Acta Psychiatrica Scandinavica 62* pp 41–7.

Goldberg, D. P., Steele, J. J., Smith, C. and Spiver, L. (1980b) 'Training family doctors to recognise psychiatric illness with increased accuracy'. *Lancet ii.* pp 521–3.

Gottlieb, B. H. (1983) *Social support strategies: guidelines for mental health practice.* Beverly Hills, Sage.

Grant, I., Mcdonald, W. I., Patterson, T. and Trimble, M. R. (1989) 'Multiple sclerosis' in Brown, G. W. and Harris, T. O. (Eds) *Life events and illness.* London, Unwin Hyman.

Griffiths, Sir R. (1988) *Community Care: Agenda for Action.* A report to the Secretary of State for Social Services. London, HMSO.

Grosskurth, A. (1984) 'From care to nowhere'. *Roof* (Shelter's housing magazine) July/August pp 11–14.

Harris, J. and Kelly, D. (1986) 'Community care and elderly people: one-way traffic?' in Phillipson, C., Bernard, M. and Strang, P. (Eds) *Dependency and interdependency in old age: theoretical perspectives and policy alternatives.* London, Croom Helm.

Harris, T., Brown, G. W. and Bifulco, A. (1986) 'Loss of parent in childhood and adult psychiatric disorder: the role of adequate parental care'. *Psychological Medicine 16* pp 641–59.

Harris, T., Brown, G. W. and Bifulco, A. (1987) 'Loss of parent in childhood and adult psychiatric disorder: the role of social class position and premarital pregnancy'. *Psychological Medicine 17* No 1 pp 163–83.

Harris, T., Brown, G. W. and Bifulco, A. (1990) 'Depression and situational helplessness in a sample selected to study parental loss'. *Journal of Affective Disorder 20* pp 27–44.

Hatfield, A. B. (1987) 'The expressed emotion theory: why families object'. *Hospital and Community Psychiatry 38* No 4 p 341.

Heinrichs, D. W. *et al.* (1985) 'Prospective study of prodromal symptoms in schizophrenic relapse'. *American Journal of Psychiatry 142:3.*

Herz, M. I. (1984) 'Recognising and preventing relapse in patients with schizophrenia'. *Hospital and Community Psychiatry 35* No 4 p 345.

Hinde, R. A. and Stevenson-Hinde, J. (Eds) (1988) *Relationships within families: mutual influences.* Oxford, Clarendon Press.

Hoeper, E. W., Kessler, L. G., Nycz, G. R., Burke, J. D. and Pierce, W. E. (1984) 'The usefulness of screening for mental illness'. *Lancet i.* pp 33–5.

Hogarty, G. E., Anderson, C. M., Reiss, D. J., Kornblith, S. J., Greenwald, P., Javan, C. D., Manonia, M. J. and the EPICS research group (1986) 'Family psychoeducation, social skills training, and maintenance chemotherapy in the aftercare treatment of schizophrenia'. *Archives of General Psychiatry 43* pp 633–42.

Hudson, F. and Dawson, N. (1987) 'Schoolgirl mothers: an issue'. Unpublished paper. Bristol, Unit for Schoolgirl Mothers.

Hughes, B. and Wilkin, D. (1980) 'Residential care of the elderly: a review of the literature'. Research Report No 2. University of Manchester, Department of Psychiatry and Community Medicine.

Ingham, R. (1984) 'Scope projects'. Unpublished paper for ACPP Study Day on Interventions with Young Families, 30 November 1984.

Jenkins, A. (1987) 'Recognising and treating the hurt child within parents' in Whitefield, R. and Baldwin, D. (Eds) *Families matter*. London, Collins Fount.

Johnson, J. E. (1984) 'Psychological interventions and coping with surgery' in Baum, A., Taylor, S. E. and Singer, J. E. (Eds) *Handbook of psychology and health. Vol IV*. Hillsdale, New Jersey, Lawrence Erlbaum Associates.

Jones, E. F., Forrest, J. D., Goldman, N., Henshaw, S. K., Lincoln, R., Rosoff, J. I., Westoff, C. F. and Wulf, D. (1985) 'Teenage pregnancy in developed countries: determinants and policy implications'. *Family Planning Perspectives 17* No 2 pp 53–63.

Kanter, J., Lamb, H. R. and Loeper, C. (1987) 'Expressed emotion in families: a critical review'. *Hospital and Community Psychiatry 38* No 4 pp 374–80.

Kasl, S. V. and Berkman, I. F. (1981) 'Some psychosocial influences on the health status of the elderly' in McGaugh, J. L. and Keisler, S. B. (Eds) *Aging: biology and behaviour*. New York, Academic Press.

Koperski, M. (1989) 'Health education using video recordings in a general practice waiting area: an evaluation'. *Journal of the Royal College of General Practitioners 39* pp 328–30.

Kreitman, N. (1986) 'Alcohol consumption and the prevention paradox'. *British Journal of Addiction 81* pp 353–63.

Langer, E. and Rodin, J. (1976) 'The effects of choice and enhanced personal responsibility for the aged: a field experiment in an institutional setting'. *Journal of Personality and Social Psychology 34* pp 191–8.

Lazar, I., Darlington, R., Murray, H., Royce, J. and Snipper, A. (1982) 'Lasting effects of early education: a report from the consortium for Longitudinal Studies', *Monographs of the Society for Research in Child Development, serial no. 195. 47* pp 2–3.

Lee, P., Wickham, C., Lewis, E., Barker, W. and Kevany, J. (1983) 'Anthropometric and dietary assessment of disadvantaged Dublin infants'. *Irish Medical Journal 76* No 5 pp 226–9.

Leff, J. P. and Vaughn, C. E. (1980) 'The influence of life events and relatives' expressed emotion in schizophrenia and depressive neurosis'. *British Journal of Psychiatry 136* pp 146–53.

Leff, J. P. and Wing, J. K. (1971) 'Trial of maintenance therapy in schizophrenia'. *British Medical Journal 3* pp 599–604.

Leff, J., Kuipers, L., Berkowitz, R. and Sturgeon, D. (1985) 'A controlled trial of social intervention in the families of schizophrenia patients: two-year follow-up'. *British Journal of Psychiatry 146* pp 594–600.

Leff, J., Kuipers, L., Berkowitz, R., Eberlein-Vries, R. and Sturgeon, D. (1982) 'A controlled trial of social intervention in the families of schizophrenia patients'. *British Journal of Psychiatry 141* pp 121–34.

Leighton, A. (1982) *Caring for mentally ill people: psychological and social barriers in a historical context*. Cambridge, Cambridge University Press.

Lesser, A. L. (1981) 'The psychiatrist and family medicine. A different training approach'. *Medical Education 15* pp 398–406.

Lesser, A. L. (1985) 'Problem-based interviewing in general practice: a model'. *Medical Education 19* pp 299–304.

Leverton, T. J. and Elliot, S. A. (1988) 'Antenatal intervention for post-natal depression'. Unpublished paper presented at the Royal College of Psychiatrists

Autumn Quarterly Meeting, 27 October 1988.

Levine, M. (1981) *The history and politics of community mental health.* New York, Oxford University Press.

Luckett, R. and Chessum, R. (1985) 'Gateshead Community Care Scheme'. Paper for DHSS Seminar, 14 and 15 March 1985.

Lupton, C. (1985) 'Moving out: older teenagers leaving residential care'. Report No 12. Portsmouth, Social Services Research and Intelligence Unit.

MacCarthy, B., Kuipers, L., Hurry, J., Harper, R. and LeSage, A. (1989) 'Counselling the relatives of the long-term adult mentally ill: 1 Evaluation of the impact on relatives and patients'. *British Journal of Psychiatry 154* pp 768–75.

McKechnie, A. A., Philip, A. E. and Ramage, J. G. (1981) 'Psychiatric services in primary care: specialized or not?' *Journal of the Royal College of General Practitioners 31* pp 611–14.

Marshall, M. and Hargreaves, M. (1979) 'So you want to try GP attachment?' *Social Work Today 10* No 42, July pp 25–6.

Martin, E. and Martin, P. M. C. (1985) 'Changes in psychological diagnosis and prescription in a practice employing a counsellor'. *Family Practice 2* No 4 pp 241–3.

Millard, P. H. (1983) 'Depression in old age'. *British Medical Journal 287* No 6389 pp 375–6.

Mitchell, A. R. K. (1985) 'Psychiatrists in primary care settings'. *British Journal of Psychiatry 147* pp 371–9.

Mitchell, R. G. (1975) 'The incidence and nature of child abuse'. *Dev Med Child Neurology 17* pp 641–6.

Mulvey, T. (1977) 'After-care – who cares?' in *Concern.* London, National Children's Bureau.

Murphy, E. (1982) 'Social origins of depression in old age'. *British Journal of Psychiatry 141* pp 135–42.

Murphy, E. (1984) 'Preventing mental illness'. *Geriatric Medicine* February pp 75–9.

Neilson, E., Brown, G. W. and Marmot, M. (1989) 'Myocardial infarction' in Brown, G. W. and Harris, T. O. (Eds) *Life events and illness.* London, Unwin Hyman.

Newton, J. (1988) *Preventing mental illness.* London, Routledge.

Newton, J. and Craig, T. (1991) 'Prevention' in Bennett, D. and Freeman, H. (Eds) *Community Psychiatry.* Edinburgh, Churchill Livingstone.

Office of Population Censuses and Surveys (1982) *General Household Survey 1980.* London, HMSO.

Olds, D. L., Henderson, C. R., Chamberlin, R. and Tatelbaum, R. (1986a) 'Preventing child abuse and neglect: a randomised trial of nurse home visitation'. *Pediatrics 78* No 1 pp 65–78.

Olds, D. L., Henderson, C. R., Tatelbaum, R. and Chamberlin, R. (1986b) 'Improving the delivery of prenatal care and outcomes of pregnancy: a randomised trial of nurse home visitation'. *Pediatrics 77* No 1 pp 16–28.

Osofsky, H. J., Osofsky, J. D., Kendall, N. and Rajan, R. (1973) 'Adolescents as mothers: an interdisciplinary approach to a complex problem'. *Journal of Youth and Adolescence 2* No 3 pp 233–49.

Ounsted, C., Roberts, J., Gordon, M. and Milligan, B. (1982) 'Fourth goal of perinatal medicine'. *British Medical Journal 284* pp 879–82.

Palfreeman, S. (1982) 'Working with families: services or support?' in Pugh, G. (Ed.) 'Parenting Papers' 5. Unpublished papers from NCB study day.

Parkes, C. M. (1981) 'Evaluation of a bereavement service'. *Journal of Preventive Psychiatry 1* No 2 pp 179–88.

Parkes, C. M. (1988) 'Evaluation of Tower Hamlets Crisis Intervention Service'. Unpublished final report to DHSS, London Hospital Medical College.

Patmore, C. and Weaver, T. (1991) 'Community mental health teams: lessons for planners and managers', manuscript available from Good Practices in Mental Health, London.

Paykel, E. S. (1978) 'Contribution of life events to causation of psychiatric illness'. *Psychological Medicine 8* pp 245–53.

Paykel, E. S. (1979) 'Recent life events in the development of the depressive disorders' in Depue, R. A. (Ed.) *The psychobiology of the depressive disorders*. London, Academic Press.

Peace, S. (1983) 'A pleasure to live in?'. *Community Care* 24 March pp 19–21.

Pearlin, L. I. and Schooler, C. (1978) 'The structure of coping'. *Journal of Social Health and Behaviour 19* pp 2–21.

Peterson, L. and Brownlee-Duffeck, M. (1984) 'Prevention of anxiety and pain due to medical and dental procedures' in Roberts, M. C. and Peterson, L. (Eds) *Prevention of problems in childhood*. New York, Wiley.

Pettigrew, S. (1987) 'Building on experience' in *St Michael's Fellowship*, (booklet). London, St Michael's Fellowship.

Pound, A. and Mills, M. (1985) 'A pilot evaluation of Newpin'. *Association for Child Psychology and Psychiatry Newsletter 7*: 4 p 13.

Pugh, G. (1987) 'Pen Green Centre for Families, Corby' in Pugh, G., Aplin, G., De'Ath, E. and Moxan, M. *Partnerships in action*. London, National Children's Bureau.

Pugh, G. and De'Ath, E. (1984) *The needs of parents: practice and policy in parent education*. Basingstoke, Macmillan.

Pugh, G., Aplin, G., De'Ath, E. and Moxan, M. (Eds) (1987) *Partnerships in action*. London, National Children's Bureau.

Quinton, D. and Rutter, M. (1983) 'Parenting behaviour of mothers raised "in care" ' in Nicol, A. R. (Ed.) *Practical lessons from longitudinal studies*. Chichester, Wiley.

Quinton, D., Rutter, M. and Liddle, C. (1984) 'Institutional rearing, parenting difficulties and marital support'. *Psychological Medicine 14* pp 107–24.

Raine, J. P. (1985) 'Young people leaving care'. Fieldwork sub-committee document. Bradford Directorate of Social Services.

Raphael, B. (1977) 'Preventive intervention with the recently bereaved'. *Archives of General Psychiatry 34* pp 1450–54.

Robins, L. N. (1966) *Deviant children grown up*. Baltimore, Williams & Wilkins.

Robson, M. H., France, R. and Bland, M. (1984) 'Clinical psychologist in primary care: controlled clinical and economic evaluation'. *British Medical Journal 288* pp 1805–8.

Rodin, J. (1983) 'Behavioural medicine: beneficial effects of self-control training in aging'. *International Review of Applied Psychology 32* pp 153–81.

Rodin, J. (1986) 'Health, control and aging' in Baltes, M. M. and Baltes, P. B. (Eds) *Aging and the psychology of control*. Hillsdale, New Jersey, LEA.

Rodin, J., Cashman, C. and Desiderato, L. (1987) 'Psychosocial interventions in aging focusing on enrichment and prevention' in Riley, M., Baum, A. and Matarazzo, J. (Eds) *Perspectives on behavioural medicine IV*. New York, Academic Press.

Rose, G. (1981) 'Strategy of prevention: lessons from cardiovascular disease'. *British Medical Journal 282* pp 1847–51.

Rutter, M. L. (1966) *Children of sick parents: an environmental and psychiatric study. Maudsley Monograph No 16*. London, Oxford University Press.

Rutter, M. L. (1981) *Maternal deprivation reassessed.* Harmondsworth, Penguin.

Rutter, M. L. (1985) 'Resilience in the face of adversity: protective factors and resistance to psychiatric disorder'. *British Journal of Psychiatry 147* pp 598–611.

Rutter, M. L., Quinton, D. and Liddle, C. (1983) 'Parenting in two generations: looking backwards and looking forwards' in Madge, N. (Ed.) *Families at risk.* London, SSRC/DHSS/Heinemann.

Saunders, R. (1982) 'Innovations in social work: a community care scheme for the elderly using voluntary agencies'. Unpublished paper produced by the Community Care Organiser. Dover, Kent County Council.

Sayce, L. (1988) 'Community mental health centres in the UK', manuscript, London, Research and Development in Psychiatry.

Sharpe, S. (1987a) 'A safe arbour'. *The Guardian* 14 October 1987.

Sharpe, S. (1987b) *Falling for love: teenage mothers talk.* London, Virago Upstarts.

Shinman, S. (1981) *A chance for every child? Access and response to pre-school provision.* London, Tavistock.

Siddy, K. (1986) 'Surgery libraries: GPs try a novel approach to education in the surgery'. *Medeconomics* April pp 28–30.

Silver, R. and Wortman, C. (1980) 'Coping with undesirable life events' in Garber, J. and Seligman, M. E. P. (Eds) *Human helplessness.* New York, Academic Press.

Sixsmith, A. (1986) 'Independence and home in later life' in Phillipson, C., Bernard, M. and Strang, P. (Eds) *Dependency and interdependency in old age: theoretical perspectives and policy alternatives.* London, Croom Helm.

Smith, J. V. E. and Birchwood, M. J. (1985) 'Understanding schizophrenia 1–4'. West Birmingham Health Promotion Unit, Health Education Council.

Smith, J. and Birchwood, M. (1990) 'Relatives and patients as partners in the management of schizophrenia'. *British Journal of Psychiatry 156* pp 654–60.

Smith, J., Birchwood, M. and Cochrane, R. (1991) 'Family intervention: effects on burden, stress and coping'. Manuscript, All Saints Hospital, Birmingham.

Spencer, B., Morris, J. and Thomas, H. (1986) 'Family workers – social support during pregnancy'. *Bulletin of the Maternity Alliance 27* pp 6–7.

Stein, L. I. and Test, M. A. (Eds) (1978) *Alternatives to mental hospital treatment.* New York, Plenum Press.

Stein, M. (1983) 'Leaving care: a personal and political issue'. *Youth and Policy 2* No 3 pp 10–12.

Stein, M. (1987) 'Young single and homeless'. *Social Services Insight* 19 June pp 18–19.

Stein, M. and Carey, K. (1986) *Leaving care.* London, Blackwell.

Strathdee, G. and Williams, P. (1984) 'A survey of psychiatrists in primary care: the silent growth of a new service'. *Journal of the Royal College of General Practitioners 34* pp 615–8.

Tarrier, N., Barrowclough, C., Vaughn, C., Bamrah, J. S., Porceddu, K., Watts, S. and Freeman, H. (1988) 'The community management of schizophrenia: a controlled trial of a behavioural intervention with families to reduce relapse'. *British Journal of Psychiatry 153* pp 532–42.

Taylor, B., Wadsworth, J. and Butler, N. (1983) 'Teenage mothering: admission to hospital and accidents during the first 5 years'. *Archives of Disease in Childhood 58* pp 6–11.

Tennant, C., Bebbington, P. and Hurry, J. (1981) 'The role of life events in depressive illness: is there a substantial causal relation?' *Psychological Medicine 11* pp 379–89.

Tod, J., Mervyn, R., Kerr, F. and Thompon, D. (1985) *Someone to talk to: self-help directory.* London, Mental Health Foundation.

Toynbee, P. (1983) 'The counsellor in the doctor's chair'. *The Guardian* 25 July 1983.

Tuckett, D. *et al.* (1985) *Meetings between experts: an approach to sharing ideas in medical consultation.* London, Tavistock.

Varnavides, C. K., Zermansky, A. G. and Pace, C. (1984) 'Health library for patients in general practice'. *British Medical Journal 288* pp 535–7.

Vaughn, C. E. and Leff, J. P. (1976) 'The influence of family and social factors on the course of psychiatric illness: a comparison of schizophrenic and depressed neurotic patients'. *British Journal of Psychiatry 129* pp 125–37.

Wadsworth, J., Taylor, B., Osborn, A. and Butler, N. (1984) 'Teenage mothering: child development at 5 years'. *Journal of Child Psychology and Psychiatry 25* pp 305–14.

Warner, R. (1985) *Recovery from schizophrenia: psychiatry and political economy.* London, Routledge.

Waydenfeld, D. and Waydenfeld, S. W. (1980) 'Counselling in general practice'. *Journal of the Royal College of General Practitioners 30* pp 671–7.

Wells, N. (1983) *Teenage mothers.* Liverpool, Children's Research Fund.

Wenger, G. C. (1986) 'What do dependency measures measure? Challenging assumptions' in Phillipson, C., Bernard, M. and Strang, P. (Eds) *Dependency and interdependency in old age: theoretical perspectives and policy alternatives.* London, Croom Helm.

Wing, J. K. and Brown, G. W. (1970) *Institutionalism and schizophrenia.* Cambridge, Cambridge University Press.

Wing, J. K., Bennett, D. H. and Denham, J. (1964) 'The industrial rehabilitation of long-stay schizophrenic patients'. Medical Research Council Memo No 42. London, HMSO.

Wolmar, C. (1980) 'Out of care'. *Roof* (Shelter's housing magazine) March/April pp 48–51.

World Health Organization (1984) 'Health promotion: a discussion document on the concept and principles'. Copenhagen, WHO Regional Office for Europe.

Name index

Abramson, L. Y. 7, 8
After-Care Team 81
Albee, G. W. 10
Alberman, E. 4
Anderson, R. 47
Ariety, S. 141

Balint, E. 107
Barker, W. 47
Barnard, K. E. 30, 33
Bebbington, P. 10
Beck, A. 17
Berkman, L. F. 166
Berry, C. 4
Birch, D. 82
Birchwood, M. 158, 160
Birley, J. L. T. 16, 129
Blackwell, B. 103
Boardman, A. P. 203
Bohm, L. C. 165
Booth, T. 170, 178
Bowlby, J. 17, 26
Bowling, A. 166
Briscoe, M. E. 112
Bronfenbrenner, U. 12, 31
Brook Advisory Centres, 84
Brown, G. W. 5-8, 16-22, 26, 62-3, 99-
    101, 129-31, 164, 203
Brown, P. 203
Brownlee-Duffeck, M. 114
Button, E. J. 112

Caplan, G. 10, 25, 119
Carey, K. 62, 64, 65
Cartwright, A. 166
Challis, D. 182-3, 192-6
Chapman, J. 159
Chessum, R. 181, 188

Child Development Programme, 47
Child Development Project, 48
Children Act, 61, 201
Clare, A. 136
Clark, E. 95
Cohen, S. 17
Cooper, B. 164
Corney, R. H. 112
Costello, C. G. 17
Cox, A. D. 56, 57, 205
Craig, T. K. J. 25, 99
Creed, F. 99
Cutting, J. 129

Davies, B. 183, 193-4, 196
Davis, J. M. 17, 24, 128
Davis, K. 15
Dawson, N. 83, 97
Department of Health, 64
Dixon, S. 171, 177-9, 204
Docherty, J. 159
Dohrenwend, B. P. 16, 17, 99
Dohrenwend, B. S. 16, 17, 99
Drake, M. 66

Earll, L. 112
Elliot, S. A. 29, 36, 37
Epstein, S. 114
Evans, G. 178
Eyken, W. van der, 10-11, 34-5

Falloon, I. R. H. 16, 132
Feinmann, J. 111
Fenton, F. R. 127
Finlay-Jones, R. 17, 99
First Key, 66-7
Freeman, G. K. 112

Garber, J. 7

Subject index